Epworth

Gen
Ivor

The Epistles

Epworth Commentaries

Already published

The Epistles of
PETER AND JUDE

DAVID G. HORRELL

EPWORTH PRESS

Extracts from the Revised English Bible are © 1989
by the Delegates of the Oxford University Press and the
Syndics of the Cambridge University Press and are used
by permission

0 7162 0523 8

First published 1998
by Epworth Press
20 Ivatt Way
Peterborough, PE3 7PG

Typeset by Regent Typesetting, London
Printed and bound in Great Britain by
Biddles Ltd, Guildford and King's Lynn

CONTENTS

Contents

GENERAL INTRODUCTION

The *Epworth Preachers' Commentaries* that Greville P. Lewis edited so successfully in the 1950s and 1960s having now served their turn, the Epworth Press has commissioned a team of distinguished academics who are also preachers and teachers to create a new series of commentaries that will serve the 1990s and beyond. We have seized the opportunity offered by the publication in 1989 of the Revised English Bible to use this very readable and scholarly version as the basis of our commentaries, and we are grateful to the Oxford and Cambridge University Presses for the requisite licence. Our authors will nevertheless be free to cite and discuss other translations wherever they think that these will illuminate the original text.

Just as the books that make up the Bible differ in their provenance and purpose, so our authors will necessarily differ in the structure and bearing of their commentaries. But they will all strive to get as close as possible to the intention of the original writers, expounding their texts in the light of the place, time, circumstances, and culture that gave them birth, and showing why each work was received by Jews and Christians into their respective Canons of Holy Scripture. They will seek to make full use of the dramatic advance in biblical scholarship world-wide but at the same time to explain technical terms in the language of the common reader, and to suggest ways in which scripture can help towards the living of a Christian life today. They will endeavour to produce commentaries that can be used with confidence in ecumenical, multi-racial, and multi-faith situations, and not by scholars only but by preachers, teachers, students, church members, and anyone who wants to improve his or her understanding of the Bible.

Ivor H. Jones

PREFACE

The letters of Peter and Jude occupy a somewhat neglected corner of the canon. That is understandable, but it is also a shame. From a historical perspective they offer much interesting insight into the character of early Christianity; from a contemporary perspective they raise pressing questions about how Christians are to regard the Bible, and what kind of authority they should accord to it. How are modern readers to deal with texts that time and again display their original location in a world very different from our own, and in which their authors express views which, to say the least, present some difficulties for many of us? In the course of this commentary I have tried not to avoid such questions, conscious of the aim of the *Epworth Commentary* series to provide material relevant to the needs of readers in today's multi-racial, multi-faith society. In view of this contemporary context certain stylistic decisions also seem to me important. First, in the commentary I refer not to 'the Old Testament' but to 'the Jewish scriptures'. While it may certainly be maintained that the term Old Testament is appropriate within the context of Christian theology (see Moberly 1992), I consider it valuable, through the choice of terminology, to remind Christian readers that these books of their Bible are also the scriptures of members of another living faith tradition, Judaism, for whom the description 'old covenant/testament' is deeply problematic (see Sawyer 1991). Secondly, I label dates not with the conventional BC/AD but with the increasingly standard BCE/CE (Before the Common Era/ Common Era). A dating system which assumes and thus imposes the validity of the Christian faith seems inappropriate in a pluralistic, multi-faith society, in which the adoption of a more widely acceptable system demonstrates tolerance, courtesy and respect for others. Thirdly, in view of the need to avoid portraying God as male, I have used personal pronouns for God as little as possible, and where they are necessary have alternated between he and she, his and her, etc. I confess that using feminine pronouns for God does not come naturally or easily to me (some readers may also find that they jar) but I take this merely as an indication of how deeply ingrained are the conventions of using masculine terminology. Perhaps the occasional feminine pronoun may help to reveal and then to question any implicit presupposition of God's maleness.

I would like to thank those who have played their part in enabling this commentary to be written. Ivor Jones, editor of the series, deserves acknowledgment and thanks, not only for inviting me to write this volume, and for encouraging comments along the way, but also for his part in introducing me to New Testament studies in the first place. Paul Priest and Arne Meyer have read my drafts with interest and care, and their comments have helped me considerably. In particular, Arne's own work on the household code in I Peter helped me to clarify the circular structure of the passage. Louise Lawrence helped to compile the bibliography. I should also like to acknowledge my profound indebtedness to the authors of previous books and commentaries, much more learned and lengthy than my own, especially those of J. Ramsey Michaels and Richard Bauckham, whose insights have helped me far more than I have been able to indicate in the limited space available for references. Even less visible on the pages of the commentary, though no less important, is the love and support of family, friends and colleagues too numerous to name but to whom I am extremely grateful. I would like, however, to express my thanks to Carrie, for honesty and love, and to dedicate this book to her.

January 1998

ABBREVIATIONS

ANRW	*Aufstieg und Niedergang der römischen Welt*, H. Temporini & W. Hasse (eds); Berlin, New York: Walter de Gruyter.
BAGD	Bauer, W., Arndt, W.F., Gingrich, F.W. and Danker, F.W., *A Greek-English Lexicon of the New Testament and Other Early Christian Literature*, Chicago and London: University of Chicago Press.
CBQ	*Catholic Biblical Quarterly*
I Clem	*I Clement*
II Clem	*II Clement*
EKK	Evangelisch-Katholischer Kommentar zum Neuen Testament
ExpT	*Expository Times*
Eusebius *EH*	Eusebius, *Ecclesiastical History*
ICC	International Critical Commentary
JBL	*Journal of Biblical Literature*
JSNT	*Journal for the Study of the New Testament*
JTS	*Journal of Theological Studies*
LXX	Septuagint (the Greek translation of the Hebrew scriptures)
NAB	New American Bible
NIV	New International Version
NJB	New Jerusalem Bible
NovT	*Novum Testamentum*
NRSV	New Revised Standard Version
NTS	*New Testament Studies*
REB	Revised English Bible
TynBul	*Tyndale Bulletin*
WBC	Word Biblical Commentary
ZNW	*Zeitschrift für die neutestamentliche Wissenschaft*

BIBLIOGRAPHY

Throughout this book other commentaries are referred to simply with the author's name and relevant page numbers. Other works are indicated by the author's name and the date of publication. All are listed below. Non-biblical ancient texts such as the Apostolic Fathers (the *Didache*, *I Clement* etc.), Eusebius, Josephus, and other Greek and Roman writers can be found in the *Loeb Classical Library* series. Jewish and Christian Pseudepigrapha (such as *I Enoch*) and Apocrypha mentioned in the commentary are collected in Charlesworth (1983; 1985) and Hennecke (1963; 1965). For translations of the Dead Sea Scrolls, see García Martínez 1994 and Vermes 1995.

References in the text to, e.g., Ch. IV 2(iv) etc. indicate other sections of this commentary where further relevant information may be found (see Contents).

The references to secondary literature in the commentary are restricted, and the list below is selective. For fuller, up-to-date bibliographies on I Peter see Achtemeier and Casurella 1996, and on Jude and II Peter see Neyrey and Vögtle. For detailed commentary on the Greek text readers should consult Michaels, Achtemeier and Bauckham. For more general interest Kelly is still one of the best commentaries, packed with insight. A number of good, small-to-medium length evangelical commentaries have been published in recent years, including Grudem, Marshall and Davids. For introductions to the letters see Chester and Martin 1994, Knight 1995, and the valuable collection of essays in Talbert 1986.

Bigg, C., 1910: *A Critical and Exegetical Commentary on the Epistles of St Peter and St Jude*, ICC; Edinburgh: T. & T. Clark.

Brox, N. 1979: *Der erste Petrusbrief*, EKK 21, Zürich: Benziger and Neukirchen-Vluyn: Neukirchener.

Cranfield, C.E.B., 1950: *The First Epistle of Peter*, London: SCM Press.

Davids, P. 1990: *The First Epistle of Peter*, New International Commentary on the New Testament; Grand Rapids, MI: Eerdmans.

Frankemölle, H., 1987: *1. und 2. Petrusbrief. Judasbrief*, Neue Echter Bibel 18/20; Würzburg: Echter Verlag.

Goppelt, L., 1993: *A Commentary on I Peter*, Grand Rapids, MI: Eerdmans.

Grudem, W.A. 1988: *1 Peter*, Tyndale NT Commentaries; Leicester: Inter-Varsity Press.

Kelly, J.N.D., 1969: *A Commentary on the Epistles of Peter and Jude*, Black's NT Commentaries; London: A. & C. Black.

Knoch, O., 1990: *Der Erste und Zweite Petrusbrief. Der Judasbrief*, Regensburger Neues Testament; Regensburg: Friedrich Pustet.

Marshall, I.H., 1991: *1 Peter*, Leicester: Inter-Varsity Press.

Michaels, J.R., 1988: *1 Peter*, WBC 49; Waco, TX: Word Books.

Neyrey, J.H., 1993: *2 Peter, Jude*, Anchor Bible 37C; New York: Doubleday.

Perkins, P., 1995: *First and Second Peter, James, and Jude*, Interpretation; Louisville, KY: John Knox Press.

Reicke, B., 1964: *The Epistles of James, Peter and Jude*, Anchor Bible 37; New York: Doubleday.

Selwyn, E.G. 1952: *The First Epistle of St Peter*, 2nd edn, London: Macmillan.

Spicq, C., 1966: *Les Épitres de Saint Pierre*, Sources Bibliques; Paris: Gabalda.

Vögtle, A., 1994: *Der Judasbrief. Der zweite Petrusbrief*, EKK 22; Zürich: Benziger and Neukirchen-Vluyn: Neukirchener.

Other books and articles

Balch, D.L., 1981: *Let Wives Be Submissive: The Domestic Code in I Peter*, Atlanta, CA: Scholars Press.

—, 1986: 'Hellenization/Acculturation in I Peter', 79–101 in Talbert (ed) 1986.

Barclay, J.M.G., 1995: 'Deviance and Apostasy: some applications of deviance theory to first-century Judaism and Christianity', 114–127 in *Modelling Early Christianity*, P.F. Esler (ed), London: Routledge.

Barker, M. 1990: 'Pseudonymity', 568–571 in *A Dictionary of Biblical Interpretation*, R.J. Coggins and J.L. Houlden (eds), London: SCM Press.

Bauckham, R.J., 1980: 'The Delay of the Parousia', *TynBul* 31, 3–36.

—, 1988a: '2 Peter: An Account of Research', *ANRW* II.25.5, 3713–3752.

—, 1988b: 'The Letter of Jude: An Account of Research', *ANRW* II.25.5, 3791–3826.

—, 1988c: 'James, 1 and 2 Peter, Jude', 303–317 in *It is Written: Scripture Citing Scripture*, D.A. Carson and H.G.M. Williamson (eds), Cambridge: Cambridge University Press.

—, 1988d: 'Pseudo-Apostolic Letters', *JBL* 107, 469–494.

—, 1990: *Jude and the Relatives of Jesus*, Edinburgh: T. & T. Clark.

Benko, S., 1985: *Pagan Rome and the Early Christians*, London: Batsford.

Best, E., 1969: 'I Peter II, 4–10 – A Reconsideration', *NovT* 11, 270–293.

—, 1970: 'I Peter and the Gospel Tradition', *NTS* 16, 95–113.

Birdsall, J.N., 1963: 'The Text of Jude in 𝔓⁷²', *JTS* 14, 394–399.

Boobyer, G.H., 1959: 'The Indebtedness of 2 Peter to 1 Peter', 34–53 in *New Testament Essays: Studies in Memory of T. W. Manson*, A.J.B. Higgins (ed), Manchester: Manchester University Press.

Bornemann, W., 1920: 'Der erste Petrusbrief – eine Taufrede des Silvanus?' *ZNW* 19, 143–165.

Brown, R.E., Donfried, K.P., Reumann, J., 1973: *Peter in the New Testament*, Minneapolis: Augsburg.

—, Maier, J.P., 1983: *Antioch and Rome: New Testament Cradles of Catholic Christianity*, New York and Ramsey, NJ: Paulist Press.

Campbell, R.A., 1994: *The Elders: Seniority within Earliest Christianity*, Edinburgh: T. & T. Clark.

Casurella, A. 1996: *Bibliography of Literature on First Peter*, Leiden: E.J. Brill.

Caulley, T.S., 1982: 'The False Teachers in Second Peter', *Studia Biblica et Theologica* 12, 27–42.

Cavallin, H.C.C., 1979: 'The False Teachers of 2 Pt as Pseudo-Prophets', *NovT* 21, 263–270.

Charles, R.H. (ed), 1913: *The Apocrypha and Pseudepigrapha of the Old Testament, Vol II. Pseudepigrapha*, Oxford: Clarendon 1968.

Charles, J.D., 1990: '"Those" and "These": The Use of the Old Testament in the Epistle of Jude', *JSNT* 38, 109–124.

— 1991a 'Jude's use of Pseudepigraphical Source Material as Part of a Literary Strategy', *NTS* 37, 130–145.

Charles, J.D., 1991b: 'Literary Artifice in the Epistle of Jude', *ZNW* 82, 106–124.

—, 1993: *Literary Strategy in the Epistle of Jude*, Scranton: University of Scranton Press, and London & Toronto: Associated University Presses.

—, 1997: *Virtue amidst Vice: The Catalog of Virtues in 2 Peter 1*, Sheffield: Sheffield Academic Press.

Charlesworth, J.H. (ed), 1983: *The Old Testament Pseudepigrapha, Vol 1: Apocalyptic Literature and Testaments*, London: Darton, Longman and Todd.

—, 1985: *The Old Testament Pseudepigrapha, Vol 2: Expansions of the 'Old Testament' and Legends, Wisdom and Philosophical Literature, Prayers, Psalms and Odes, Fragments of Lost Judeo-Hellenistic Works*, London: Darton, Longman and Todd.

Corley, K., 1995: 'I Peter', 349–360 in *Searching the Scriptures, Vol 2: A Feminist Commentary*, E. Schüssler Fiorenza (ed), London: SCM Press.

Cothenet, E., 1988: 'La Première de Pierre: bilan de 35 ans de recherches', *ANRW* II. 25.5, 3785–3712.

Cross, F.L., 1954: *I Peter: A Paschal Liturgy*, London: Mowbray.

Cullmann, O., 1962: *Peter: Disciple, Apostle, Martyr*, 2nd edn, Philadelphia: Westminster Press.

Dalton, W.J., 1965/1989: *Christ's Proclamation to the Spirits: A Study of I Peter 3:18–4:6*, 2nd fully revised edn 1989, Analecta Biblica 23, Rome: Pontifical Biblical Institute.

—, 1979: 'The Interpretation of 1 Peter 3,19 and 4,6: Light from 2 Peter', *Biblica* 60, 547–555.

Davies, M., 1996: *The Pastoral Epistles*, NT Guides; Sheffield: Sheffield Academic Press.

Downing, F. G., 1988: 'Pliny's Prosecutions of Christians: Revelation and I Peter' *JSNT* 34, 105–123.

DSR 1986: *Accept and Resist: A Study of Civil Disobedience in Christian History and Today*, London: Division of Social Responsibility, The Methodist Church.

Dunn, J.D.G., 1975: *Jesus and the Spirit*, London: SCM Press.

—, 1987: *The Living Word*, London: SCM Press.

—, 1990: *Unity and Diversity in the New Testament*, 2nd edn, London: SCM Press.

Elliott, J.H., 1966: 'The Elect and the Holy: An Exegetical Examination of I Peter 2:4–10 and the Phrase *basileion hierateuma*', Leiden: Brill.

—, 1969: 'A Catholic Gospel: Reflections on "Early Catholicism" in the New Testament', *CBQ* 31, 213–223.

—, 1976: 'The Rehabilitation of an Exegetical Step-Child: I Peter in Recent Research', *JBL* 95, 243–254, cited from reprint in Talbert (ed) 1986.

—, 1981: *A Home for the Homeless: A Sociological Exegesis of I Peter, Its Situation and Strategy*, Philadelphia: Fortress; London: SCM Press.

—, 1986: 'I Peter, its situation and strategy: a discussion with David Balch', 61–78 in Talbert (ed) 1986.

Ellis, E.E., 1978: 'Prophecy and Hermeneutic in Jude', in *Prophecy and Hermeneutic in Early Christianity*, Tübingen: Möhr Siebeck.

Feldmeier, R., 1992: *Die Christen als Fremde*, Tübingen: Möhr Siebeck.

Fornberg, T., 1977: *An Early Church in a Pluralistic Society: A Study of 2 Peter*, Lund: C.W.K. Gleerup.

Fossum, J., 1987: 'Kyrios Jesus as the Angel of the Lord in Jude 5–7', *NTS* 33, 226–243.

García Martínez, F. 1994: *The Dead Sea Scrolls Translated: The Qumran Scrolls in English*, Leiden: Brill.

Green, G.L., 1993: 'The Use of the Old Testament for Christian Ethics in I Peter', *TynBul* 41, 276–289.

Gundry, R.H., 1967: '"Verba Christi" in I Peter: Their Implication concerning the authorship of I Peter and the Authenticity of the Gospel Tradition', *Biblica* 13, 336–350.

—, 1974: 'Further Verba on Verba Christi in First Peter' *Biblica* 55, 211–232.

Gunther, J.J., 1984: 'The Alexandrian Epistle of Jude', *NTS* 30, 549–562.

Hagner, D.A., 1973: *The Use of the Old and New Testaments in Clement of Rome*, Leiden: Brill.

Harrisville, R.A., Sundberg, W. 1995: *The Bible in Modern Culture: Theology and Historical-Critical Method from Spinoza to Käsemann*, Grand Rapids, MI: Eerdmans.

Hennecke, E., 1963: *New Testament Apocrypha, Vol 1: Gospels and Related Writings*, W. Schneemelcher, R. Mc.L. Wilson (ed), London: Lutterworth Press; reissued SCM Press 1973.

—, 1965: *New Testament Apocrypha, Vol 2: Writings relating to the Apostles, Apocalypses and Related Subjects*, W. Schneemelcher, R. Mc.L. Wilson (ed), London: Lutterworth Press; reissued SCM Press 1974.

Horrell, D.G., 1996: *The Social Ethos of the Corinthian Correspondence: Interests and Ideology from I Corinthians to I Clement*, Edinburgh: T. & T. Clark.

Horrell, D.G., 1997a: 'Whose faith(fulness) is it in I Peter 1:5?', *JTS* 48, 110–115.

—, 1997b: 'Leadership Patterns and the Development of Ideology in Early Christianity', *Sociology of Religion* 58.4, 305–323.

Karris, R.J. 1973: 'The Background and Significance of the Polemic of the Pastoral Epistles', *JBL* 92, 549–564.

Käsemann, E., 1964: 'An Apologia for Primitive Christian Eschatology', 169–195 in *Essays on New Testament Themes*, London: SCM Press.

Knight, J., 1995: *2 Peter and Jude*, Sheffield: Sheffield Academic Press.

Kubo, S., 1981: 'Jude 22–23: Two-division Form or Three?', 239–252 in *New Testament Textual Criticism*, E.J. Epp and G.D. Fee (eds), Oxford: Clarendon Press.

Kümmel, W.G., 1975: *Introduction to the New Testament*, 2nd edn, London: SCM Press.

Landon, C., 1996: *A Text-Critical Study of the Epistle of Jude*, Sheffield: Sheffield Academic Press.

LaVerdière, E.A., 1974: 'A Grammatical Ambiguity in I Peter 1:23', *CBQ* 36, 89–94.

Maier, G. 1985: 'Jesustradition im I. Petrusbrief?', 85–128 in D. Wenham (ed), *Gospel Perspectives, vol 5: The Jesus Tradition Outside the Gospels*, Sheffield: JSOT Press.

Marshall, I.H., 1980: *Last Supper and Lord's Supper*, Exeter: Paternoster Press.

Martin, R.P. 1994: 'The Theology of Jude, 1 Peter, and 2 Peter', in A.N. Chester and R.P. Martin, *The Theology of the Letters of James, Peter and Jude*, Cambridge: Cambridge University Press.

Martin, T.W., 1992a: *Metaphor and Composition in I Peter*, Atlanta, GA: Scholars Press.

—, 1992b: 'The Present Indicative in the Eschatological Statements of I Peter 1:6, 8', *JBL* 111, 307–312.

McCartney, D.G., 1991: 'λογικός' in I Peter 2,2', *ZNW* 82, 128–132.

Metzger, B.M. 1975: *A Textual Commentary on the Greek New Testament*, corrected edn, London: United Bible Societies.

Meade, D.G., 1986: *Pseudonymity and Canon*, Tübingen: Mohr Siebeck.

Michaels, J.R., 1967: 'Eschatology in I Peter III.17', *NTS* 13, 394–401.

Mitton, C.L. 1951: *The Epistle to the Ephesians: Its Authorship, Origin and Purpose*, Oxford: Clarendon Press.

Moberly, W., 1992: '"Old Testament" and "New Testament": The Propriety of the Terms for Christian Theology', *Theology* 95, 26–32.

Moule, C.F.D., 1957 'The Nature and Purpose of I Peter', *NTS* 3, 1–11.

Neyrey, J.H., 1980a: 'The Form and Background of the Polemic in 2 Peter', *JBL* 99, 407–431.

—, 1980b: 'The Apologetic Use of the Transfiguration in II Peter 1:16–21', *CBQ* 42, 504–519.

Osburn, C.D., 1972: 'The Text of Jude 22–23', *ZNW* 63, 139–144.

—, 1977: 'The Christological Use of I Enoch 1:9 in Jude 14,15', *NTS* 23, 334–341.

—, 1981: 'The Text of Jude 5', *Biblica* 62, 107–115.

Parker, D., 1994: 'The Eschatology of I Peter', *Biblical Theology Bulletin* 24, 27–32.

Perkins, P., 1994: *Peter: Apostle for the Whole Church*, Columbia, South Carolina: University of South Carolina Press.

Pietersen, L.K., 1997: 'Despicable Deviants: Labelling Theory and the Polemic of the Pastorals', *Sociology of Religion* 58.4, 343–352.

Piper, J., 1980: 'Hope as the Motivation of Love: I Peter 3:9–12', *NTS* 26, 221–231.

Polkinghorne, J.C. 1989: *Science and Providence: God's Interaction with the World*, London: SPCK.

Reichert, A., 1989: *Eine Urchristliche praeparatio ad martyrium: Studien zur Komposition, Traditionsgeschichte und Theologie des I. Petrusbriefes*, Frankfurt: Lang.

Reicke, B., 1946: *The Disobedient Spirits and Christian Baptism: A Study of I Pet. III.19 and Its Context*, Copenhagen: Ejnar Munksgaard.

Richardson, P., 1969: *Israel in the Apostolic Church*, Cambridge: Cambridge University Press.

Ross, J.M., 1989: 'Church Discipline in Jude 22–23', *ExpT* 100, 297–298.

Rowston, D.J., 1975: 'The Most Neglected Book in the New Testament', *NTS* 21, 554–563.

Rowland, C.C., 1990: 'Apocalyptic', 34–36 in *A Dictionary of Biblical Interpretation*, R.J. Coggins and J.L. Houlden (eds), London: SCM Press.

Sawyer, J.F.A., 1991: 'Combating Prejudices about the Bible and Judaism', *Theology* 94, 269–278.

Schutter, W.L., 1989: *Hermeneutic and Composition in I Peter*, Tübingen: Mohr Siebeck.

Sellin, G., 1986: 'Die Häretiker des Judasbriefes', *ZNW* 77, 206–225.

Snodgrass, K.R., 1978: 'I Peter II.1–10: Its Formation and Literary Affinities', *NTS* 24, 97–106.

Snyder, G.F., 1977: 'The *Tobspruch* in the New Testament', *NTS* 23, 117–120.

Soards, M.L., 1988: '1 Peter, 2 Peter and Jude as Evidence for a Petrine School', *ANRW* II.25.5, 3827–3849.

Spicq, C., 1994: *Theological Lexicon of the New Testament*, 3 vols, Peabody MA: Hendrickson.

Talbert, C.H., 1966: 'II Peter and the Delay of the Parousia', *Vigiliae Christianae* 20, 137–145.

—(ed), 1986: *Perspectives on First Peter*, Macon, GA: Mercer University Press.

Theissen, G., 1982: *The Social Setting of Pauline Christianity*, Edinburgh: T. & T. Clark.

—, 1993: *Social Reality and the Early Christians*, Edinburgh: T. & T. Clark.

Thiede, C.P., 1986: 'Babylon, der andere Ort: Anmerkungen zu I Petr 5,13 und Apg 12,17', *Biblica* 67, 532–538.

Thompson, M.B., 1991: *Clothed with Christ: The Example and Teaching of Jesus in Romans 12.1–15.13*, Sheffield: Sheffield Academic Press.

Thurén, L., 1990: *The Rhetorical Strategy of I Peter: With Special Regard to Ambiguous Expressions*, Åbo: Åbo Academy Press.

—, 1995: *Argument and Theology in I Peter: The Origins of Christian Paraenesis*, Sheffield: Sheffield Academic Press.

—, 1997: 'Hey Jude! Asking for the Original Situation and Message of a Catholic Epistle', *NTS* 43, 451–465.

Townsend, M.J., 1979: 'Exit the Agape', *ExpT* 90, 356–361.

Vermes, G. (ed), 1995: *The Dead Sea Scrolls in English*, 4th edn, London: Penguin.

Watson, D. F., 1988: *Invention, Arrangement and Style: Rhetorical Criticism of Jude and 2 Peter*, Atlanta, GA: Scholars Press.

Watson, F.B., 1986: *Paul, Judaism and the Gentiles: a sociological approach*, Cambridge: Cambridge University Press.

—, 1992: 'Strategies of Recovery and Resistance: Hermeneutical Reflections on Genesis 1–3 and its Pauline Reception', *JSNT* 45, 79–103.

—, 1994: *Text, Church and World: Biblical Interpretation in Theological Perspective*, Edinburgh: T. & T. Clark.

White, J. L., 1972: *The Form and Function of the Body of the Greek Letter*, Montana: University of Montana.

Wiles, M., 1986: *God's Action in the World*, London: SCM Press.

Wisse, F., 1972: 'The Epistle of Jude in the History of Heresiology', 133–143 in *Essays in the Nag Hammadi Texts in Honour of A. Böhlig*, M. Krause (ed), Leiden: Brill.

I

GENERAL INTRODUCTION TO THE
EPISTLES OF PETER AND JUDE

1. The 'catholic' epistles

The letters of Peter and Jude are traditionally included among the so-called 'catholic' epistles, a label applied since at least the fourth century to the letters of James, Jude, I and II Peter, I, II and III John (Eusebius *EH* 3.23.25). The label 'catholic' (meaning 'general' or 'universal') indicates that the letters were regarded as 'addressed to the church at large rather than to a specific community' (Perkins, 1). However, the description 'catholic' is hardly an appropriate term to distinguish these letters from others in the New Testament. On the one hand, they were probably written with particular situations in view (I Peter is explicitly addressed to Christians living in certain Roman provinces); on the other hand, other New Testament epistles also address themselves to a wider audience (e.g. I Cor. 1.2; Col. 4.16), or give no indication of a specific audience (Hebrews).

2. I Peter, Jude, II Peter – in that order?

There is a certain logic in dealing with I Peter, II Peter and Jude together, but we should be wary of failing to regard each of them as distinctive in their own right. I Peter certainly has a character distinct from that of Jude and II Peter; and while Jude and II Peter share a good deal of material in common, nevertheless they use that material differently and to confront somewhat different problems (see the introductions to each of the letters). In the commentary I deal with I Peter first. Then, however, I depart from canonical order and turn to Jude. It is clear that there is some literary relationship between Jude and II Peter and, like most modern scholars, I believe that Jude is the earlier letter, used by II Peter as one of its main sources. It therefore makes sense to comment on the earlier letter first, before examining the way in which Jude's material is taken up in II Peter. The earliest preserved text of all three letters is in the Bodmer Papyrus known as $\mathfrak{P}^{72}$, which dates from the third or fourth century.

3. Difficult issues

(i) Pseudonymity

Studying I Peter, II Peter and Jude raises certain controversial issues. One is that of pseudonymity – that is, the practice of writing under someone else's name, the resulting texts being known as 'pseud-epigrapha' (see Barker 1990). Scholars are almost unanimous that II Peter was not written by Peter himself, and many, including myself, take the view that I Peter and Jude are probably also pseud-onymous. The notable differences between I and II Peter surely indicate the work of two different authors, so even if Peter did write I Peter, he cannot have written both letters. Some readers will wish strenuously to avoid this conclusion, since, at least from our twentieth-century perspective, it seems to suggest that these letters are deceitful about their origin and authorship. However, the presence of pseudonymity in the Bible can hardly be completely denied. It is impossible to maintain the traditional view that Moses was the author of the Pentateuch (the first five books of the Bible), since his death is recorded in Deut. 34.5–12. The book of the prophet Isaiah almost certainly contains material from at least two distinct historical periods. In the New Testament, II Peter is probably the clearest case of pseudonymity, but most scholars would also regard the Pastoral Epistles (I and II Timothy, Titus), for example, as pseud-onymous writings (see Bauckham 1988d). Furthermore, we have many examples from around the time of Christian origins of both Jewish and Christian literature which was written in the name of a figure long since dead. Jewish examples include writings in the name of Enoch, Abraham, Moses, Solomon, etc. (see Charlesworth 1983; 1985); Christian writings of the second and third century include Gospels attributed to various apostolic figures and records of their Acts – Peter, Paul, Philip, Thomas, Mary etc. (see Hennecke 1963; 1965).

We should acknowledge that, at that time, writing in the name of revered and honoured predecessors was seen as a legitimate way of presenting their teachings to a new generation, bringing their tradition to bear upon the present (and, we should add, claiming their authority and power). (A useful discussion of the issue of pseudonymity may be found in Dunn 1987, 65–85; further Meade 1986.) It is of course open to debate whether and to what extent the teaching of these epistles is in fact in line with Peter's or Jude's. This is an important question, though one which is difficult to answer, since we have no other written records of their teaching (on Peter in the New Testament see Cullmann 1962; Brown et al. 1973; Perkins 1994). The example of the Pastoral Epistles, written in Paul's name some years after his death, suggests that the problems and per-spectives of later years certainly brought about a development, some would say a corruption, of the apostle's teaching (cf. Davies 1996). Combined with the pseudonymous character of such letters, ques-tions about their content certainly underscore, in my view, the need for a careful and critical reading of their teaching (see below).

(ii) Biblical authority

Another difficult issue which arises in the study of I and II Peter and Jude, at least for Christians who regard the Bible as their holy canon, concerns the nature of biblical authority. What are we to do with I Peter's instruction that wives should submit to and obey their husbands (I Peter 3.1–6)? Should we accept Jude's picture of a God who condemns the disobedient to eternal darkness? Will the day of the Lord really come 'like a thief' and the world be dissolved in a judgment of fire (II Peter 3.10)? Is the vicious polemic of Jude and II Peter in any way a model for communication between Christians who disagree? These are just a few of the questions which are raised in the course of the commentary.

Some readers will feel that all biblical teaching, carefully and cor-rectly understood, should be affirmed and obeyed; any criticism or rejection will be viewed as a rejection of the Bible's authority. I want to insist that a Christian approach to the Bible can, and indeed should, involve a critical and discerning reading which seeks to hear the word of the gospel in the words of the Bible, but which does not assume that every text will provide enduring or equal witness to that gospel. Lest this be regarded as a modern aberration it is worth illus-trating how such an approach may be derived from the work of the great reformer Martin Luther (see Watson 1994, 231–36). Luther, as is well known, expressed rather negative views about the letters of James, Jude and Revelation etc., and believed, for example, that

3

Hebrews 6.4 was wrong to deny the possibility of a second repentance (Harrisville and Sundberg 1995, 15). Luther drew a sharp distinction between 'law' and 'gospel', but this did not imply an equation of the Jewish scriptures ('Old Testament') with law and the New Testament with gospel. Rather, Luther believed that words of scripture, even words of Jesus, could be true, or false, in their presentation of the gospel of Christ. Francis Watson argues that

> Luther's distinction between the true and the false Christ of holy scripture is of genuine hermeneutical significance, for it provides theological justification for the interpreter who wishes to resist the plain, literal meaning of scriptural texts where that meaning is oppressive and tyrannical . . . Luther makes it theologically possible and necessary to be willing to resist even the gospels (Watson 1994, 234).

The basic point is that Luther 'never equated the gospel with the written word' (Harrisville and Sundberg 1995, 15–16); and 'the authority of the gospel is greater than the authority of the text' (Watson 1994, 234).

A Christian reading of scripture, according to this approach, will seek to be both receptive and critical, requiring both appreciation and suspicion, obedience and resistance. Of course, our understanding of the gospel is founded upon scripture and so there is a certain circularity involved in using our conception of the gospel as the basis for a critical reading of the Bible. Nevertheless, such a discerning approach, even if it unavoidably remains open and provisional, is an important basis both for a responsible presentation of the gospel and a responsible engagement with the world in which we live. The *Epworth* commentary series explicitly recognizes that our contemporary context is a multi-racial, multi-faith one. In such a context a Christian community must be prepared to listen and hear as much as to speak, and must be critical and cautious in the difficult but central task of discerning the word of the gospel among the diverse words of scripture. I hope that the commentary which follows may offer some help in that task.

II

INTRODUCTION TO I PETER

1. The significance of I Peter

I Peter is the first of the two short epistles in the New Testament attributed to the apostle Peter, one of the most prominent followers of Jesus and leaders of the early church. Even though, as we shall see, it is unlikely that Peter himself wrote either I or II Peter, these letters demonstrate something of the influence and authority which his name was felt to convey (see 2(i) below).

In the early church I Peter was clearly accepted and valued as a genuine and canonical epistle. Eusebius, who in the late third to early fourth century became the first person to compile a history of the church, lists the first epistle of Peter among the undisputed canonical writings of the New Testament, though he expresses doubts about II Peter (*EH* 3.3.1–3.4.3; 3.25.2; 6.25.8). The absence of a mention of I Peter in the Muratorian Canon, a second-century document from the Roman church, is puzzling, but there is no reason to suspect that there was any general doubt about the genuineness or authority of the epistle.

In the contemporary world, and certainly among biblical scholars, at least until recently, I Peter may be said to have suffered (though a good deal less than II Peter and Jude) from 'benign neglect' (Elliott 1976, 4). Although it contains much that is well-known and loved – consider 2.9–10 and 5.7, for example – it does not receive the same attention as the longer and more influential Pauline letters. Now, however, a considerable number of recent books and commentaries suggest that interest in I Peter is showing signs of healthy growth.

2. *Historical questions*

(i) *Who wrote I Peter?*

Perhaps the most obvious question about any piece of correspondence is that of authorship. In this case the letter clearly indicates that its author is the apostle Peter. However, scholars have long debated whether in fact the evidence supports this conclusion, or whether the letter is pseudonymous – written in Peter's name by someone else, claiming Peter's authority for a presentation of his teaching to a new generation of Christians (see Ch. I 3(i) above).

Evidence in favour of Peter's authorship of I Peter is the clear statement in 1.1, and also the phrase in 5.1, where the author describes himself as 'a witness of the sufferings of Christ'. It is of course possible that such phrases are merely a deliberate attempt to add touches of authenticity. Moreover, 5.1 probably does not intend to make a claim to special eye-witness status by the author at all, but rather to stress the calling and responsibilities which he and all the elders share in common (see on 5.1).

The reference to writing the letter 'through Silvanus' (5.12) is sometimes used to defend a modified form of Petrine authorship against some of the points raised as objections (see below). Peter, it is suggested, could have communicated the ideas to Silvanus, who wrote them in his own style (cf. Davids, 6–7); or perhaps Silvanus wrote the letter after Peter's death (Knoch, 22–25). The greater the role ascribed to Silvanus, of course, the greater the distance from Peter's own supposed 'authorship' and this hypothesis is perhaps something of a 'device of desperation' (Beare, 209) to save some kind of authenticity for the epistle (see Achtemeier, 9; further on 5.12).

Evidence concerning the date of the epistle (outlined in (iv) below) counts against the likelihood of Petrine authorship. If a date somewhat after 70CE is accepted as most likely, then unless (like Michaels) we reject the evidence suggesting that Peter died in the 60s CE, it is clear that the apostle Peter cannot have been the author of I Peter. Other evidence which points away from Peter's authorship includes the elegant Greek and the influence of Pauline language within the epistle – both perhaps unlikely features in a letter written by Peter the Galilean fisherman (see Achtemeier, 2–9; contrast Grudem, 24–33). These features could be explained by reference to the influence of Silvanus, if he actually wrote the letter, since he was a co-worker of Paul's (I Thess. 1.1; II Cor. 1.19; see on 5.12). However, the character, content, and apparent date of the letter may point instead to a somewhat later author, a leading member of the church at Rome, a man (I think we may assume, given the teaching contained in the epistle), who wrote in the name of Peter and also included mention of co-workers of Paul's (Mark and Silvanus; see on 5.12–14).

Of particular significance is the complete lack of evidence in I Peter that relations between Jews and Christians pose any theological problem. The letter simply applies to Christians terms which are clearly descriptions of Israel (e.g. 2.1–10; see esp. Achtemeier, 69–73) – so much so that Eusebius takes it as a Christian writing addressed to Jews (*EH* 3.1.2; 3.4.2). Paul could never forget the sharp theological problem presented by the apparent 'failure' of the Jews to respond to God's action in Christ, nor could he ignore their continued existence and particular status (Rom. 9–11). The Roman church in the 50s itself apparently faced the problem of tensions between Gentile and Jewish Christians (Rom. 14.1–15.13; see Watson 1986, 94–105). It seems unlikely that Peter, a Galilean Jew, pillar of the Jerusalem church (Gal. 2.9), apostle specifically to the circumcised (Gal. 2.7), who sided with the Jewish believers at Antioch (Gal. 2.11–16), if he were the author of I Peter, could have so completely transferred to the Christian community essentially Jewish self-identity descriptions, without at least some recognition of the pressing issue of God's promises to the ethnic people of Israel. The development of Christian self-identity, in other words, seems to have moved beyond that of the period during which Peter and Paul were alive.

If the assumption of pseudonymity is correct – and the evidence does not allow a firm conclusion either way – then why did the author(s) choose to write in the name of Peter? The answer probably lies in the increasing regard for Peter (especially after his martyrdom in Rome in the 60s) as the most significant leader of the earliest church (cf. Matt. 16.18). He was later listed as the first bishop of Rome (see Brown et al. 1973; Perkins 1994). The attribution of the letter to Peter is most likely intended, then, to strengthen its apostolic authority and its claim to be heeded (see Achtemeier, 41–42).

(ii) Where was I Peter written?

The letter seems clearly to indicate that it was written in Rome. While it is certainly possible to dispute this, most commentators agree that this is indeed the most likely point of origin for I Peter. The main pieces of evidence for this are the following:

(a) the use of the term Babylon in 5.13, a coded designation for Rome used in both Jewish and Christian literature after 70CE (see further (iv) below and on 5.13). Eusebius records explicitly this understanding of the reference to Babylon in I Peter (*EH* 2.15.2);

(b) the reference to Mark in 5.13, a co-worker of Paul's (see on 5.13) also connected in early church tradition with Peter in Rome. The second-century bishop Papias described Mark as Peter's 'interpreter', referred to them both being in Rome, and viewed the Gospel of Mark as essentially Peter's recollections (*EH* 3.39.15; 2.15.2);

(c) early church tradition which records that Peter ended his life in Rome (*I Clem* 5.4);

(d) I Peter's affinities with other documents connected with Rome; notably Paul's letter to the Romans, and especially *I Clement*, a letter sent from Rome to Corinth in the last decade of the first century.

(iii) To whom was I Peter sent?

I Peter names its addressees as the Christian believers scattered throughout the Roman provinces in northern Asia Minor (approximately the area of present-day Turkey), a wide geographical area (see further on 1.1–2). The intended recipients are apparently Gentile Christians (1.14, 18; 2.10; 3.6; 4.3–4; see commentary). I Peter is therefore a genuine letter, a 'circular' letter addressed to a dispersed group of Christian congregations (see further (v) and 3.(i) below).

(iv) When was I Peter written?

As with many of the New Testament writings, there is little indisputable evidence from which the date of I Peter can be ascertained. Some commentators (e.g. Cranfield, 10; Bigg, 87; Grudem, 35–37) argue for an early date (in the 60s CE). Others, such as F.W. Beare (28–38) suggest a date early in the second century. Many scholars favour a date somewhere between 70 and 100CE.

An early date would almost certainly be indicated if Peter himself were the author of the letter. Early church tradition points to the martyrdom of Peter (and Paul) in Rome during the reign of Nero, which ended in 68CE (see John 21.18–23; II Peter 1.13–14; *I Clem* 5.4; *EH* 2.25.6). Although it is possible to dispute this evidence and to argue that Peter may have lived in Rome beyond the death of Nero (so Michaels, lvii–lxi), the tradition seems most likely to be correct on this point. Therefore, if Peter was the author, the letter must have been written by 67CE at the latest. Conversely, if the letter should be dated somewhat later than this, for reasons outlined below, then Peter was almost certainly not personally responsible for writing it.

The main argument for a late (second-century) date is the possible link between the hostility towards Christians recorded in I Peter (suffering for 'the name of Christ'; see on 4.12–16) and the correspondence written around 110CE between Pliny, the governor of Bithynia (one of the provinces to which I Peter is addressed), and Trajan, emperor from 98–117, describing charges brought against Christians and their punishment merely for admitting being a Christian (Pliny, *Letters* 10.96–97; see Downing 1988). However, while the links are certainly notable, the kind of hostility I Peter refers to need not indicate official state persecution, nor does the Pliny-Trajan correspondence imply that accusations against Christians had only just begun to occur (cf. Michaels, lxvi).

There is considerably more evidence to support a date somewhere between 70 and 95CE, some of which points away from a later date, some away from an earlier date. Against a late (second-century) date are the following points:

(a) the lack of evidence for the emergence of the position of *episkopos* (overseer/bishop) in I Peter. *I Clement* (c.96CE), like I Peter, refers to 'presbyters' but also mentions the 'strife for the name of *episkopê*' (44.1; cf. 44.4). The letters of Ignatius (very early second century) clearly show that a system of monepiscopacy (oversight by one bishop, under whom are presbyters and deacons) is emerging, and Ignatius seeks to strengthen the position and authority of the bishop (e.g. Ignatius *Philadelphians* 7.1).

(b) I Peter may be known by *I Clement* (see Hagner 1973, 239–46) though their similarities may not prove literary dependence. Polycarp's epistle to the Philippians (early second century) certainly seems to know and cite I Peter (see Michaels, xxxii–iv). II Peter 3.1 also attests to the existence of an earlier letter attributed to the apostle. I Peter, then, is not likely to have been written any later than the early 90s, at least a short while before the writing of *I Clement*.

However, other evidence points away from an early date:

(a) The use of the term Babylon as a coded designation of Rome is most likely to have emerged only after the fall of Jerusalem to the Romans in 70CE (otherwise Thiede 1986). Only then do the analogies with the Babylonian exile make sense (see on 5.13).

9

(b) The references to 'presbyters' in 5.1–5 are significant, since this term for those in positions of leadership only appears in later New Testament writings (Acts 11.30; 14.23; 15.2 etc., dated probably to around 80–90CE; I Tim. 4.14; 5.17, 19; Titus 1.5, letters generally reckoned to have been written some time after Paul's death). I Peter, then, seems to reflect a time towards the end of the first century, when structures of leadership are developing in the church.

(c) The use in I Peter of the 'household code' form of instruction (2.18–3.7) also seems to suggest a later date. Such instruction is found only in the later New Testament letters (its earliest New Testament form is almost certainly Col. 3.18–4.1, which many regard as a post-Pauline letter). I Peter may have known Ephesians, generally regarded also as post-Pauline, and, if this is the case, must be later than Ephesians (see Mitton 1951, 176–97).

(d) The combination of sources in I Peter – Jewish scriptures, synoptic gospel traditions, Pauline formulations (see 3(ii) below) – points also to a time in which various strands of Christian material and tradition were being brought together and in which Pauline and Petrine perspectives, often in conflict in the earlier period, were being drawn together (a characteristic also of *I Clement*; cf. Frankemölle, 10–11).

(e) The name *Christianos* only appears three times in the New Testament: in Acts 11.26; 26.28; I Peter 4.16. Its absence from so many New Testament writings, its linguistic form and New Testament uses, and its adoption in later writings as a Christian self-description, seem to suggest that it originated as a hostile label for Christians in the later part of the New Testament period (see on 4.16). The hostility directed towards Christians – labelled *Christianoi* – which is evident in I Peter indicates their increasing recognition as a distinct group (as opposed to an inner-Jewish sect).

(f) Also relevant is the lack of evidence in I Peter that relations between Jews and Christians pose any theological problem; the Christian self-identity reflected in the epistle seems to have developed beyond that of the period during which Peter and Paul were alive (see 2(i) above).

While none of these points are indisputable, the weight of evidence seems to favour the period 75–95CE as the approximate date for I Peter.

(v) Why was I Peter written?

As the commentary itself will detail, the author's major concern was to instruct and encourage Christians who, because of their faith, were experiencing hostility, persecution and suffering (see also 4 below). The situation was not (yet) one of organized imperial persecution against Christians but rather one in which believers encountered hostility and accusation from their contemporaries because they were seen as rejecting the established patterns of religious and social life (see on 4.16). Women and slaves who became Christians independently of their head of household would be the cause of particular criticism and suspicion (see on 2.18–3.6). Informal criticism and accusation, moreover, could at times have resulted in Christians being brought before their local magistrates' courts and facing charges. In view of this difficult context the author sought to encourage his readers by affirming their Christian identity as the people of God (e.g. 2.4–10) and assuring them of the certain hope of salvation. He was also concerned that they should live upright and good lives even in the face of criticism and hostility.

I Peter, like *I Clement,* thus reveals the developing concern of the Roman church to act as a voice of encouragement and instruction to Christians dispersed across the empire, a concern which also represents the beginnings of a concentration of, and a claim to, power in Rome (see further Brown and Maier 1983).

3. Literary issues

(i) Style and genre

In the earlier part of this century various scholars developed theories about I Peter's origin as a baptismal homily or liturgy (e.g. Bornemann 1920), or more specifically, as part of the Easter baptismal eucharist used in the Roman church (Cross 1954). The integrity and unity of the letter were also questioned. The apparent break at 4.11, where a doxology appears, could indicate the juxtaposition of two originally separate documents, or, perhaps, the addition of a 'postscript' to an originally shorter writing. As evidence supporting this partition theory it was suggested that these two parts of I Peter reflected different situations, with 4.12–5.14 indicating an outbreak of real and severe persecution which was only a hypothetical possibility in the earlier parts of the letter (e.g. Moule 1957, 7–11; see overview in Achtemeier, 58–60; Cothenet 1988). However, recent scholarship has almost unanimously rejected these proposals. It is now widely agreed that I Peter is a genuine letter (albeit one which uses a variety of traditional materials and sources; see Reichert 1989; Martin 1992a). In J.N.D Kelly's words: 'it is, and always has been, a genuine unity, with a single consistent message, and was written as a real letter to the churches named in the address' (Kelly, 20; see further Reichert 1989). Its *genre* is therefore 'circular letter', a (pseudonymous) letter written to be delivered to a group of congregations spread over a wide geographical area, rather like the Jewish 'diaspora letters' sent to the people in exile (Jer. 29.4–23; II Macc. 1.1–10; for Christian examples see Acts 15.23–29; James 1.1).

I Peter is written in Greek of a quality somewhat more refined than that found in most of the New Testament (for analysis of its style and rhetoric see Thurén 1990; Martin 1992a). Its style is flowing, with many long sentences, linked to the next with a relative pronoun. The vocabulary includes 62 words found nowhere else in the New Testament, though a good many of these are found in the Septuagint (Achtemeier, 4; Bigg, 2–3).

(ii) Sources

The most obvious of I Peter's sources is indeed the Septuagint (LXX). Among the New Testament writings I Peter is one of the most saturated with citations from and allusions to the Jewish scriptures (see Best 1969, 217–75; Schutter 1989; Green 1993). Direct citations from the LXX include 1.16 (Lev. 19.2), 1.24–25 (Isa. 40.6–8) and 2.6 (Isa. 28.16), each of which is explicitly introduced as a quotation. Allusions are not always so easy to discern, but clear examples include the use of Isa. 53.4–12 in 2.22–25, and of Gen. 18.12 in 3.6. (For a fuller list see Davids, 24. Other citations and allusions are mentioned throughout the commentary.) In some cases it is clear that the passages to which I Peter alludes had already been the subject of Christian thought and reflection (e.g. Isa. 28.16 and 8.14, which are also linked together in Rom. 9.33).

A second clear source for I Peter is the Gospel tradition. As in most other early Christian epistles, including those of Paul, clear citations of this tradition are very rare (there are none in I Peter). References are made only by allusion (see Thompson 1991, 37–63). There is disagreement over the extent of the allusions to Gospel sayings and narratives in I Peter, but it is generally accepted that there are at least some examples (compare Gundry 1967; 1974 and Best 1970; more recently Maier 1985). Whether the author knew of these traditions specifically as Jesus-traditions or only as Christian teaching derived initially from such sayings is hard to determine. The clearest allusions are to parts of the Sermon on the Mount. Examples include: 2.12 (Matt. 5.16), 2.19–20 (Luke 6.32–34), 3.14 (Matt. 5.10; Luke 6.22), 4.14 (Matt. 5.11–12). The presence of allusions to both Matthew's and Luke's form of the sermon may suggest that I Peter is drawing on an earlier ('Q') version of this tradition (Michaels, xli).

Also to be mentioned as a source for I Peter is Pauline theology, though the extent of Pauline influence on I Peter is much debated. While some emphasize the 'Paulinism' of the author of I Peter (e.g. Beare, 44–45; Kümmel 1975, 423), much recent scholarship prefers to stress the distinctive contribution and theology of I Peter; it 'argues positively for the liberation of I Peter from its "Pauline bondage"' (Elliott 1976, 9). Certainly I Peter must not be viewed as a post-Pauline restatement of Pauline theology; after all, it is written in the name of Peter, not Paul! Yet neither should the links with Pauline theology and phraseology be ignored. The context from which I Peter was written should not be seen as comprising an exclusively 'Petrine school' (against Elliott 1976, 9; Soards 1988). In I Peter a variety of early Christian traditions are brought together and woven into new forms of theology and instruction (cf. Goppelt, 22). There are similarities between I Peter and the Pauline letters, especially Romans and Ephesians (see Michaels, xliii–xlv; Mitton 1951, 176–97). It would hardly be surprising if the author did indeed know Paul's letter to the Romans, though most commentators agree that the parallels do not provide clear evidence of literary dependence. The same is true of Ephesians, and indeed of James and Hebrews, other New Testament epistles which have points of close contact with I Peter. Nevertheless, whether our author directly knew any of Paul's letters or not, the influence of Pauline thought and language is clear (cf. Knoch, 17–18). Examples include 2.13–14 (Rom. 13.1–4), 2.24 (Rom. 6.11, 18), 4.6 (Rom. 8.10; 14.9; I Cor. 5.5), 4.7–11 (Rom. 12). Also to be noted are the instances of the typically Pauline 'in Christ' formula (3.16, 5.10, 5.14).

Pauline influence, then, should be neither denied, nor artificially elevated above the other various Christian traditions upon which I Peter draws. In the words of Ceslas Spicq, 'I Peter may be characterized as an "epistle of tradition"' (Spicq, 15). In many places the epistle takes up developing forms of Christian teaching and expressions of faith which also appear elsewhere. There are notable parallels with the pattern and content of instruction found in the letter of James (e.g. see on 5.5–9; compare James 4.6–10). The three major christological sections of the letter (1.18–21; 2.21–25; 3.18–22) utilize traditional credal statements concerning the person and achievement of Christ. The form of ethical instruction found in 2.18–3.7, known as the 'household code', is clearly based an established pattern of Christian teaching (cf. Col. 3.18–4.1).

All of these various sources show their influence upon the epistle, yet it does not lose its character as a genuine piece of correspondence. It is certainly not a 'scrapbook' of earlier fragments, nor should its creativity and originality be denied.

4. Content: themes and theology

The first epistle of Peter is indeed theological in the true sense of the word: its central focus and the foundation for all of its teaching is *God*. God the Father, the Holy One (1.15), in grace and mercy has chosen and called a holy people to inherit a glorious salvation (1.1–9; 2.4–10). God's power and might will ensure that his purposes are fulfilled – God is in control – and salvation will come very soon (1.5; 4.7, 11; 5.11). However, even though this provides the believers with a sure and certain ground for hope, they should regard God with reverent fear, for he is an impartial judge who stands ready to judge the whole world (1.17; 4.5). Indeed the evidence of God's judgment is already visible, particularly in the sufferings of the church (4.17).

The saving work of God is accomplished through his Son, *Jesus Christ*, who was destined before the foundation of the world (1.20) but appeared 'in this last period of time' (1.21). He suffered and died a sacrificial death for others, and was raised and vindicated at the right hand of God (see 1.18–21; 2.21–25; 3.18–22). A particular emphasis in I Peter is upon Christ as example; the calling of the Christian is to follow in his footsteps, through suffering to glory (2.21). Christ suffered without resisting his accusers, yet was ultimately vindicated by God, and his followers are to do the same, confident of the same eschatological reward (2.21–25; 4.1, 13).

In spite of the trinitarian expression found in 1.2, the *Spirit* is mentioned little in the rest of the epistle. The emphasis upon the Spirit's activity and upon the Spirit as the sign of new life in Christ, found in the Pauline epistles and in Luke-Acts, are absent here. Even the charismatic gifts, briefly mentioned in 4.10–11, are not attributed to the Spirit, as they are in I Cor. 12.4ff. In 3.18 and 4.6 being 'in the spirit' is contrasted with being 'in the flesh', and in 4.14 we find the assurance that the Spirit of God rests on those who are 'reviled for being Christians'. A particularly interesting reference is found in 1.11 where the Spirit ('of Christ') is said to have testified to the prophets of old concerning Christ. The following verse speaks of the Spirit's activity in the proclamation of the gospel.

For the believers whom I Peter addresses, life in the world is characterized by experiences of hostility and suffering and the author is concerned to offer hope and encouragement. The hope he offers is based on the conviction that their suffering will only be for a short time, for the time of final judgment and salvation is very near (4.7). Indeed, their sufferings are a sign that the final judgment has already begun (4.17) and will shortly encompass the whole world. Once they have faithfully borne their sufferings – which are described as God's will (3.17; 4.19) – they will receive the glory of eternal salvation (1.9; 5.4), an inheritance which is 'kept in heaven' (1.4). Thus I Peter, like much of the New Testament, is characterized by a sense of imminent expectation, by the conviction that the end of the ages had arrived. And this imminent expectation is presented as the ground for hope and endurance under conditions of difficulty and suffering.

The response of Christians to their present difficulties, however, is not only to be one of expectancy. They are also to live good lives, so as, hopefully, to silence the criticism and abuse of those who currently revile them (2.12; 3.1; 3.9–17). One of the letter's main aims is to exhort Christians to holy and upright living – to 'do good'. The foundation and motivation for this exhortation is manifold (see Thurén 1995): it is theological, rooted in the character of God (see 1.15–16); christological, rooted in the example of Christ (2.21–25); and it is based on assertions about Christian identity. Using terms and concepts drawn from the Jewish scriptures the author describes his readers as chosen, holy, a royal priesthood, and so on (see esp. 2.1–10). This *is* their Christian identity; therefore they must live as the people they are, and be holy in all their conduct. Many of the terms used describe the believers as a corporate community, bound together as the new-born children of God, and hence as a community alienated and estranged from the world.

Doing good, for I Peter, means submitting quietly and obediently within the social structures of the time, even when one is treated harshly or unjustly (2.13–3.6; note 2.18–20 and 3.6), in so far as that is possible without abandoning commitment to Christ. Such submissive conduct is urged especially upon slaves and wives, who were particularly likely to encounter harsh treatment and physical abuse, especially if they embraced a religion different from that followed by the head of their household. This pattern for Christian behaviour is 'based on the model of Jesus as a servant or slave who submits himself to unjust suffering and achieves vindication' (Corley 1995, 356).

The message of the letter may therefore be summarized: God, the God of power and grace, is the source of a great and glorious salvation, a new life, which Christians have entered by baptism and rebirth. Christians should not be surprised when they suffer, for Christ, whose path they follow, suffered too. Like him, they should endure undeserved suffering quietly and humbly, confident in the ultimate vindication of God, demonstrated already in the resurrection of Christ – a sure ground for hope. They must do good, and live a holy life, for it is better, if need be, to suffer (innocently) for doing good than (deservedly) for doing evil.

The first epistle of Peter therefore has its own contribution to make to the variegated theology of the New Testament. However, in spite of the lavish praise which it often receives (e.g. Marshall, 12), its theology, in my view, must be critically appraised by Christians living in a multi-racial, multi-faith context, and who are concerned to live responsibly and to see justice enacted in the world. Space does not permit a detailed discussion, let alone a resolution, of the relevant issues, but the following questions may encourage readers to think further for themselves.

First, on the question of Christian identity. I Peter describes the Christian community in thoroughly Jewish (scriptural) terms: the Christian church is God's chosen people, God's spiritual house, and so on. It does so without giving any indication of the fact that these self-descriptions belong to another faith-community – to the Jews (see Richardson 1969, 171–75; Achtemeier, 67–73). It does not, therefore, explicitly deny the Jewish people their own identity, nor explicitly claim that the church has superseded Israel as God's chosen people. Yet the implication, surely, is that 'the Church has taken over the inheritance . . . of Israel' (Richardson 1969, 174). So, can Christians who understand their identity as God's people in terms suggested by I Peter still find ways of respecting the faith and identity of their Jewish neighbours? Can they avoid the implication that they have simply 'replaced' Israel as the people 'claimed by God for his own' (see further on 1.10–12 and 2.4–10)?

Secondly there is the question of suffering. I Peter clearly indicates that the suffering experienced by the believers in Asia Minor should be seen as the will of God, even though its immediate cause is the hostile and wicked people in the world. So does God 'will' suffering, even innocent and unjust suffering? This may be linked with the question of election: I Peter not only presents the positive side of election, the choosing of the believers as God's own, but also hints at the negative side to this doctrine, divine appointment to a fate of 'stumbling' (see on 2.8). Like much of the biblical literature, I Peter holds in an awkward tension the twin poles of human responsibility and divine sovereignty. The author wishes to affirm that God is sovereign – the world is in no way out of control – but in so doing he raises the difficult question of God's responsibility for, even God's will for, innocent suffering and unbelief. Should we not insist that the suffering which human beings inflict upon one another is contrary to, an offence against, the will of God (see on 3.17)?

Thirdly there are the difficulties raised by the imminent expectation which characterizes I Peter and indeed many of the New Testament writings. The author urges his readers to quiet submission and patient endurance on the grounds that the end will soon come and with it an end to suffering. Of course the end did not come, and there is no more sign now than there was then that the agonies of the world are nearing an end. II Peter recognizes the problem, but its answer is hardly a comfort for those longing for an end to their suffering and oppression (II Peter 3.3–9). The issue is not only whether the hope which the author encouraged is merely 'pie-in-the-sky' but also whether using such a hope as a motivation for quiet submission amid the injustices and sufferings of the world does not place I Peter rather firmly into the role of 'opiate of the masses', to use Karl Marx's phrase. In other words, isn't the impact of I Peter's teaching to encourage the poor and oppressed to accept (joyfully!) the agonizing conditions of their lives, comforted by the thought that glory and peace await them in heaven? It is no answer to such criticism merely to assert that I Peter's hope is not 'pious optimism' but 'a deep conviction about the return of Christ', not 'an irrelevant opiate to dull the pain' but 'a careful evaluation of present behavior in the light of future goals and an unseen reality' (Davids, 19, 66). Christian hope can only obviate Marx's criticism, it seems to me, when its eschatological vision becomes not a reason for quietly accepting the world as it is, but precisely a vision which contradicts the world as it is and functions as a real and pressing demand for change. The vision of the kingdom of God is meant, as it did in the ministry of Jesus, to invade the present, and to transform it, just as Martin Luther King's 'dream' was not intended as an opiate to pacify the black masses, but as a vision of the future which inspired and demanded real change (see further on 2.18–25; 3.22).

This issue is linked with a fourth, which concerns the social teaching of I Peter. Good conduct, for I Peter, means submitting quietly and obediently within the social structures of the time, even when one is treated harshly or unjustly. And this teaching is directed especially to slaves and wives – to those who are already in a socially weaker position. Whether commentators and theologians regard this teaching favourably or not depends a good deal on their own sympathies and commitments. Ralph Martin, for example, correctly sees that in I Peter 'there is no bid to overthrow the social order . . . no call to disobedience, whether civil or activist . . . The ethical admonitions operate within the limit of "what is possible" . . . to stay within the contemporary social structures as submissive and peace-making' (Martin 1994, 130). The epistle, for him, may therefore have relevance in 'several parts of the world to which the Christian gospel is introduced as a provocation to resistance, a disturbance within the social order' (p.90). It is hardly a surprise, therefore, to find a rather different judgment in a recent feminist commentary: 'The basic message of I Peter does not reflect God's liberating Word' (Corley 1995, 357). Kathleen Corley draws attention especially to the dangers inherent in I Peter's use of Jesus, presented as the silent, submissive, suffering servant, as a model for Christians, especially women and slaves, to imitate. In her view, 'such imitation merely perpetuates a cycle of victimization, violence, and abuse in domestic situations' (p.354). Her penetrating critique of I Peter offers important reasons why the letter's theology should not be uncritically absorbed (see further on 2.11–3.12).

It is my hope, therefore, that those who study this epistle will do so carefully, critically, and responsibly, not unaware of the dangers as well as the value of its theology. Such an interpretative stance, as I suggested in the general introduction to the three epistles, should not be seen as un-Christian. On the contrary, it represents a Christian commitment to discern within the varied witnesses of scripture the word of the gospel for today.

5. The structure of I Peter

III

COMMENTARY ON I PETER

Opening greetings
   1.1–2

The normal form for the opening of a Greek letter was a simple statement giving the name of the sender(s), the name of the recipient(s),
and the single word 'greetings' (*chairein*; for New Testament
examples see Acts 15.23; 23.26; James 1.1). Like most other New
Testament epistles, I Peter broadly follows this pattern but expands
it somewhat.

1.1   The opening verses of I Peter reveal what kind of writing it is:
a letter sent from *Peter* to the Christians scattered throughout the
provinces of northern Asia Minor. *Peter* (the Greek translation of the
Aramaic 'Cephas') is identified as *apostle of Jesus Christ*, a concise
designation which 'is intended to cloak the message of the epistle in
an authority derived from Christ' (Achtemeier, 80). The recipients
are described using three terms, all of which reflect important
themes developed in the letter. First they are referred to as *chosen*,
'elect', a label often used of Israel (e.g. Deut. 4.37; 7.6–8; Ps. 78.68;
135.4; Isa. 41.8–9; 44.1) and in the New Testament of Christians
(Rom. 8.33; Col. 3.12; I Thess. 1.4; Titus 1.1). Secondly, they are said
to be *living as aliens*, or 'exiles', people who live temporarily in a
foreign land (cf. Gen. 23.4; Ps. 39.12; passages which may well
underlie the author's form of expression here and in 1.17 and 2.11).
The writer is referring not to the social or political status of the letter's recipients (against Elliott 1981, 21–100; see Feldmeier 1992), but
rather to his conviction that as Christians they are now 'strangers
and aliens' in the world (cf. Heb. 11.13), abused and misunderstood
by those amongst whom they live. The consequence of their election
by God is their alienation from the world. Thirdly the readers are
described as *scattered*, a translation of the Greek noun *diaspora*, used

in Jewish literature as a technical term for those Jews dispersed among the nations, in exile from their true home in Jerusalem (e.g. Deut. 28.25 [LXX]; 30.4; Ps. 147.2; Isa. 49.6; II Macc. 1.27; note James 1.1). Here, as in much of I Peter, Jewish terms are used to describe the situation of the (Gentile) Christians addressed.

Next the areas to which the letter is being sent are listed. The names probably refer to the Roman provinces in Asia Minor north of the Taurus mountains. The only puzzle is why *Pontus* and *Bithynia* should be listed separately, since they comprised a single province after 64BCE. A possible explanation is that the order in the list reflects the travel route intended for the messenger who delivered the letter, a roughly circular tour which ended up back in the same province. Whether these provinces had ever been evangelized by Peter, or by those connected closely with him, is impossible to determine, but they comprise an area in which Paul's activity was limited (Acts 16.6–10 describes Paul being prevented from entering Asia and Bithynia; note also II Tim. 1.15). Perhaps the geographical destination of the letter explains in part why it was sent in Peter's name.

1.2   The author proceeds briefly to spell out the basis of his readers' election (not the basis of Peter's apostleship, though this is grammatically possible) and in doing so introduces the themes which are developed in more detail in 1.3–2.10. Here he makes a threefold declaration which has a notably trinitarian shape, though it does not reflect the later form of the doctrine of the Trinity: their status as Christians is founded upon *the foreknowledge of God the Father, the consecrating work of the Holy Spirit,* and their *sprinkling with* the *blood* of *Jesus Christ.* God's foreknowledge implies not mere knowledge in advance, but divine purpose and choice (cf. Acts 2.23; Rom. 8.29; 11.2). (For a discussion of the negative side to this idea see on 2.8.) God is father both in relation to Jesus Christ his son, and also to all those who have received new birth (1.3). The work of the Spirit (not specifically described here as 'holy'; 'holy' is added by the REB) is sanctification, holiness, 'setting apart' (cf. I Cor. 1.30, I Thess. 4.4, II Thess. 2.13). The purpose, and in a sense the result, of this divine work of salvation, is *obedience* (which should stand on its own and not be linked with Jesus Christ, as in REB, and many other translations: *obedience to Jesus Christ*; see Kelly, 43–44; Michaels, 11–12). Accepting the gospel, which cannot be conceived of apart from living a holy (obedient) life, may be described as an act of obedience (1.22; cf. Acts 6.7; Rom. 1.5). Conversely, I Peter describes those who do not believe as 'disobedient to the word' (2.8; also 3.1; 4.17). The third part of this pre-trinitarian formulation points to the saving effect of Christ's death. The result of this death for the believer is here described as a 'sprinkling with the blood of Jesus Christ', an image of cleansing and purification which recalls the operation of the Jewish sacrificial system. Exodus 24.3–9 records the covenant sacrifices made by Moses at Sinai: 'He took the blood and flung it over the people' (v.8). Notably this follows the people's affirmation that they will be obedient (vv.3, 7). So I Peter implies that a new covenant community has been created, sealed by obedience and the sprinkling of the blood of Christ. The specific language of sprinkling derives from the ritual described in Numbers 19, where blood (v.4), ashes (v.9) and water (vv.13, 20, 21) are all sprinkled for the purposes of purification. This sacrificial imagery of Christ's death is developed further in Heb. 9.11–27, where the parallels with Ex. 24.3–9 are more explicit.

Instead of the concise greetings frequently found in Greek letters, I Peter uses the characteristic Christian phrase *grace and peace to you*, used in Paul's epistles and other early Christian writings (e.g. I Cor. 1.3; II Cor. 1.2; Gal. 1.3). The standard Greek *chairein* is replaced by the favourite Christian term *charis* (grace) and linked with the Jewish greeting *shalom* (peace, Gk: *eirene*). The precise form of the greeting here shows close similarity to Jewish letter-writing. The verb used by the author (not found in Paul's greetings) has earlier Jewish parallels (Dan. 4.1 and 6.26 [LXX]), and is found in the Christian greeting in Jude 1, II Peter 1.2 and *I Clement*. The mood of the verb – expressing a wish, in effect a prayer – is best preserved in a translation like the NRSV: 'may grace and peace be yours in abundance.'

Foundations of the Christian life
1.3–2.10

Thanksgiving for a glorious salvation
1.3–12

I Peter's opening greetings are followed by a thanksgiving. Ancient letters often followed their opening greetings with an expression of concern for the health and wellbeing of the recipients, sometimes declaring gratitude to the gods for their welfare and the prayer that it would continue (cf. Kelly, 46; White 1972). Here the thanksgiving takes a clearly Christian form – a blessing of God for all he has done – which serves as an introduction to the main body of the letter. In these verses (vv.3–12) a major theme of the letter is made clear: 'hope and joy despite distress' (Knoch, 41). The whole passage from v.3 to v.12 comprises 'one complete sentence-thought, structured with stylistic care in a series of relative clauses' (Goppelt, 79). It divides into four short sections (vv.3–5, vv.6–7, vv.8–9, vv.10–12), each of which is linked to what precedes by a relative pronoun.

1.3 The exclamation of praise with which the author opens his thanksgiving is based upon a form of blessing common in the Jewish scriptures (e.g. Ps. 72.18: 'Blessed be the LORD God'; cf. Gen. 24.27; I Sam. 25.32; etc.; note Luke 1.68 and II Cor. 11.31) and found in the second-person form in Jewish liturgy ('Blessed are you, Lord our God, King of the universe . . .'). I Peter adopts the Christianized Pauline form of this blessing as it appears in II Cor. 1.3 and Eph. 1.3, where *God* is identified as *Father of our Lord Jesus Christ*. God is here praised specifically for the *new birth* granted to all believers. By specifying that it was given to *us*, the author underlines the common experience which is his own and that of his readers, whereas in the rest of the passage he refers to 'you', that is, the readers of the letter. This new birth has been given according to God's *great mercy* – probably a reference to God's steadfast kindness and covenant-love described by the Hebrew word *ḥesed*, which is translated in the LXX by the Greek word for mercy (*eleos*) used here (cf. Ex. 20.6; 34.6; Joel 2.13 etc.).

I Peter describes God's merciful action in 'causing us to be born anew', using a verb (*anagennaô*) which appears in the New Testament only here and in 1.23. The notion that Christian initiation involves being 'born again' is, however, found elsewhere, notably in the Gospel and letters of John (John 1.13; 3.5, 7; I John 2.29; also James 1.18). In Titus 3.5–7 we also find a passage similar to I Peter 1.3–4, where mercy, new birth, and hope are linked together, as they are here. The language of new birth and the references to water and the spirit (Titus 3.5; John 3.5) suggest a link with baptism, which symbolized and enacted this act of rebirth, of leaving behind old ways of evil and corruption and becoming newborn children of obedience (see 1.13–2.3; 3.21). Yet the fact that the letter reminds its readers of their baptism, their new birth, their transformed lives, and of the consequences of God's saving action, does not mean that it should be regarded as a record of specifically baptismal teaching, as some scholars once thought (see Ch. II 3(i)). What is clear is that the author regards the saving action of God in Christ as the basis and motivation for Christian faith and conduct – as the foundations of the Christian life.

The new birth, grounded in the deep and gracious love of God, is brought about through *the resurrection of Jesus Christ from the dead*. The resurrection, for I Peter, is both a foundation and a guarantee of God's salvation, a sure ground for hope and certainty even (and especially) in suffering, for Christ himself endured suffering but was raised to glorious new life by God his father. The author now offers a threefold description of what it is that Christians have been born into. There are three phrases introduced by the Greek word *eis* (into): into a living hope (v.3), into an incorruptible inheritance (v.4), into a salvation which is to be revealed at the end of time (v.5; cf. Michaels, 19). (The REB rather obscures this structure by repeating the word 'hope' at the beginning of v.4; the NAB retains it most clearly.) The first affirmation, then, is that they have been born *into a living hope*. Hope is a key word in I Peter ; it is for the author central to Christian existence. The description of the hope as *living* is appropriate in view of the themes which have been mentioned: because of the resurrection Christ is now alive, and through their new birth, the Christian believers have begun a new life.

1.4–5   The *inheritance* which is promised is not an earthly one, like the land promised to the patriarchs (Deut. 12.9; 15.4; 19.10) or 'the earth' promised to the meek in Matt. 5.5. Rather it is *reserved in heaven for you*; it is an inheritance which lies beyond the present world with its evil and suffering. It is described with three 'negative' adjectives, all beginning *a-* in Greek: 'imperishable, undefiled, unfading' (NRSV). The inheritance cannot be spoilt or corrupted; it is kept pure in heaven. Not only the inheritance is guarded, but *you* also *are under the protection of his power*. This is where the emphasis in this phrase should fall – upon the protecting power of God, and not upon the faith of the believer, as is implied by the REB's rendering: *Because you put your faith in God* . . . God's guarding power works 'through faith/faithfulness' (Gk: *dia pisteôs*) which probably implies that Christians remain under God's protection by putting their faith and trust in God, though it might refer instead to God's sure faithfulness in continuing to guard them (Horrell 1997a). Either way the readers are assured that God is at work not only guarding their inheritance in heaven, but also, despite appearances to the contrary – the harsh realities of hardship and suffering – protecting them by his power. This is the only explicit reference to God's power, *dunamis*, in the epistle.

Thirdly, believers have been born into *salvation*, though the fulfilment and consummation of this is awaited. Salvation will mean the end of trials and suffering and entry into the promised inheritance. It remains, for the moment, a future hope, yet it is 'ready to be revealed in the last time' (NRSV). Although the difference in meaning is slight, the phrase is better understood as 'salvation . . . ready to be revealed' (NRSV), than as *salvation now in readiness*, which will be revealed (REB; see BAGD, 316; Goppelt, 87 n.28). God's salvation is indeed 'prepared', but by emphasizing the fact that it is 'ready to be revealed' the author demonstrates his conviction that *the end of time* – the day of God's decisive intervention – is very near (otherwise Parker 1994). The failure of this imminent hope to materialize, either in the first century or in any century since, has always been something of a problem for Christian faith (see Ch. II 4.; and on II Peter 3.3–9).

1.6   *This is cause for great joy* (v.6), the author asserts. But what precisely is 'this'? As often in I Peter, a sentence begins with a relative pronoun (literally 'in which/whom you rejoice . . .') without it being quite clear exactly what is referred to. Davids (p.54) is wrong to state that '"this" agrees grammatically in Greek with "hope", v.3, not "inheritance" or "salvation"', since all three nouns are feminine in Greek and the relative pronoun is masculine or neuter. The two real possibilities are that 'in which/whom' refers either to the whole of vv.3–5 (i.e. 'you rejoice in this great salvation'), or more specifically to the preceding phrase *at the end of time* (it is unlikely to refer back to God, v.3, as is occasionally suggested). REB's translation implies the former, but the latter is perhaps more likely. This requires understanding the verb 'you rejoice' as future in sense, with the meaning 'at the end of time, when your salvation is complete, you will rejoice greatly' (so Goppelt, 88–89; Martin 1992b; otherwise Achtemeier, 100). There should indeed be joy in the present, a joy which anticipates with confidence the unspeakable joy which will abound when Christ's glory is finally and fully revealed. But the time of *great joy* lies in the future, at the consummation of God's saving purposes on the final day. This distinction is made clear in 4.13 (note also 1.8;

these are the three places in I Peter where the verb *agalliaô*, 'to rejoice exceedingly', is found. In the LXX and the New Testament it often has an eschatological reference, looking forward to the time when God is revealed as Lord and Judge, and when salvation comes; e.g. Ps. 96.12; 97.1; 98.4; Isa. 12.6.).

Great joy is anticipated *even though for a little while* yet the readers of the letter must *suffer trials of many kinds*, the first mention in the letter of the theme of suffering. These trials are no merely hypothetical possibility, but are actually occurring now. It is not that the believers *may have had to suffer*, as the REB renders this phrase, suggesting that the trials may already lie in the past. Rather, 'for a short time yet' (NJB) they must endure the trials which have already begun and will indeed continue. The author is convinced, however, that it will only be for a little while, for the day of salvation is surely close. These trials are a part of what 'must be' (cf. Mark 13.7). They come under the control of God; they may even be regarded as God's will – 'divine necessity' (Michaels, 29). While there is perhaps some comfort intended in the affirmation that God remains in control of the whole process of history, the ultimate goal of which is salvation, this theology of suffering raises some difficulties (see Ch. II 4 and on 3.17).

1.7 For the author, these trials are also serving a purpose; they are testing the genuineness of the readers' *faith*. Effectively as a parenthesis (see NRSV; NIV) he compares faith to *gold*, pointing out both difference and similarity: faith is *much more precious than perishable gold*; yet, like gold, faith too is tested by *fire* (cf. I Cor. 3.12–15). The reasoning is from the lesser to the greater: if it is important for gold – a perishable material substance – to be tested, how much more important is it for faith to be tried? And faith which proves itself genuine, faith which endures, will result in *praise, glory, and honour*. While these things are rightly and usually accorded to God, those who have been faithful will themselves receive praise, glory and honour from God at the end, *when Jesus Christ is revealed*.

I Peter's way of describing the positive role of trials in testing genuine faith is closely paralleled in James 1.2–4, though there are differences (and James 1.13 is careful to insist that God does not 'test' anyone; contrast Wisd. 3.5–6). The linguistic similarities seem to point to shared Christian tradition, a way of interpreting persecution and suffering which both letters share in common (cf. also Matt. 5.11–12; Rom. 5.1–5; 8.18; II Cor. 4.17). The roots of these ideas are found in the Jewish scriptures, in passages such as Ps. 66.10 and

Prov. 17.3, though they develop most clearly in Jewish writings dating from the second and first centuries BCE. Wisd. 3.4–6 and Sirach 2.1–5 form especially close parallels to I Peter 1.6–7.

1.8–9 The mention of Jesus Christ, and of the expectation that he will be revealed, forms the link into v.8. What is yet to be revealed is now unseen. Indeed, this is the very nature of faith and hope, and the writer makes the point about the lack of sight twice: *You have not seen him* (in the past), *yet you love him*. Even *now without seeing him* (this time the verb is in the present tense) you are *trusting* (putting your faith) *in him*. Only the first generation of disciples could claim to have seen Christ (John 1.14; 20.29), though Paul also records his seeing the risen Christ 'last of all . . .' (I Cor. 15.8). And even for the 'eye-witnesses' (Luke 1.2) the glory that is yet to be remains unseen – it is a matter of hope (Rom. 8.24–25; I Cor. 2.9; II Cor. 4.16–5.10). So marvellous is what is anticipated that it is the cause for *a glorious joy too great for words*. In a sense this boundless joy belongs primarily to the future (see on 1.6; 4.13; Michaels, 34; Martin 1992b), it awaits the consummation, 'but for the writer the joy of the End overflows into the present' (Kelly, 57). Here we meet the Christian paradox: 'already but not yet', salvation now, yet still awaited. The paradox is evident also in v.9. Already, in a sense, *you are reaping* (attaining, receiving) *the harvest of your faith*. But this 'goal' (a better rendering of the Greek word *telos* than REB's 'harvest') has not yet been reached. Because of his sense of eschatological expectancy the writer can blur the distinction between present and future; 'the hoped for salvation is already in process of being realized' (Kelly, 58). The goal, he believes, will soon be attained, and the goal is *salvation for your souls*. I Peter's reference to 'souls' should not be taken to imply a dualistic view of the human person – a body which dies, a soul which lives on. Here the word 'soul' (Gk: *psuche*) means the self, the whole person (3.20; 4.19; cf. Gen. 2.7; Matt. 6.25; Rom. 13.1; see Achtemeier, 104).

1.10–12 After his description of the great and glorious salvation which is already but not yet the possession of the Christian believers, the writer looks back to the past, when the prophets of old glimpsed the divine plan of salvation through Christ. In so doing he emphasizes both the fact that God's foreknown plan was always for this time of salvation (cf. 1.2) and especially that it is now 'to you', the readers of the epistle, that this anticipated grace has been given: 'his concern throughout is to assure his readers that they belong to the age of fulfilment even though they are still waiting for their salvation' (Michaels, 39). For *this salvation was the subject of intense search* (the author emphasizes the intensity and diligence of the inquiry by using two Greek verbs which convey essentially the same meaning) *by the prophets*. The prophets I Peter has in mind are clearly the prophets of the Jewish scriptures, the Christian Old Testament, and not Christian prophets prophesying after the time of Christ's death and resurrection, as has sometimes been suggested (e.g. Selwyn, 134). The only reason for assuming the latter is the reference to *the spirit of Christ in them,* which is a striking way to speak of Jewish prophets before the time of Christ. Nevertheless, as we shall see below, this is indeed what the writer does. If the prophets were Christian prophets then clearly they cannot have been predicting the sufferings of Christ and the glories which would follow (v.11). Rather, as the REB unfortunately suggests, they must have been talking of *the sufferings in Christ's cause* which are the lot of the readers of the letter. However this is a most unlikely interpretation, not least in view of the contrast between 'the prophets' and 'those who brought you the gospel' (v.12; see below).

Throughout vv.10–12 the author is presenting a Christian, indeed a christological, reading of the Jewish scriptures; their purpose is to point to Christ. Indeed, a central claim of the early Christians was that what had happened to Jesus was 'in accordance with the scriptures' (Luke 24.27; I Cor. 15.3–4). The focus and content of the prophetic message of scripture, according to I Peter, was *the grace of God* to be given in Christ at the eschatological time of salvation, to be given 'to you'. The particular concern of the prophets, according to the author, was with *the time and the circumstances* in which these things would happen. Attempts to interpret prophecy in this way, discerning clues as to the timing of the fulfilment of the eschatological vision, are found in Jewish literature dating from the last two centuries BCE and the first century CE (see Dan. 9.1–27; 12.6–13; II Esd. 4.33–46; 4QpHab 7.1–13, the commentary found at Qumran on the book of Habbakuk). The author of I Peter shares with such literature the belief that the focus of the ancient prophecies was indeed the 'end-time'. According to I Peter, however, the foresight which the ancient prophets had was given by *the spirit of Christ in them.* The idea that prophecy is inspired and enabled by God's spirit is frequently found in both Jewish and Christian literature (e.g. Num. 11.25–29; I Sam. 10.6–13; Neh. 9.30; Joel 2.28; Luke 1.67; Eph. 3.5 etc.). But here the writer specifically names it 'the spirit of *Christ*' (a phrase found only here and at Rom. 8.9). This indicates both an apparent, if undeveloped, belief in Christ's preexistence (cf. esp. John 1.1–14) and, coupled with this, a 'reading back' of Christ's presence into the life of ancient Israel (cf. I Cor. 10.4). Moreover, what the spirit of Christ *foretold* – that to which the prophets pointed – was specifically 'the sufferings destined for Christ' (NRSV) and *the glories to follow* (cf. I Peter 2.21–25, reading Isa. 53.4–12 as a description of the sufferings of Christ). These *glories* refer to the resurrection and heavenly vindication of Christ, and to his final revelation and the consummation of salvation, for which the readers eagerly wait. For *it was disclosed to* the prophets of old that their ministry (the Greek verb *diakoneô* was *not for their benefit but for yours* (v.12; note the emphasis again on 'for you'). But *now*, according to the author, is the time of fulfilment and of revelation, for *now* these things *have been openly announced to you* ('for you' again!), by those who proclaimed *the gospel*. This proclamation too was empowered by the spirit, this time described as *the Holy Spirit sent from heaven*.

The greatness and wonder of the things which have been proclaimed to the readers of the epistle is further emphasized: not only were they foreseen by the prophets of old but even *angels long to glimpse* them. The readers stand at the climactic point in history, when the mysterious saving purposes of God are finally being brought to completion, and the angels, like the prophets before, yearn to see the plan laid bare.

So the author claims that the goal, the fulfilment, to which Jewish prophecy pointed was the Christ-event, and that the recipients of grace and salvation are his Gentile readers. Clearly this constitutes a christological claim over the Jewish scriptures, the Christian 'Old Testament'. Christ is the one to whom the scriptures point and the Christians are the ones whose is the benefit. This may seem an arrogant and presumptuous claim; certainly it is a claim which makes dialogue and understanding between Christians and Jews difficult. But it is clearly a claim the New Testament writers make: the (Jewish) scriptures were written for *our* instruction, Paul insists, for *we*, the believers in Christ, are the ones on whom the ends of the ages have arrived (I Cor. 10.11). Christians today must somehow come to terms with the fact that the first century CE did not turn out to be 'the end of the ages' – at least not in the way the first Christians expected. They must also, if they wish to respect and understand their Jewish neighbours, find some way of holding the Christian belief that the biblical story reaches its goal in Christ while not denying that it may be read in other ways too. How else can they avoid the conclusion that the Jews have simply 'missed the point' (cf. Rom. 9.30–10.21)?

A Call to Holiness
1.13–25

After outlining the greatness of the hope, the inheritance, and the salvation which are God's gracious gift to those who believe, the author proceeds, for the first time in the letter, to exhortation and instruction based upon and motivated precisely by this great work of God. The themes and ideas of 1.1–12 are picked up again, only now the emphasis is upon the Christians' responsibility to live a life worthy of that calling.

1.13   The fact that the writer is now going to draw out the implications which follow from what precedes is shown by the word *therefore*, which is the first word of v.13 in the Greek. The readers are instructed to prepare their minds *for action*. The image is literally that of gathering up the long main garment and fastening it around the waist, thus being ready to move quickly (REB's *stripped for action* does not quite convey this picture; cf. Ex. 12.11; Luke 12.35). As part of this readiness they are also to be *fully alert* (see on 4.7). But the main imperative in this verse is to *fix your hopes on the grace which is to be yours when Jesus Christ is revealed* (cf. the 'living hope' described in 1.3). As the REB's translation shows, the focus of this hope lies in the future (although a present tense verb is used; as in 1.6, 1.8 and 1.9). Indeed 1.7 clearly points forward to the time when praise, glory and honour will be received, using the same phrase: 'when Jesus Christ is revealed'. Although Jesus Christ has already appeared, in one sense, in this, the last of the ages (1.20), the salvation and revelation of the last day are still eagerly awaited (1.5).

1.14   The phrase which the REB renders *Be obedient to God your Father* is neither an imperative nor does it mention God the Father. Literally translated v.14 begins: 'As children of obedience'. This is a characteristically semitic form of words using a noun which refers to 'an essential property or role of the persons described' (Kelly, 67; cf. Michaels, 56. For examples see Deut. 13.13; I Kings 6.13; II Sam. 7.10; Isa. 17.3, 9; Hos. 10.9; Matt. 9.15; Mark 2.19; Eph. 2.3). Obedience should characterize the readers of this epistle, for this is an essential feature of their new status as God's chosen ones (1.2). On this basis they are given two closely-linked instructions, one negative (v.14), one positive (v.15). The first is *not to let your characters be shaped any longer by the desires you cherished in your days of ignorance* (v.14). The only other use of this verb in the New Testament is in Rom. 12.2, where a similar instruction is given. The word translated 'desires' is used in the New Testament both of good and of sinful desires (cf. Phil. 1.23 and Gal. 5.16). Here the desires are clearly those of a former life which must be left behind (cf. 4.3). I Peter elsewhere specifies such desires as 'fleshly desires' (2.11), 'human desires' (4.2). The description of the readers' past as *days of ignorance* points to their status as Gentiles and not Jews: in both Jewish and Christian writings 'it is a routine characterization of the Gentiles' who 'do not know God' (Kelly, 68).

1.15 The positive command of v.15 is grounded in the character of God. *He who called you is holy*. The Greek words might also be understood slightly differently: 'like the Holy One who called you . . .' (see Michaels, 51, 58; Bigg, 114; NJB). The difference in meaning is not great, but if the latter interpretation is correct we have here an example of the use of a Jewish title for God, 'the Holy One', found elsewhere in the New Testament only at I John 2.20 (see II Kings 19.22; Job 6.10; Prov. 9.10 etc.). God's holiness is affirmed throughout the Bible (e.g. Isa. 6.3; Rev. 4.8 – the two occurrences of the phrase 'holy, holy, holy'). To be holy means to be 'separate', 'marked off', distinct from what is common and in ordinary use (Cranfield, 35). To be set apart for God, holy like God, implies exclusive loyalty, devotion and dedication, and also, in conformity with God's character, ethical and pure behaviour. Hence the instruction: *be holy in all your conduct*. Central to early Christian self-understanding was the notion of being 'holy ones' (Gk: *hagioi*, 'saints'; see e.g. Acts 9.13; Rom. 1.7; I Cor. 1.2; Heb. 3.1), though the term later came to be applied only to specific and venerated figures. A similar self-understanding was also characteristic of the community at Qumran (1QS 8.20; CD 20.2).

1.16 As is often the pattern in I Peter, having made his point, the author backs it up with a quotation of scripture. The precise quotation comes from Lev. 19.2 (LXX), though the phrase runs 'like a refrain through the book of Leviticus' (Kelly, 69; Lev. 11.44, 45; 20.7, 26). Leviticus 17–26 is often labelled the 'law of holiness', or Holiness Code, intended to direct 'Israel in a way of life other than that of the people in whose midst they dwell', a concern which is central to I Peter too (Achtemeier, 122). The future tense (*you shall be holy*) functions here as an imperative: 'Be holy'. The quotation from Leviticus, from the commands given to Moses for all the people of Israel, is a further example of the subtle but frequent use of 'Exodus imagery' throughout this passage (1.13–25): clothing gathered up in readiness (Ex. 12.11), obedience and holiness, and, as we shall see below, allusions to God's work of redemption and to the Passover lamb (vv.18–19).

1.17 A further reason for living an obedient, holy life is given in v.17, which stands as a somewhat distinct unit of thought. For the first time in the epistle the author sounds a note of warning, even·of threat (Thurén 1995, 113). For the one whom Christians call upon as *Father* (cf. Matt. 6.9; I Cor. 1.2 etc.) is one *who judges everyone impartially*. God's impartiality is often asserted in the Bible (Deut. 10.17; Eph. 6.9; Col. 3.25); here it serves as a warning not to become presumptuous or complacent because of a relationship with God as Father. For everyone will be judged *on the basis of what they have done* (cf. Ps. 62.12). It would be easy to contrast this idea with the Pauline theme of 'justification by faith'. Paul, however, pronounces similar warnings against complacency and sin (see Rom. 11.20; I Cor. 3.13–14; 6.9–11). The consequence of God's impartial judging is that all people, Christians included, *must live in awe of him* (Gk: *phobos*, 'fear, awe, or reverence'; cf. Rom. 11.20). Fear of God is a motivation for upright living *during your time on earth* (cf. Prov. 1.7). Time on earth, the author reminds his readers, is but a temporary phase of 'living as aliens' (see 1.1; 2.11) and their pattern of life in the world should be shaped by fear of divine judgment as well as the hope of heavenly glory.

1.18 Following two motivations for living good lives – the imitation of God's holiness and the fear of judgment – the author proceeds to a third: the believers' knowledge of the costliness of their redemption, which should produce an 'awed thankfulness' (Kelly, 72). He reminds them of things which they *know well*. Indeed vv.18–21 seem to contain common Christian tradition, material which is acquiring some sort of credal form. The statements go beyond what the author needs to make his point (and thus indicate his incorporation of traditional material) and encapsulate concisely the story of what God has accomplished in Christ (cf. 3.18–22; II Tim.

1.9–10; Titus 2.14). Further traditional christological material is found in 2.21–25 and 3.18–22, where, as here, the example of Christ serves as a motivation for Christian living.

For the second time in the epistle an unfavourable comparison is made with *gold* (see 1.7; here linked with *silver* too), which is *of passing value*. That which was used to purchase the Christians' freedom is of much greater worth. The Greek verb used here, *lutroô* ('to set free, redeem, deliver'), was used, for example, to refer to the financial transaction by which slaves were freed. In the LXX it is used both of everyday transactions such as the 'redeeming' of a piece of property or land (Lev. 25.24–32), compensation for a crime (Ex. 21.30), freedom for a captive or slave (Lev. 25.47–55), and of God's redeeming work – paradigmatically in liberating his people from slavery in Egypt (Ex. 6.6; Deut. 15.15). The New Testament speaks of Christ's death in this way, as a 'ransom' (*lutron*). If Mark 10.45 is an authentic saying of Jesus (and this is certainly debatable) then Jesus himself interpreted his mission in these terms (cf. also I Tim. 2.6). Here the effect of redemption is described as liberation *from the futility of your traditional ways*, a further indication of the Gentile status of the recipients of the epistle. Their former way of life is as a whole portrayed as empty and pointless (see also 4.3).

1.19   They have been *set free by Christ's precious blood*, blood shed in a sacrificial death (see on 1.2). Here again the writer uses Exodus imagery as he compares Christ with *a lamb without mark or blemish* (the author, as usual, indicates that he is using a metaphor). The words 'like a lamb' are found in Isa. 53.7, a passage which may well be in the author's mind here, as it clearly is in 2.21–25. But the dominant image is probably of the Passover sacrifice, usually a lamb, which enabled the liberation from Egypt and forms a central part of the ritual celebration of that great act of deliverance (see Ex. 12; I Cor. 5.7). The animal offered for the Passover sacrifice, as for other sacrifices too, had to be perfect, without blemish (Ex. 12.5; Lev. 22.17–25; Heb. 9.14).

1.20   Having spoken of the redemption effected by Christ's blood, the author presents a concise credal affirmation concerning Christ, probably dependent upon established Christian tradition, perhaps a form of 'christological hymn' (cf. Phil. 2.5–11). *He was predestined* ('foreknown'; the same word-group used in 1.2) *before the foundation of the world* (v.20; cf. John 17.24). God's purposes for Christ were planned and known before creation. *But in this last period of time* (again the recurring conviction that little time remains) *he has been revealed*, made manifest (cf. II Tim. 1.10). These words, like those in 1.11, suggest a belief in Christ's pre-existence. And again we find the author emphasizing to his readers not only that this is 'the last of the ages' but also that this amazing redemptive work of God in Christ is *for your sake*.

1.21   Despite the christological focus of these verses it is clear that the foundation and centre of faith, for I Peter, is God. The result of Christ's redemptive work is that *through him*, that is Christ, *you have come to trust* (have faith, believe) *in God*. It was God who, in the words of a Christian formula already well-established by this time, *raised him from the dead* (Rom. 4.24; 8.11; Gal. 1.1; Acts 2.32 etc.). The affirmation of the resurrection is at the heart of the earliest Christian confession (Rom. 10.9; I Cor. 15.3–4) together with the belief in God's vindication, exaltation and glorification of Christ (*God . . . gave him glory*; cf. John 17.1ff.; Phil. 2.9–11; I Tim. 3.16). The focus for Christian *faith and hope* is *God*: for just as God raised and glorified Jesus, so, the author of I Peter is convinced, God will vindicate and honour those who follow in Jesus' footsteps.

1.22   The author now returns to the theme of exhortation, but he does so by first stating what is the case; indicative and imperative are here closely linked. The readers are reminded: *You have purified your souls by obedience to the truth*, by responding to the gospel (echoes of the themes of obedience and sanctification from 1.2, 14–15). The word *souls* here effectively means 'yourselves' (see on 1.9). The product and goal of these purified lives is *sincere affection towards your fellow-Christians*, that is, *philadelphia* – love for the brothers and sisters (it is hard to find an inclusive equivalent for the term 'brotherly love') – a love focussed inwards upon the community which was characteristic of early Christianity and other close-knit sectarian groups such as that at Qumran (Rom. 12.10; Heb. 13.1; I John 3.11, 14; 1QS 1.9–11). The command to love one another 'was from the beginning a conspicuous part of Christian ethical instruction' (Michaels, 176). The exhortation here is effectively an instruction to continue and to deepen this love. A similar indicative-imperative pattern is found in I Thess. 4.9–10: 'you . . . love one another . . . Yet we appeal to you . . . do better still.' The author of I Peter urges his readers to love *with all* their *strength*, 'with total commitment' (Goppelt, 125), and 'from a pure heart'. Most translations, like the REB, follow the ancient texts which omit the adjective 'pure'; hence the translation *wholeheartedly* (cf. 'from the heart'; NRSV). However, the textual evidence for the inclusion of the word 'pure' (*katharas*) is strong and it should probably be accepted as original (cf. Davids, 77 n.6).

1.23   Having urged the readers to love one another the author makes another statement indicating what is the case, and what therefore provides another motivating basis for this loving behaviour. Indeed he surrounds the imperative – 'love one another' – with two statements of what has already taken place: 'having purified your souls' . . . 'having been born again' (cf. the 'new birth' of 1.3). It is because of this new status that they can, and should, fulfill the demands of the imperative to love. Their love can (and must) be genuine and pure because their new birth has come about 'not from perishable or corruptible but from imperishable, incorruptible seed'; they are children of purity, holiness, and obedience.

The Greek words for 'seed' can be used to refer either to human procreation or to plants, so there is a link (obscured by the REB's rendering of 'seed' as *parentage*) between the imagery here – that of imperishable seed – and that in the following verse (v.24), with its contrast between the perishable, fading glory of plants of the field and the abiding word of God. It is *through the living and enduring word of God* (which is more likely here than 'through the word of the living and enduring God', though this is grammatically possible; see La Verdière 1974; Achtemeier, 140) that their new birth has come about.

1.24–25   Characteristically, having made his point, the author illustrates it from *scripture*, quoting almost exactly the LXX of Isa. 40.6–8 (which basically omits v.7 from the Hebrew text). The prophet elaborates what I Peter has just mentioned, namely the contrast between perishable human seed and the imperishable word of God. *All mortals* (the Greek word here is *sarx*, 'flesh') *are like grass*. Human beings and their 'glory' – including the might and splendour of the Roman empire – are temporary and passing, like flowers and grass which wither and fall in a season. What *endures for evermore* is *the word of the Lord*. This last phrase contains the most significant variation from the text of Isaiah, where both the Hebrew and LXX texts have 'the word of our God'. Assuming that the change from *theos*, God, to *kurios*, Lord, was made for a reason, it seems likely that the author intended to apply the phrase to Christ (referred to as *kurios* in

I Peter and the New Testament generally). The phrase would then mean either 'the word spoken by [Christ] the Lord' or 'the word which is about [Christ] the Lord' (cf. Mark 1.1), probably the latter, which would make good sense of the following sentence, in which the author adds his own conclusion to the scripture quotation: *And this 'word' is the gospel which was preached to you* (cf. Isa. 40.9). The final two words of the chapter (not that such divisions were part of the original document) sound a refrain which has already been frequently heard: the glorious saving purposes of God, planned from before the foundation of the world and brought to fruition in this last age – all this is 'for you'.

Christian identity
2.1–10

This section of the letter, full of a wide range of images and metaphors which describe the status and calling of the people of God, is strongly linked with what has preceded in 1.3–25, both in its exhortations and its affirmations. Specifically, the description of their 'new birth', not of corruptible, mortal seed, but through the living and enduring word of God (1.23) forms the basis for the appeal which is made in 2.1–3.

2.1 Beginning with the Greek word *oun*, 'therefore', or *then* (cf. James 1.21), verses 1–2 spell out what should be consequences of that new birth. The first imperative which follows from their status as those born of the incorruptible word of God is that they must 'put away' all that is wicked and which corrupts and spoils brotherly / sisterly love (1.22). The term used for 'putting away' seems to have become a standard word in early Christian vocabulary to describe the leaving behind of sinful ways and 'old selves' (Rom. 13.12; Eph. 4.22, 25; Col. 3.8), sometimes linked with baptism (Rom. 6.1–14; Gal. 3.27; Col. 3.5–17).

A number of places in the New Testament contain lists of 'vices', wicked things to be avoided, often contrasted with 'virtues', qualities which should characterize the lives of those called to be holy (e.g. Rom. 1.29–31; Gal. 5.19–23; Eph. 4.31; Col. 3.8; Titus 3.3). Similar lists are also found in Jewish and Hellenistic literature of the period (e.g. 1 QS 10.21–23; 4.2–11). So I Peter's list here is somewhat standard, and should therefore not be taken as an indication that the author thought his readers particularly guilty of these sins. The first two terms are all-encompassing: *all wickedness and* all *deceit* (the word 'all' is repeated in the Greek). The next three terms, all plural in the Greek, refer more specifically to vices which corrupt human relationships and are thus destructive of mutual love (*philadelphia*): *hypocrisy and jealousy and malicious talk*.

2.2   Having told his readers what they should avoid – the 'old' things they should 'put away' – the writer now gives them a positive instruction, based upon the fact that they are *new born infants* (cf. 1.3, 23). They are to *crave for pure spiritual milk*. The contrast is clear in I Peter's language: they are to put away all deceit (Gk: *dolos*) and crave milk which is 'pure', without deceit (Gk: *adolos*). The word translated *spiritual* is the Greek word *logikos*, found elsewhere in the New Testament only at Rom. 12.1. It was generally used in Greek literature to describe things connected with speech or reason, to distinguish what was 'rational' or 'spiritual' from what was merely material or natural, and sometimes to denote something as metaphorical, as opposed to 'literal' (see Michaels, 87; BAGD, 476; Achtemeier, 146). By describing the milk which the Christians should crave as *logikos* the author may seek to indicate that it is the 'right kind' of milk, appropriate to nourish people to salvation, hence the translation *spiritual*. More likely, the description of the milk as *logikos* is meant to link it with the reference to Christians being born through the living word (*logos*) of God (1.23). We might translate the phrase: 'pure milk of the Word' (McCartney 1991; Kelly, 85; Elliott 1966, 204; Achtemeier, 147). Those who are born through the word of God are nourished by the milk of the word.

The purpose of craving for this milk is *that you may thrive on it and be saved*. There is no hint here that 'milk' is only for those who are spiritually immature, as there is in I Cor. 3.1–2 and Heb. 5.13. Drinking pure spiritual milk will enable them 'to grow up to salvation' (a more literal rendering of the Greek). Here again, as in 1.3–5, we see I Peter's focus upon the final outcome of the saving work of God. Salvation remains a future hope, the goal towards which believers look and the outcome of their faith (cf. 1.5, 9). Yet the nearness and certainty of that final salvation fills the present with hope and joy, in spite of trials and suffering.

2.3   Indeed the new-born infants who are to crave spiritual milk have *surely* already *tasted that the Lord is good*. As is often the pattern in I Peter, an assurance or exhortation is given and then followed by a citation from the Jewish scriptures (e.g. 1.15–16; 1.23–25). Here in 2.3 the phrase comes from Ps. 34.8, a psalm which is quoted again in 3.10–12 and which some have argued was in the author's mind throughout the letter (e.g. Bornemann 1920; Kelly, 87). 2.4 makes it clear that it is Christ the Lord who is referred to here in v.3, as is the case with many of the New Testament uses of *kurios*. But there is also a word-play in the Greek which the epistle's readers could hardly have missed, even though it is impossible to bring out in an English translation. The word translated 'good' (or 'kind') is *chrêstos* in the Greek, almost identical to the word *Christos*, Christ. So when the recipients of the letter heard the words of the psalm, 'the Lord is *chrêstos*', they would also have been reminded of the confession so central to early Christian faith: 'Jesus Christ is Lord' (Rom. 10.9; II Cor. 4.5; Phil. 2.11). A reference to the Lord's supper or eucharist might be seen here (with the image of tasting), but probably was not intended and narrows the author's concerns too specifically.

The image which the author presents in these verses then, is one in which the believers are to crave 'the milk of the word', the sustenance of Christ, just as new born babies crave their mother's milk. I Peter does not develop this imagery in any detail, nor specify whether God or Christ is the maternal figure who provides the milk, but similar imagery is found at Qumran (1QH 9.35–36; 7.20–21) and most notably in the *Odes of Solomon*, a Jewish-Christian writing of the first or second century CE. There we find the following description: 'Christ speaks: I fashioned their members and my own breasts I prepared for them, that they might drink my holy milk and live by it' (8.14; cf. also 19.1–4; in Charlesworth 1985). Perhaps the variety of metaphors found in I Peter, and in other Jewish and Christian writings, might encourage us not to be too restrictive in the range of images and terms, both female and male, which we use to depict God and Christ.

2.4–10   I Peter's imagery changes abruptly at the beginning of v.4; Christ is now described as *the living stone*. Vv. 4–10 comprise a passage which is both intricate in construction and of great importance for the epistle as a whole. Here the status of the believers as the elect and holy people of God is made clear, thus forming the climax of the affirmations and the exhortations found in 1.3–2.10 and the foundation for the instruction which is to follow in the second major section of the letter (2.11–4.11). We have already noted the connection in

I Peter between indicative ('this is what you are') and imperative ('so you must do this'; see e.g. on 1.22). 'Here' in 2.4–10, John Elliott writes, 'the fundamental indicative for the entire epistle has been spoken' (1966, 217).

The whole section from 4–10 may be characterized loosely as a *midrash*, a Jewish-style piece of exegesis, not unlike the *pesharim* from Qumran, in which texts from the Jewish scriptures are cited and interpreted, with vv.4–5 serving as an introduction to the exegesis (see Bauckham 1988c, 310–12; and on Jude 4–19). The scriptural texts in vv.6–8 are linked together by the keyword 'stone' (*lithos*), those in vv.9–10 by the keyword 'people' (*laos*). The structure of the passage is as follows (following Bauckham 1988c, and see in more detail Elliott 1966, 16–49):

> vv.4–5 Introduction
>> v.4 Jesus the elect *stone*
>> v.5 The church the elect *people* of God
> vv.6–10 Midrash
>> vv.6–8 The elect *stone*: three texts plus
>> interpretative comments (Isa. 28.16;
>> Ps. 118.22; Isa. 8.14).
>> vv.9–10 The elect *people*: three texts (Isa. 43.20–21;
>> Ex. 19.5–6; Hosea 2.23, plus phrases drawn
>> from Hosea 1.6; 1.9; 2.1)

Vv.4–5 introduce vv.6–10, briefly stating the themes which are drawn out in the texts and comments which follow. More specifically, v.4 introduces the texts and comments about Christ the stone in vv.6–8, and v.5 introduces and summarizes vv.9–10. Vv.6–10 thus contain the primary sources of the ideas which are summarized in 4–5 (see Bauckham 1988c, 310–11; Elliott 1966, 48).

2.4   There is in fact, as is typical in I Peter, no real break in the flow of the Greek between vv.3 and 4. The opening words of v.4 may be a further echo of Ps. 34 (LXX 33.6). The phrase is probably better understood as a statement rather than an imperative, and translated 'as you come to him' (against REB, NRSV, etc.). The one to whom they are coming is Christ, *the living stone* – 'living' because God has vindicated him and raised him from death (cf. 1.3 and the phrase 'living hope'). Echoing the texts which he will cite in vv.6–8, the writer contrasts human and divine perspectives on this 'living stone': on the one hand he *was rejected by* people, yet with God – in God's sight and through God's action – he is *chosen* and *of great worth*.

2.5   As Christ is the living stone, so those who come to him are also *living stones*, which are being built (again the indicative interpretation of the verb is to be preferred to REB's imperative rendering) into a 'spiritual house'. The author does not actually call the building a 'temple', and there is debate as to whether this is the implication of his phrase 'spiritual house' or not (Elliott 1966 argues that it is not). The adjective *spiritual* shows that this is no ordinary house; it is a building which belongs to God and where the Spirit is to be found. And given the mention of priesthood and sacrifices in the words immediately following, the image of the house as a temple cannot be far from the author's mind (cf. I Cor. 3.16; Eph. 2.21). Yet Elliott may be right to argue that his primary intention is to designate the community here as the 'household of God' (Elliott links this with the interpretation of *basileion* as 'the house of the king' in v.9, see below; Elliott 1966, 149–59; 1981, 168–70). The description of the believers as *a holy priesthood*, which immediately follows, is a change of image, though not unconnected with what precedes: first new-born infants, then living stones built into a house, now a priesthood – the inhabitants of the spiritual house/temple? – whose purpose is *to offer spiritual sacrifices acceptable to God through Jesus Christ*. What precisely these 'sacrifices' are the author does not specify, though in the light of v.9 and of the epistle as a whole, we may suggest that what is implied is living a life of holy obedience, 'doing good', in the sight of God and in the world (see Elliott 1966, 159–98; and cf. Rom. 12.1). This is a life of both worship and witness – the two are inseparable – 'proclaiming God's glorious deeds' (v.9; see below). However, the phrase *acceptable to God through Jesus Christ* suggests that worship, orientation towards God, is primary (Michaels, 101–102) and that such acceptable offering is possible only through Jesus Christ. Some have suggested that the eucharist may be in view here, as it later came to be regarded as an 'offering' (see Kelly, 92). However, I Peter does not make any such indication and it is more likely that, as in Rom. 12.1, it is the offering of believers' lives in service to God which constitutes the holy and acceptable sacrifice.

Throughout verse 5 the author has described the identity of the Christians as a *corporate* entity, using terms based upon the texts which he will cite in vv.9–10. We shall explore the meaning of those terms further below (on vv.9–10), in particular the description of the community as a 'priesthood'.

2.6   The quotations from the Jewish scriptures which are the foundation for the ideas expressed in vv.4–5 are formally introduced in v.6: *For you will find in scripture* . . . The author proceeds first to quote Isa. 28.16 (LXX), but with a number of variations and omissions from the LXX text. The differences may indicate that the author knew a different text-form of the LXX here, possibly one derived 'from earlier Jewish or Jewish Christian adaptations of the Isaiah texts' (Michaels, 103). The initial phrase of the quotation, *I am laying in Zion*, differs from the LXX yet matches Paul's quotation of the same verse in Rom. 9.33. However, it is unlikely that the author of I Peter derived his use of Isa. 28.16 directly from Romans, since there it is amalgamated with a part of Isa. 8.14, which I Peter quotes separately. Both Paul and the author of I Peter, then, were separately aware of the significance of these two 'stone' texts. The most likely explanation is that in both Jewish and Christian circles these two texts were seen as messianic texts of particular significance (e.g. at Qumran; see Snodgrass 1978; Elliott 1966, 26–33). The early Christians also found in Ps. 118.22 (also quoted here by I Peter) a significant text which appeared to foreshadow the surprising reversal of Jesus' apparent fate: rejected by people, but vindicated and honoured by God (note its use in Mark 12.10 and Acts 4.11). It is uncertain whether the early Christians developed written or oral collections of scripture texts which were deemed to be of particular significance, but such written collections, known as *testimonia*, have been found at Qumran (e.g. 4Q *Testimonia*).

The text from Isa. 28.16 refers to God's action in laying a stone, clearly, for I Peter, Christ, which is described as *chosen, of great worth,* and a *corner-stone* – best interpreted here as a foundation stone. Those who *have faith in it*, or 'in him' – the Greek can mean either, and the author is clearly speaking of Christ here – are promised vindication. This is the meaning of the negative expression *will not be put to shame*. Here again the themes and concerns of the epistle are clear: salvation and vindication will come to those who place their faith in God, in spite of their present hardships.

2.7–8   The author then adds his own interpretative comment, making the meaning he is drawing from the scriptural quotation clear. 'This honour therefore belongs to you who believe' (v.7a). This is a rather different translation of v.7a from that of the REB and of most other standard translations. However, most commentators agree that the author is referring here not to the 'honour' or value of Christ the stone, but to the 'honour' which is 'for you' (Michaels, 104; Goppelt, 145, etc.). The author is emphasizing both the honoured status of the believers, a status he will outline more fully in vv.9–10, and the promise of their vindication; they will be held in honour (by God) and will not be put to shame (cf. Kelly, 93). This is in stark contrast to the fate of *those who have no faith*. Their situation is described in the words quoted from Ps. 118.22, the second of the 'stone' texts cited here; they are among those who *rejected* the stone which *has now become the corner-stone*. And so, to them, this stone has become, in words from Isa. 8.14, *a stone to trip over, a rock to stumble against*. The writer of I Peter then adds his own interpretation of these texts, applying them to those who do not believe: *they trip because they refuse to believe* (literally: they disobey) *the word*. The author then asserts that *this is the fate appointed for them*. The passive verb here clearly indicates that this is the action of God (the same verb used in v.6; *tithêmi*): God 'places' a stone in Zion, and God 'places', or 'appoints' the unbelievers to their fate. But does God appoint them to their destiny of disbelief and stumbling, or does God decree that because they choose to disbelieve they are destined to stumble? Although theologically difficult, the former seems most likely. The writer hardly offers an answer to the difficult problem of reconciling human freedom and divine sovereignty, but as elsewhere in the New Testament (e.g. Rom. 9.10–21; I Thess. 5.9) he seems to express the idea that God 'appoints' both believers and unbelievers to their fate, whether that be vindication or stumbling. There are the seeds here of the doctrine of 'double predestination' which developed in some strands of the Calvinist tradition, namely the idea that God elects some to salvation and some to damnation. There has always been strong opposition to this doctrine, however, from those who regard it as utterly incompatible with the idea of a God of love who gave his Son for the salvation of the world. Those who stand in the Arminian tradition have always insisted that the offer of salvation is genuinely open to *all* (hence one of the 'four alls' of Methodism: 'all *can* be saved'). It is notable that, in the extended passage where Paul wrestles with similar ideas in connection with the fate of Israel (Rom. 9–11), where he also speaks of divine will and divine hardening, the ultimate *purpose*, according to Paul, of God's sovereign plan, is that God may 'show mercy to all' (Rom. 11.32). As in I Peter, Paul wants to insist that God is in control. In the context when I Peter was written Christians were a hard-pressed minority in an often hostile environment. In such a situation it was perhaps understandable that the believers would encourage one another with the notion that God would ultimately vindicate them and put their enemies to shame. But we may well want now to reject aspects of the theology which emerged from that context, namely the idea that God appoints certain people to a 'fate' of disobedience and unbelief.

2.9 The author now returns to the status of the believers; their privileged position stands in sharp contrast to those who are destined to stumble. *But you are . . .* This second midrashic section comprises phrases drawn from a number of scriptural texts and expands some of the ideas expressed in v. 5. The phrase *chosen race* is taken from Isa. 43.20 and highlights again I Peter's emphasis on the theme of election. The next two words in the Greek, from Ex. 19.6 (LXX), are generally understood, as in the REB, as an adjective and noun: *a royal priesthood.* Elliott has argued, however, that they are best taken as two separate nouns, *basileion* and *hierateuma*, meaning 'royal dwelling place' and 'body of priests' (Elliott 1966; Kelly, 82, 96–98. Best 1969, 288–91, suggests the translation 'body of kings' for *basileion*. Cf. also Rev. 1.6; 5.10). On balance, however, the traditional translation is probably to be preferred (cf. Achtemeier, 164–65). The quotation of Ex. 19.6 continues with *a dedicated* ('holy') *nation,* followed by a phrase based on words from Isa. 43.21, *a people claimed by God for his own* (a similar phrase, though less closely parallel to I Peter's formulation, is also found in Ex. 19.5; cf. also Mal. 3.17).

The dependence on Isa. 43.21 (cf. also Isa. 42.12) continues in the words which follow, a declaration of the task to which this elect and holy people is called: *to proclaim the glorious deeds etc.* Their corporate calling is to declare the saving acts of God. This is fundamentally an act of worship, yet equally an act of witness and proclamation (cf. Ps. 9.1ff. 57.9–11; 96.1ff.). It is the gracious election of God which has taken them from the *darkness* of their former lives into God's *marvellous light* – an image of conversion and transformation often found in early Christian literature (e.g. Acts 26.18; I Thess. 5.4–5).

2.10 The images of change and transformation continue into v. 10. Indeed it would be hard to draw a stronger contrast than the one found here, based on words from Hosea 1.6, 1.9, 2.1 and 2.23. As with the Isaiah stone texts, the same texts are used by Paul in

Romans (9.25–26), though here again I Peter's usage is unlikely to be directly dependent on Romans. The terms are taken from the names Hosea was instructed to give to his children, names which illustrated Israel's rejection by God because of her unfaithfulness. The daughter was named 'Lo-ruhamah', which means 'not loved', or 'not shown mercy', the son 'Lo-ammi', which means 'not my people'. Yet the prophet's message was that God would once again restore his relationship to his people: 'I shall show love to Lo-ruhamah and say to Lo-ammi, "You are my people".' (Hosea 2.23; cf. 2.1) Here in I Peter the terms are applied not to Jews restored to a right relationship with God, but to Gentiles who were previously not God's people at all but who now have been chosen as God's holy nation.

Several points are notable in these well-known verses (vv.4–10). First, it is striking that the author applies to the Christian community terms taken from the Jewish scriptures which designate the Jews as God's own people without showing any explicit awareness of the continuing existence of Jewish communities. The terms are used 'as if they were applicable to Christians alone and had never had any other reference' (Michaels, 107). The author never discusses the questions concerning the relationship between Israel and the church or God's promises to his original covenant people (cf. Knoch, 62). This observation is relevant to discussion concerning the date and authorship of the letter and raises certain questions for Christians who wish to be sensitive to their multi-faith context (see Ch. II 2(i); 4).

Second, all the descriptions of the people of God found in these verses are essentially corporate descriptions. It is the identity and character of the people of God as a body, a community, which are described. This must be borne in mind when considering the implications of I Peter's description of the community as a 'holy priesthood' (vv.5 and 9). These verses have provided the most important New Testament evidence in support of the Reformation doctrine of the 'priesthood of all believers'. I Peter, however, does not seek to develop ideas about the 'priestly' function of the church, but rather to describe the elect and holy status of the people of God (so Elliott 1966). And the priestly function, in so far as I Peter does describe it, primarily involves holy living and proclamation of God's saving acts. I Peter describes the status and calling of the community as a corporate body and is simply not concerned about the rights and functions of individual believers in relationship to God; that was Luther's concern in the sixteenth century (see further Elliott 1966; Goppelt, 141–42; Knoch, 65–66). That is not to say that I Peter opposes such a doctrine, or is incompatible with it, merely that it is not the author's concern, nor is it present as such in the text.

So the author of I Peter has set out the foundations of the Christian life: the saving activity of God, through the death and resurrection of Jesus Christ, who calls those who were no people at all to become his holy nation, to live a life of worship and witness. Their hope is salvation and vindication, while those who do not obey the gospel are destined to stumble and fall. Having set out this foundation, and having already set out some of the exhortations based upon it – the call to be holy (1.15) – the author proceeds to spell out in detail the behaviour which is required of God's people living in the world.

Christian life and mission in the world
2.11–4.11

Instruction to believers: the 'household code'
2.11–3.12

Here at 2.11 the second major section of the epistle begins. Having described in the first section the glorious salvation to which God has called his elect and holy people the author now deals with 'the consequences for the behavior of Christians in the structures of society' (Goppelt, 151). The first part of this major section of instruction contains material generally referred to as a 'household code', or 'domestic code' (the German word *Haustafel* is also frequently used, following Luther), in other words, instruction addressed to various social groups within the Graeco-Roman household. The clearest and most concise examples of the 'household code' are found in Col. 3.18–4.1 and Eph. 5.21–6.9 (cf. also I Tim. 2.8–15; 5.1–6.2, Titus 2.2–10). Strictly speaking it is the section 2.18–3.7 which contains 'household code' material, but the whole section 2.11–3.12 is best taken together as a structured passage of instruction and admonition; the passage begins and ends with general exhortation to all believers and concludes with a scriptural quotation (see the outline in Ch. II 5).

The origins of the household code material lie in the writings of Plato and Aristotle, Greek philosophers of the fourth century BCE, 'concerning household management' (see esp. Balch 1981). Aristotle outlined in some detail how the appropriate 'order' in the household

– masters over slaves, parents over children, husbands over wives –
was an essential part of ensuring order and stability in the city (*polis*)
and the state. This Aristotelian form influenced later Stoic philosophers such as Seneca and Hellenistic Jewish writers of the New
Testament period (e.g. Philo *The Decalogue* 165–167; Josephus *Against
Apion* 2.199–201).

There has been considerable discussion about why this form of
instruction was introduced into the New Testament letters. John
Elliott and David Balch in particular have debated the purpose of the
code in I Peter (Elliott 1981; Balch 1981; and their debate in Talbert
1986). Elliott argues that in I Peter 'the household code, like other
elements of the household theme, was used to promote both the
internal solidarity of the sectarian movement and its external distinction from Gentile motives and manners' (1981, 231). Balch's suggestion is, however, generally more convincing. He maintains that
religions and cults which were foreign to the Romans (often coming
from the East, like Judaism) were regarded with suspicion and
hostility. Their adherents were seen as immoral and seditious.
Christianity, like Judaism, provoked particular hostility because it
demanded absolute loyalty; its members refused to worship the
traditional gods and the emperor. Hostility would be even stronger
when slaves or wives who became Christians refused to follow the
religion of the head of the household. Consequently, the author of
I Peter exhorts his readers to be good citizens, to be submissive
according to their social position, in so far as this was possible without compromising their ultimate allegiance and obedience to God, in
the hope that 'good conduct' would be recognized as such and
hostility might lessen. At the same time he recognizes that suffering
for the name of Christ (4.16) will continue.

The material in the New Testament household codes raises difficult questions for Christians today. How should we regard this
teaching? Should it still be allowed to shape our domestic and social
relationships? A wide variety of answers are possible. Some would
argue that the pattern of relationships presented in the household
codes, with the husband as the head of the household, is God's
intended pattern for family relationships (though few, I suspect,
would also want to justify slavery). Others might suggest that the
instruction was formulated in a very different social context from our
own, in which slavery, for example, was accepted. While it was right
for Christians to conform then to social expectations, such expectations are very different today and so the teaching of the household

codes, while containing some points of enduring value, should not be taken as a direct pattern for contemporary human relationships. My own view is that the household codes generally serve to sustain a particular (and oppressive) social hierarchy; to urge the subordinate to remain quietly 'in their place' – for the Lord's sake! It is certainly understandable that a relatively powerless community suffering considerable hostility should seek to lessen its conflict with society by greater conformity (within limits); though not all the early Christians wanted to take this route. However, the codes' demand for subordination and conformity stands in some tension with the demands of justice and equality, and may therefore perhaps be better resisted than obeyed (cf. Watson 1992; 1994, 161–72).

Exhortation to all to pure and good conduct

2.11–12

2.11–12 The beginning of this new section of the epistle is clearly marked. The author uses the common Christian address *dear friends*, 'beloved', and makes an *appeal* to them as *aliens* and strangers *in a foreign land*. These terms have already been used in 1.1 and 1.17 and describe for I Peter an essential aspect of Christian identity. As 'strangers' in the world, and as God's holy and elect children, they are here given both a negative and a positive exhortation which serve as an introduction to the more specific instructions to follow. First they must *avoid bodily desires which make war on the soul*. The contrast between body and soul here should not be taken to imply that the author sees 'physical', sexual desires as wicked, nor that he sees a person as divided into physical and spiritual parts (see on 1.9 for comments on the word 'soul'). Rather, the phrase *bodily desires* is used to describe the kinds of human impulses which lead to wicked and harmful behaviour (cf. 2.1; 4.2) and which are contrary to the holy and good behaviour which God wills.

The positive instruction in v.12 reveals a concern for *good conduct* as an act of witness to *unbelievers*. Clearly there are cases where these unbelievers, among whom the Christians live, *malign* the believers *as wrongdoers*. This is strong language, but it reflects the reality of hatred, mistrust and accusation which the early Christians experienced (recorded, for example, by the Roman historians Tacitus [*Annals* 15.44] and Suetonius [*Nero* 16.2]). The author's hope, perhaps an over-optimistic one, is that *good deeds* on the part of the

47

Christians will lead, eventually, to their accusers giving *glory to God on the day when he comes in judgment*. The motivation for doing good expressed here is strikingly similar to that found in Matt. 5.16 and probably shows the influence of this Gospel tradition on I Peter . The final phrase ('on the day of visitation', cf. Isa. 10.3) refers to the eschatological time of God's coming; a time of both salvation and judgment, which for the author is already close at hand. It is not entirely clear whether the unbelievers' recognition of good deeds and their glorifying God implies their conversion and salvation or only that they will ultimately (and possibly to their regret) recognize and acknowledge, as will the whole creation, the sovereignty of God (cf. Phil. 2.11). The author's point is that the Christians' good deeds will eventually be acknowledged as such, if not now, then on the final day.

Instruction to all: submission to God and the state
2.13–17

2.13–14   Now the author proceeds to specific instruction, indicating more precisely what 'good conduct' he has in mind. The first two words of v.13 – *Subject yourselves* – translate a Greek verb which runs like a theme through this whole passage of instruction (see 2.18, 3.1, 3.5) and which describes the subjection of all things to Christ in 3.22. An important theme of the instruction may therefore be summarized as 'appropriate submission'. The motivation for all such submission is one's commitment to the Lord; it is done *for the sake of the Lord* and not because of any human demand (cf. the emphasis in Col. 3.18–4.1 and Eph. 5.21–6.9). It is unclear whether *the Lord* here implies God, whom the Christians serve with reverent fear (2.16–17), or Christ, whose example believers are called to follow (2.18–25).

The first instruction is a general one, to be subject *to every human authority*. Most translations, like the REB, take the Greek phrase here to imply broadly this meaning. However, it is more likely, as many recent commentators argue, that it should be translated 'to every human creature'. Like the overall instruction to 'honour everyone' in v.17, which is followed by the more specific instruction to 'honour the emperor', this verse expresses the idea that Christians should 'be subject' (in appropriate ways) to all people, followed by the specific examples of the emperor and his governors (thus emphasizing that the emperor is only a human being, albeit the pre-eminent one, in opposition to the claims of the imperial cult; see Achtemeier, 180–83). (Note the similar ideas in Eph. 5.21; *I Clem* 37.5–38.1; also in I Tim. 2.1–2 – prayers for 'all people' followed by the specific example of 'the emperor'; Titus 3.1–2.) A particular and prominent instance of appropriate submission, then, is *to the emperor as supreme,* and *to governors as his deputies.* The declared duty of these *deputies* is to enact justice: to punish *those who do wrong* and to commend *those who do right.* As in Rom. 13.3–4, there appears to be here an optimistic and positive view of Roman justice.

2.15   In v.15, as in v.12, however, there is an indication that people, in their foolishness and ignorance, may fail to recognize that the Christians are doers of good and not of wickedness. Yet *it is God's will that by doing right,* they may silence such false accusations, even though this may not happen until the 'day of judgment' when all will finally be seen in their true light (v.12). This is the reason for doing good and being appropriately submissive; 'the good and decent lives of the Christians will, our author is convinced, help overcome the hostility based on ignorance that they faced in their contemporary society' (Achtemeier, 185).

2.16   Some of the epistle's readers might have regarded the call to submission as compromising their Christian freedom, a freedom strongly asserted in the Pauline letters (e.g. Gal. 5.1, 13); indeed, some may have felt that their 'freedom' in Christ included a liberation from the subordination expected because of their social position (cf. Gal. 3.28). The author of I Peter agrees that Christians are indeed to *live as those who are free,* yet insists that they are free only, and paradoxically, in their status *as slaves in God's service* (cf. I Cor. 6.20; 7.22; 9.19). They must not, therefore, use 'freedom' as an excuse for *wrongdoing* – a misunderstanding of the gospel that Paul also had to confront (Rom. 3.8; 6.1ff.; Gal. 5.13). The instruction in this extended passage from 2.13–3.6 makes it clear that for I Peter 'wrongdoing' would include any subversive activity or refusal to be appropriately submissive according to one's social position. Whether we would agree with the labelling of such 'subversion' as wrongdoing is quite another matter. I Peter is clear that obedience to God and allegiance to Christ must be maintained, whatever the cost, but for the author, equality between husbands and wives, or slaves and masters, is not an essential part of obedience to the gospel. In our own very different social context, we might want to assess the gospel imperative differently (see Ch. II 4.).

2.17   V.17 rounds this short section off with a concise and balanced set of imperatives, formed in an ABBA (chiastic) pattern. The first imperative relates to all people: *Give due honour to everyone*; the second relates specifically to the Christian community: *love your fellow-Christians*. This second instruction reflects I Peter's emphasis upon love primarily as something shared and owed within the community, rather than something directed outward to the world (cf. 1.22; 4.8; I John 4.20–21). The final two imperatives mark a significant distinction between what is owed to God and what to the emperor (perhaps influenced by Mark 12.14–17 and/or Prov. 24.21). God should be the object of awe, of reverent fear; the emperor should be honoured. The careful distinction here shows that, for the author, ultimate loyalty, fear and awe are rightly related to God alone, while it is also right, for God's sake, to honour and submit to the emperor.

This short section urging submission to the established state authority and asserting the state's role in punishing evil and rewarding good has similarities with the instruction written earlier by Paul in Rom. 13.1–7 and that found in I Tim. 2.1–3 and Titus 3.1–3. This instruction may be influenced by Jesus' words in Mark 12.14–17 (though Jesus' reply there is rather enigmatic). I Peter's exhortation to do good even in the face of accusation and ignorance may also owe something to the instruction to love one's enemies and to respond to evil with good, found in Matt. 5.44. Unlike Paul in Rom. 13.1–7, I Peter does not insist that the emperor and his administrators are appointed by God and act as God's servants (see Achtemeier, 180–81). The danger of both passages, especially of Rom. 13.1–7, is that legitimation is offered to state power and that Christians are apparently urged to submit to this power and not to oppose it. In more recent times, therefore, some Christians have felt that obedience to the Bible requires them not to oppose the state, even when that state is manifestly unjust and oppressive, such as in Nazi Germany or apartheid South Africa. I Peter does at least indicate that God and not the emperor (or equivalent) is the rightful recipient of reverent fear and also that in spite of 'doing good' Christians may still be unjustly reviled for their unshakeable commitment to Christ. But as for guidance on the (for us) difficult question of when and why one might legitimately feel compelled to act in 'civil disobedience', little is given (cf. DSR 1986).

Instruction to specific groups within the household
2.18–3.7

To slaves: submission even in suffering, like Christ
2.18–25

2.18–19   The 'household code' proper now begins with an address to *servants*; the Greek word refers to household slaves, the author choosing a different word from the more common word for slaves, *douloi*, used in 2.16, perhaps to make clear his concern with a specific social group within the congregation. Unlike the household codes in Colossians and Ephesians, where wives and husbands, childen and fathers, slaves and masters are all addressed (in that order), here most of the household code is devoted to slaves and wives, with a short exhortation to husbands (3.7). Slaves and wives, as subordinate social groups, were most likely to suffer at the hands of their masters/husbands, especially if they adopted a new 'religion' which was not followed by the head of their household and which was the cause of suspicion. These are the groups, then, which the author is particularly concerned to urge to quiet and uncomplaining goodness. Slaves in particular exemplify the vulnerability to ill-treatment and hostility which the Christian community as a whole seems to be experiencing (cf. Achtemeier, 192).

The theme of appropriate submission continues: *servants* are urged to *submit to* their *masters with all due respect*. The word for respect is *phobos*, which might be rendered 'reverent fear'. It is not altogether clear here whether the respect or fear is directed towards God or towards the human masters, but it is probably to God, firstly because I Peter seems generally to regard 'fear' as something rightly shown only to God (cf. 1.17; 3.2, 6), as the previous verse has stated (v.17), and secondly because the following verse (v.19) explicitly mentions 'awareness of God' as a motivation for right conduct. Respectful submission, however, is to be shown to all masters, *even to those who are unjust*. This is because bearing unjust or *undeserved suffering* is a *sign of grace* – meant here in the sense of something pleasing to God, a 'credit' to someone, as in Luke 6.32–34 – if it is done *because God is in* a person's *thoughts*, or (more literally) because of their 'awareness of God'.

2.20   V. 20 spells out this point, that it is only the patient and quiet bearing of *undeserved* suffering which is a credit to someone in God's eyes. Enduring a *beating* given for doing *wrong* (not, however, actually described in the Greek as *the beating you deserve!*) is not a 'credit' to anyone (here the Greek word is *kleos*, 'fame' or 'glory', i.e. a good reputation), even though from our perspective the punishments meted out to slaves would seem disproportionately harsh for the nature of the offence. What is creditable – *a sign of grace in the sight of God* (cf. v.19) – is enduring *suffering* which comes even when one has *behaved well*. This is a major theme of the letter: 'doing good' even in the face of insult and unjust suffering, a pattern of behaviour for which Christ provides the supreme example, as the following verses will show.

2.21   Indeed it is 'to this' – not suffering itself, but 'the doing of good even when it means suffering' (Michaels, 142) – that they have been 'called' as Christians (v.21a). Though the instruction here, significantly, is addressed specifically to slaves, it is clear that for I Peter this calling, or *vocation*, belongs to all who would follow Christ.

Vv.21–25 form the second of three major christological sections in the epistle, sections which probably employ traditional, credal expressions of the salvific achievements of Christ (1.18–21; 2.21–25; 3.18–22; cf. Goppelt, 207). The phrase *because Christ himself suffered on your behalf* is very similar to the wording of 3.18 and to the traditional credal statement 'Christ died for us/for our sins' reflected, for example, in I Cor. 15.3 and II Cor. 5.14–15. The author of I Peter uses the word 'suffered' rather than 'died' because he wants to draw the instructive parallel between Christ's suffering and the suffering which his readers have to endure. Indeed, he explicitly draws out this point: Christ *left you an example in order that you should follow in his steps*. There are two images here of close and careful imitation. The first is in the Greek word *hypogrammon*, translated *example*, used elsewhere in relation to the way in which children learnt their alphabet, carefully writing over or copying the 'example' produced by the teacher. The word came to refer more generally to a moral example or model. The second image is of following in someone's footsteps, walking along exactly the same way (cf. II Cor. 12.18).

2.22–25   The nature of the example which Christ has set is detailed in this poetic passage based largely on Isa. 53.4–12. Each main phrase begins in the Greek with a relative pronoun – 'who committed no sin . . . etc.' (cf. Col. 1.15, 18; I Tim. 3.16). Many scholars have suggested that the passage, with perhaps some additions by the author of I Peter, comprises an early Christian 'hymn', similar to those sometimes identified, for example, in Phil. 2.5–11 and Col. 1.15–20. It is rather difficult to ascertain whether or not this is the case here; Michaels suggests that this text 'is adequately explained as a midrash on Isa. 53.4–12' (Michaels, 137; cf. above on 2.4–10). However, both here and in 1.18–21 and 3.18–22 it seems likely that the author is drawing on expressions of Christian faith which had already acquired a traditional form.

2.22–23 Quoting from Isa. 53.9, the author shows Christ to be the perfect example of the kind of conduct he has already urged upon his readers. *He committed no sin, he was guilty of no falsehood.* The word translated 'falsehood' is the Greek word *dolos*, 'deceit, guile', which the believers are urged to turn from in 2.1 and in 3.10, the quotation which concludes this passage of instruction. There is an emphasis, then, on avoiding the sins which are expressed in human speech (cf. 2.1; Michaels, 145). This emphasis continues in the next verse (cf. 3.9 and I Cor. 4.12): *When he was abused* (or 'insulted') *he did not retaliate* (or 'answer back'), *when he suffered he uttered no threats.* Here there is no quotation from Isaiah, though the idea is close to that found in Isa. 53.7. Christ bore insult and suffering quietly and without reviling his accusers, 'like a sheep led silently to the slaughter'. What Christ did do was to entrust his cause *to him who judges justly.* What is not clear from the Greek is whether the sense here is that he *delivered himself up* to God in this way (so REB) or whether he handed over his enemies and accusers to God's judgment (so Michaels, 147; cf. Rom. 12.18–21). The former seems most likely (cf. Isa. 53.6, 12).

2.24–25 Having focussed upon Christ's conduct as an example, particularly his conduct during his suffering and passion, which are recalled by the language of v.23, the author draws attention to the redemptive value and purpose of Christ's sufferings. In words drawn from Isa. 53.4 and 12, he declares that *he carried our sins in his own person.* In v.24 the author has shifted from second to first person plural pronouns (cf. v.21: *Christ suffered on your behalf, and left you an example*), a change perhaps influenced by the form of Isaiah 53 (see e.g. 53.4), though more likely influenced by his use of traditional credal material, since in v.24c he quotes Isa. 53.5 but alters the verb 'we were healed' to 'you were healed', and thus returns to the 'you' form which is found most often in the letter. The image here is broadly rooted in the ancient Jewish sacrificial system – e.g. the scapegoat bearing sins and being driven away into the wilderness (Lev. 16.20–22) – but it does not present the picture of a sacrificial offering made on an altar (though see Heb. 10.10–12). The dominant idea is that Christ himself carried our sins away 'to the cross'; he bore the suffering of that fate on our behalf and for our benefit (cf. Isa. 53.5). The Greek word used here is not *stauros*, 'cross' but *xulon*, 'wood' or 'tree', which can mean 'gallows' or *gibbet*, as it does in Deut. 21.22–23 (quoted in Gal. 3.13) but which is often used in the New Testament to refer to the cross (Acts 5.30; 10.39; 13.29).

The purpose of Christ's vicarious suffering, of his bearing our sins, is that we, freed from sin – having finished with it (as the Greek implies) – might *live for righteousness*. Although I Peter does not quite express the Pauline notion of dying with Christ and dying to sin (Rom. 6.1–11) the thought here is very close to that of Paul and reflects Pauline language. Because Christ has dealt with our sins and taken them away, we are finished with sin, dead to sin, and alive to God, living as his holy and new-born children. Another phrase from Isaiah 53 (v.5) expresses further the benefits received because of Christ's suffering (now back to the second person form): *by his wounds you have been healed*, using 'healed' as an expression of the restoration to wholeness which is salvation.

Continuing to draw on Isaiah 53 (v.6), the author reminds the readers of their non-Christian past – *you were* (at that time) *straying like sheep. Now*, however (contrasting the present with the past), they *have turned* back in the right direction; they have come to the one who is *the Shepherd and Guardian of* their *souls*. The source of the shepherd image is originally the Jewish scriptures, where the picture of God as the *Shepherd* of Israel is well-known (e.g. Ps. 23). In the Synoptic Gospels similar shepherd-sheep imagery is found (e.g. Matt. 9.36) and it points to the idea of Jesus as 'the good Shepherd', expressed as such in John 10.11–16 (cf. Heb. 13.20; Rev. 7.17). I Peter, characteristically, elaborates the metaphor with the more specific word *Guardian*, or 'overseer' (Gk: *episkopos*), the same term which came to be applied to those in leadership over the church (Phil. 1.1; I Tim. 3.1). Christ is the supreme pastor and overseer, keeping careful watch over his sheep, but the daily and practical task of 'shepherding the flock' falls to those who are leaders in the community (see I Peter 5.1–4). 'Soul' here means the whole person (see on 1.9).

This significant christological passage is clearly based in large part on Isaiah 53. There is considerable debate as to the extent of the influence of Isaiah 53 on New Testament christological reflection and (possibly) on Jesus' own self-understanding. It is clear at least that it became an important passage to the early Christians as they sought to understand what God had done in Christ and to interpret this in the light of their (Jewish) scriptures (see e.g. Matt. 8.17; Luke 22.37; Acts 8.32–35). Viewing Jesus as the 'servant of the Lord' of whom Isaiah had spoken was one important christological development, which may have happened quite early and in the context of Palestinian Christianity (cf. Kelly, 125–26).

The exhortation to follow in Christ's example in suffering is also found in both the Synoptic Gospels and the Pauline letters (e.g. Mark 8.34–35; Matt. 10.16–25; II Cor. 4.7–12; Phil. 2.4–8; 3.7–17). It is clear that the author of I Peter regards this vocation as the calling of each and every Christian. Yet it is not insignificant that he urges this conduct specifically upon those who are slaves. In part this is no doubt due to the fact that slaves, of whom there were probably a significant number in the congregations addressed, were more likely than most to suffer harsh and undeserved treatment either at the hands of their owners or under the legal system of their day (see Horrell 1996, 66–73; Achtemeier, 190–91). Respectful submission may have seemed the most realistic survival strategy (cf. Achtemeier, 195). However, the impact of this teaching must be critically appraised. By urging those at the bottom of the social hierarchy to be submissive and silent even in the face of unjust suffering, is I Peter not in danger of legitimating relations of exploitation, teaching those who are oppressed that it is their Christian calling to bear such suffering quietly and without complaint, extinguishing any pressure for change with the promise of reward in heaven (see further Ch. II 4)? It is notable that I Peter does not make any demands on slave-owners (contrast Col. 4.1; Eph. 6.9) except perhaps in their capacity as 'elders', well-to-do heads of households (see Campbell 1994) who have oversight of the community (5.1–4).

The Christ-like model of non-retaliation and non-violence has, nevertheless, inspired people to courageous living and radical social change. However, great figures in the history of non-violent resistance, like Mahatma Gandhi and Martin Luther King, have not accepted the ideal of quiet submission. While rejecting violence as a means of change, they have raised their voices loud and clear in protest at injustice and oppression. Christians today, living in a social context very different from that of the first century, must try to discern what it means to imitate Christ in the world today. In so doing they will undoubtedly need to study their Bibles carefully, but it may be also that they will need to distance themselves from some of the biblical injunctions.

To wives: the purity of obedience
3.1–6

The next specific group to whom instruction is given is the wives. Opening with an introductory *in the same way*, or 'likewise' (cf. 3.7), the instruction follows a similar pattern to that given to slaves: first comes the instruction to be submissive (3.1), second a comment on the kind of conduct which is pleasing to God (3.2–4), and third a precedent and motivation for the behaviour which is encouraged, here based on the example of holy women of old, particularly Sarah (3.5–6; cf. Michaels, 155).

3.1–2 The opening exhortation follows the same form as that addressed to slaves and continues the theme of appropriate submission. Wives are urged: *be subject to your husbands*. A particular purpose for this behaviour is a missionary one, to win over any husbands who may not be believers – who are 'disobedient to the word' as the author puts it, in his characteristic way (see on 2.8). It should not be assumed that all, or even most, of the wives in the Christian community were in this situation. It is expressed as a possibility ('even if some of them do not obey the word'; NRSV) which was surely a reality in at least some cases (cf. I Cor. 7.12–16). The instruction to husbands which follows in 3.7 shows that in many cases they can be addressed as believers too, and the instruction given to wives applies to them all, whether their husbands are Christian or not. However, the situation of a 'mixed marriage' would be one of particular difficulty. Wives and slaves who converted to Christianity were particularly likely to suffer hardship and accusation: slaves from perverse and unjust masters (2.18), wives from unbelieving husbands who might be angered at their wives' refusal to follow the social norms of the day and adhere to the religion of the head of the household. Even in these difficult situations, the author insists, even when unjustly treated or slandered, slaves and wives should express their Christian faith and demonstrate good conduct by submitting respectfully to their masters or husbands. The author's hope for the unbelieving husbands is that they may be *won* for the faith (cf. the use of this term in I Cor. 9.19–22) *without* the need for words of argument or persuasion, but *won over* primarily *by observing* the pure *behaviour* of their wives (the Greek word *hagnos* probably means 'pure' here in a more general sense than the specific *chaste*). This behaviour should be practised 'in fear' (REB: *respectful*), the word *phobos* again, probably indicating the reverent fear or respect for God rather than for humans (cf. 3.6) which for I Peter is the true motivation for all Christian conduct.

3.3   Now the author draws a contrast between external adornment and the inner beauty which is valued by God. For the idea that God sees and judges not external appearances but what is hidden in the heart, see I Sam. 16.7; Matt. 6.1ff.; Rom. 2.29. The contrast is drawn here first by listing typical forms of external *adornment*: *braiding the hair, wearing gold ornaments, dressing up in fine clothes.* The author's use of such a list implies that at least some of the women in the congregations addressed were not poor. Both Jewish and Graeco-Roman moralists often criticized such adornment of themselves by women, insisting that modesty and good behaviour are much more to be admired (cf. Isa. 3.18–24; Plutarch *Advice to Bride and Groom*, 141e). Such ideas were taken up in Christian teaching in the New Testament and in later writings: I Tim. 2.8–11, for example, contains words and ideas closely parallel to those found here in I Peter .

3.4   True *beauty*, then, *should lie . . . in the inmost self* (cf. Rom. 2.29; 7.22; II Cor. 4.16) where it can be *imperishable*, in contrast to ephemeral external adornment (cf. the contrast drawn between 'perishable gold' and precious faith in 1.7). What constitutes beauty with an *imperishable quality* is a *gentle, quiet spirit*. The term *spirit* here refers to the woman's own 'spirit' – her character and inner disposition – and not to the Holy Spirit. Gentleness, 'meekness', or 'humility', is seen in the New Testament and early Christian writings as a Christ-like quality to be imitated by all believers (cf. Matt. 5.5; 11.29; *I Clem* 13.1–4). Quietness too may describe a virtue applicable to all (II Thess. 3.12; I Tim. 2.2), though more often it is specifically women who are urged to be quiet, meek and submissive (I Cor. 14.34–35; I Tim. 2.11–15; Titus 2.4–5; *I Clem* 1.3; 21.6–7). Here the kind of inner beauty which wives are urged to display is said to be *of high value in the sight of God*.

3.5–6   The author now gives an example which will, he hopes, demonstrate the rightness of women submitting to their husbands.

He points back to *past days*, to Israel's earlier history, as he does in 1.10–12 and 3.20–21, specifically to *the women of God's people* – literally 'the holy women' – *whose hope was in* God. Though living before the time of Christ these women are nevertheless examples of holiness, hope and faith (cf. Heb. 11.1ff.). Drawing together the thoughts of vv.1–4 and the two ideas of appropriate submission and valuable adornment, the author here defines true adornment or beauty as wifely submission (cf. Michaels, 163). The holy women of old, he states, *used to make themselves attractive* by *submitting to their husbands*. Quite possibly the author is thinking particularly of the four great matriarchs of Jewish tradition: Sarah, Rebecca, Rachel and Leah. In any case, he now moves to the specific example of *Sarah, who obeyed Abraham and called him master*. This assertion is derived from Gen. 18.12 where Sarah, on hearing the news that she is to bear a son to Abraham, laughs and says 'my master is old' ('master', or 'lord'; *adoni* in the Hebrew text, *kurios* in the LXX). Her obedience, then, is only implied in the use of the term 'master', and this was a customary form of address, rather like 'sir'. Rabbinic interpreters had, like I Peter, drawn attention to the deference of Sarah to Abraham implied in the address 'lord' (see Goppelt, 224 n.45). However, some Rabbinic commentators had also noticed the apparent cheek which Sarah showed in laughing and saying that her husband was too old – 'past it'. God, they suggested, kept the peace between Sarah and Abraham by not passing on her comment about Abraham's age, but referring only to Sarah's age (Gen. 18.13; see Balch 1986, 94). The fact that the author of I Peter has read a text very selectively in order to back up his own point is suggested not only by these other interpretative angles on Gen. 18.11–15, where Sarah's 'obedience' is not in any case explicitly mentioned, but also by the reference in Gen. 16.2 where the LXX reads: 'and Abraham obeyed the voice of Sarah' (using the same verb, *hupakouô*, as here in I Peter 3.6 and in Col. 3.20, 22; Eph. 6.1, 5). How different his instruction might have been, had the author of I Peter chosen to focus on this scriptural text!

As is often the case, both then and now, our author has read an authoritative text (his scriptures) in a selective way in order to back up the instruction which he wishes to give. Any reading of texts, or of history, is of course partial and selective and presents its own perspective. But critical suspicion is appropriate when, as here, a certain reading of history is used to justify the subordination of a particular social group in the present. In effect the author is saying: 'the best women in the past did it like this, so you should do so too'!

The Christian women addressed by I Peter *have become* Sarah's *daughters* (the Greek word is *tekna*, children), either *by doing good and showing no fear* (as the REB suggests) or through their conversion and baptism (cf. Paul's declaration that all who believe, both men and women, are 'sons of Abraham'; Gal. 3.7). Either way, they must now show themselves to be Sarah's daughters through conduct like hers. Here again is the author's characteristic emphasis on 'doing good', which for wives means being submissive and obedient. His exhortation that they should show *no fear*, 'fear no intimidation' (NAB), suggests a recognition on the part of the author that even good submissive wives might suffer under their husbands (see Corley 1995), especially under those who regard their wives' commitment to Christianity as in itself a subversive act and a rejection of their household's religion. By telling them not to fear such human threats the author implicitly reiterates his belief that God alone is to be feared and that commitment to God is the ultimate motivation for all Christian conduct. Furthermore, unlike in much moral instruction of the time, wives are here addressed directly, as subjects who can and must take their own moral responsibility. Their commitment to God must stand firm, even when accusation and suffering result.

In a hostile social context the author believes that Christian wives should display the quality of quiet submission, even though this will not guarantee freedom from suffering. I have already suggested that this pattern of instruction raises certain difficulties, and many Christians today would prefer to picture the marriage relationship in terms of a partnership between equals. This is to a large extent a modern emphasis, though Paul comes close to it in in I Cor. 7.1–16, where he stresses the equal and parallel responsibilities which both husband and wife have towards one another (note especially v.4). I Peter does not have this view of marriage, but the epistle does at least give instruction to husbands as well as to wives; they too are reminded of their responsibilities.

To husbands: respect for the weaker partner
3.7

Husbands, like the other social groups addressed by the author, are instructed *in the same way*. Though this section is much shorter than those addressed to slaves and wives, a similar pattern is found: address, imperative, then the purpose or basis for the instruction. *Husbands* are told how they should conduct themselves in their *married life*. The Greek word means 'living with' and, not unlike the English word 'cohabit', may imply all aspects of the shared relationship including the sexual (cf. Deut. 22.13; 25.5; Sirach 25.8; Isa. 62.5). Husbands are to live with their wives with a certain *understanding*, the basis for which the author then spells out. Firstly that the woman is *physically weaker*. This is a better translation than 'the weaker sex' (NRSV) which might be taken to mean that the woman is weaker in all senses: morally, physically, psychologically, emotionally (as was often asserted at the time). The author's use of the word *skeuos*, 'vessel', implies that he is thinking of the physical body (cf. I Thess. 4.4). Then, as to a lesser extent now, it was common proverbial 'knowledge' that women were physically weaker than men, even though, as Kelly rightly points out, this assumption is 'only partially correct' (Kelly, 133).

The second basis for the husbands' understanding is that their wives are co-heirs of *God's gift of life*. This does not mean merely that they all share the gift of being alive, as the REB's translation might imply, but rather that the women, as much as the men, are heirs to salvation, the 'inheritance' of eternal life which awaits them (cf. 1.4). The use of the word 'life' probably anticipates the same word in the quotation of Ps. 34 in v. 10.

Husbands are to *treat* their *wives with respect* and honour. It is not quite clear from the Greek whether this *respect* is based on the knowledge both of their wives' physical weakness and of their status as co-heirs of salvation, or only on the latter. Certainly the author implies that the husband must not use his position of physical and social strength to abuse his wife; she must be treated with honour and respect. She is not a mere physical object; she is an equal sharer in the gift of grace which is new life. The husbands' behaviour in this matter is important in order to ensure that their *prayers will not be impeded*. It is not clear whether this refers to the prayers of the husband and wife together (cf. I Cor. 7.5; Michaels, 171) or to the prayers of the men of the Christian community (cf. I Tim. 2.8; Davids, 123). In either case an important point is being made: that proper conduct in relationship to others is essential for a right relationship with God (cf. Matt. 5.23–24; 18.19–35; Luke 11.4; I Cor. 11.17–34). Husbands who fail to treat their wives with respect cannot expect to pray with integrity.

Although the author of I Peter has not challenged the patriarchal pattern of marriage prevalent in his time, nor insisted that the Christian community must shape its relationships in a decisively different way, he does urge that the Christian values of respect and honour for the weak should characterize the relationship of husband to wife. The assumptions of male dominance are not challenged, patriarchal power is not challenged or deposed, but the men are given a responsibility of respect and care which infuses patriarchy with love (cf. Eph. 5.25–33). Gerd Theissen's term 'love patriarchalism' seems an appropriate description of the ethos of I Peter (Theissen 1982, 107).

Summary instruction to all
  3.8–9

3.8–9   The opening of v. 8 – *Finally* – makes it clear that the long passage of instruction which began at 2.11 is being brought to a conclusion. Indeed, having started with a general instruction to all Christians, then addressing specific groups within the congregation, the author now comes full circle and speaks once more *to all of you*. What follows in vv.8–9 is to some extent a summary of the preceding instruction: an exhortation to a pattern of conduct both in relation to believers and to non-believers, motivated by the hope of God's blessing and supported by the quotation of scripture in vv.10–12. These verses also serve as a transition into the next section of the letter. Although the household codes elsewhere do not end with a section of general instruction, it is notable that Romans 13 exhibits a somewhat similar pattern: the instruction to be submissive to governing authorities (vv.1–7) is followed by a general exhortation to love and to right conduct (vv.8–14).

There are particularly close parallels between I Peter 3.8–9 and Romans 12, especially Rom. 12.9–17 (see Michaels, 174; Piper 1980, 218–23). There is a similar progression, with instruction given first in relation to conduct among Christians (3.8; Rom. 12.3–13) and then to conduct with unbelievers and enemies (3.9; Rom. 12.14–21). There is also considerable similarity in the language used in the two passages. This may reflect I Peter's dependence on Romans, but it is perhaps equally likely that both letters are dependent on a common pattern of Christian teaching rooted originally in the Gospel traditions, especially the Sermon on the Mount.

The qualities which are urged upon the believers in v.8 relate primarily (though not exclusively) to their relations with one another; those in v.9, on the other hand, relate mainly to their relations with outsiders. The first two terms in v.8 are found only here in the New Testament, though similar ideas are conveyed in slightly different language elsewhere. The Christians are to be *united in thought* – 'of one mind' (cf. Rom. 12.16; I Cor. 1.10) – and *united in feeling*, that is, 'sympathetic' (cf. Rom. 12.15; I Cor. 12.26). They are to be *full of brotherly affection* (cf. on 1.22) – the author's characteristic emphasis on Christians' 'love for one another' (NRSV) which we have already seen in 1.22 and 2.17. The list continues with 'compassionate', or 'tender-hearted' (*kindly* is perhaps a bit weak; cf. Eph. 4.32) and *humble*, a Christian virtue particularly because of the example of Christ, who 'humbled himself' (Phil. 2.8; Col. 3.12).

In v.9 the focus of the instruction shifts to the responsibilities of Christians towards outsiders, especially towards those who accuse and wrong them. The opening words reproduce almost exactly the words of Rom. 12.17a: *do not repay wrong with wrong* (cf. also I Thess. 5.15). I Peter's emphasis on the wrongs of accusation and slander continues with the further elaboration, *or abuse with abuse*. This refusal to counter insult with insult is precisely how Christ responded to his abusers, as the author has already shown (2.23). Indeed, *on the contrary*, abuse should be countered with *blessing* (cf. Rom. 12.14; I Cor. 4.12). *Blessing* here means more than simply speaking well of someone (its normal meaning in Greek literature); it has the distinctively Jewish-Christian content of wishing God's blessing upon someone, which implies wishing for them the inheritance of salvation.

This Christian teaching of non-retaliation, of responding to insult with blessing, has its roots in the Sermon on the Mount (on the Plain in Luke; see Luke 6.28; Matt. 5.44). The author of I Peter may have known some of these Gospel traditions directly as 'words of Jesus', though mostly they were probably known through the developing Christian teaching based in these traditions and passed on to new converts for their instruction (see Ch II 3(ii); also the debate between Gundry 1967; 1974 and Best 1970).

The Jewish scriptures also teach that one should resist the temptation to revenge (Lev. 19.18; Prov. 20.22; 24.29; cf. Rom. 12.17–21; see Davids, 126), though prayers expressing the desire for vengeance and for God's destruction of the wicked are also found, notably in the Psalms (e.g. Ps. 69.20–29; 139.19–22; 140.10–12; cf. II Peter 2.3–22; Jude 5–19). An attitude of love for neighbour and hatred for enemy may be found in the Qumran literature (1QS 1.9–10; 9.21–22). Such an attitude is reported and rejected by Jesus in Matt. 5.43–45.

The last phrase of v.9 gives the ground and motivation for this behaviour, for responding to evil and abuse with blessing. However, the precise interpretation of the Greek is disputed. Rather literally translated, the phrase runs: 'for you were called to this, that you might inherit a blessing'. To what does 'this' refer? It might refer forwards to the blessing God intends the believers to inherit (as the REB's translation implies, and cf. 4.6). The sense would then be: God has called you to inherit a blessing, so this is a reason why you too should bless others (cf. Kelly, 137; NRSV). Alternatively, 'this' may refer back to the conduct they have been urged to display. This, I think, is more likely: it follows closely the pattern of 2.21 and makes a more logical connection with the scriptural quotation which follows, where those who would inherit life are urged to keep themselves from evil and deceit (see Michaels, 178; Piper 1980, 224–29). The sense, then, is this: God has called you to this pattern of conduct – responding to abuse with blessing – so that you might inherit a blessing (cf. NJB). The hope of their future inheritance is a motivation for ethical conduct.

Supporting quotation of Ps. 34: scriptural proof and promise
  3.10–12

3.10   A lengthy quotation from Ps. 34.12–16 (LXX 33.13–17) now provides further foundation for the preceding instruction. The author has already quoted from this psalm in 2.3 and some have argued that it was a foundation and source for the whole epistle (Bornemann 1920). This is unlikely, though the psalm is important for the author of I Peter, especially here, and its theme – the hope of the afflicted righteous in God's deliverance – is particularly relevant to the whole epistle.

The author introduces the quotation with a single word: 'For . . .' Thus he shows that the citation gives a further reason for the pattern of conduct to which the Christians are called. Although what follows is of course a quotation from scripture, the author does not in fact say so, and the REB has added the words *as scripture says*.

The writer of I Peter has adapted the psalm slightly to fit his context; for example, he omits the words which make the phrase a question (see Ps. 34.12). The word 'love' here – *if anyone wants to love life* – is probably used in the sense of desiring or choosing (cf. Kelly, 138), though there is a parallel in Sirach 4.12: 'whoever loves wisdom loves life'. In the psalm the references to 'life' and 'good days' refer to a long and happy earthly life; here in I Peter the terms take on an eschatological colouring and point to the life which is to be inherited, the glorious salvation of God, which is tasted and anticipated now but is still eagerly awaited.

The person who wishes to inherit this blessing, life with God, *must keep his tongue from evil and his lips from deceit*. Here the author follows the LXX text almost exactly, only changing the imperative from second to third person singular. The psalm is so appropriate for the author because it focusses on the sins of speech against which he warns his readers (cf. esp. 2.1; 2.22–23; also James 1.26; 3.1–12). Unlike those who accuse and revile them, the Christians are not to engage in slander and deceit.

3.11   However, it is not only sins of speech with which the author is concerned. He continues to quote the LXX of Ps. 34, which offers an appropriate summary of so much of his ethical teaching: *turn from wrong and do good*. Here we see again the fundamental antithesis between evil and good and the repeated call of I Peter to 'do good'. The readers are also to *seek peace and pursue it*. The words of the psalm are thus an appropriate summary of I Peter's ethic, and also relate specifically to the preceding instructions in the household code. Slaves, wives, indeed all citizens, are to *do good* and to *seek peace* by quietly and humbly submitting to those over them, accepting suffering, and refusing to trade abuse for abuse or insult for insult. By so doing, the author hopes, they will win over their opponents and accusers, who will be compelled to acknowledge their good conduct.

3.12   The final part of the quotation provides for the author a further reason for adopting this pattern of good behaviour. He demonstrates this link by adding 'for . . .' to the psalm text as the first word of v.12 (omitted by the REB). Christians should devote themselves to peace and keep themselves from evil because *the Lord has eyes for the righteous* (literally, his eyes are 'upon' them), *and ears open to their prayers; but the face of the Lord is set against wrongdoers*. In spite of the present experiences of affliction and hardship, then, God's attention and care are devoted to the righteous, while he opposes the wicked (cf. 5.5). Ultimately, the suffering believers will inherit the blessing of salvation. Yet the author also believes that those who at present oppose them will come to recognize the truth and perhaps also find salvation (cf. 2.12). He leaves the question of their fate rather open, but it is notable where he ends his quotation from Ps. 34.16 (. . . *against wrongdoers*), choosing not to include the final phrase: 'to wipe out the memory of them from the earth'. This is not because he is addressing Christians, 'whom he hardly wants to threaten with God's wrath' (Davids, 128), but rather because of a certain 'reluctance to fasten in detail on the fate of the ungodly' (Michaels, 182; cf. 3.16; 4.5, 18). Perhaps the author leaves the possibility of salvation open: for God is an impartial judge (1.17), and the purpose of the Christians' humble testimony and good behaviour is that unbelievers may realize their error of judgment and acknowledge God (2.12; 3.1–2; 3.15–16; cf. II Peter 3.9). God's impartiality as judge of good and evil requires from Christians continuing humility: they must never become complacent or arrogant, nor must they dare to judge those they regard as ungodly.

Exhortation to all believers to holy living
3.13–4.11

Doing good even in suffering, ready to give an account
3.13–17

Although the quotation of Ps. 34 in 3.10–12 serves to conclude the preceding section of instruction, it also serves as a transition to the discussion of suffering and vindication which follows. 'The writer now brings the Scripture quotation of vv.10–12 directly to bear on the situation of his readers' (Michaels, 184).

3.13   A concise conclusion, phrased as a question, is drawn from the psalm: 'then' (the linking word in the Greek is not translated by the REB) *who is going to do you harm if you are devoted to what is good?* In view of the hardship and suffering which the Christians already seem to be facing, this might seem a rather naive question. The possibility of suffering is indeed confronted in the following verse, but here the writer expresses confidence in the (ultimate) vindication and protection of those who do good – persecution cannot remove them from God's favour (cf. Achtemeier, 230). This confidence may be found throughout the Bible, often expressed in situations where harsh reality seems to contradict the claim, and it is grounded in the assurance that God cares for the righteous (cf. 5.6–7). 'If God is for us, who is against us?', exclaimed Paul (Rom. 8.31; cf. Ps. 91; Isa. 50.7–11).

3.14 The writer's assurance of God's blessing and vindication is reinforced in what follows. Even *if* they *should suffer* (the uncommon mood of the Greek verb shows that suffering is possible but not inevitable) *for doing good,* they are blessed. There is probably an allusion here to one of the 'beatitudes' from the Sermon on the Mount, where Jesus announces God's blessing upon those who are persecuted for righteousness' sake (Matt. 5.10; cf. Matt. 5.11; Luke 6.22; James 1.2–3). The same word appears there as is used here (and in 4.14): *makarioi,* 'blessed'. The assurance of God's blessing is rather more certain than is implied by the translation *you may count your-selves happy,* and the idea of blessedness is more profound than the word *happy* might suggest.

Given this sure knowledge of God's blessing and ultimate vindi-cation the believers need not fear anyone except God. To reiterate this point the writer adapts slightly a quotation from Isa. 8.12–13. *Have no fear of other people* (this is the more likely meaning of the ambiguous Greek than 'do not fear what they fear' [NRSV] though this is possible). *Do not be perturbed,* or intimidated. Although I Peter urges Christians to accept their social position with quiet submis-sion, the epistle also maintains that people are not to be feared. It is not always exactly clear whether the word *phobos,* 'fear', refers to relations towards humans or only towards God (e.g. 2.18; 3.2), but the evidence of the letter as a whole makes it clear: God alone is the rightful object of reverent fear, and no human being or institution (see 1.17; 2.17; 3.6).

3.15 Indeed, the counterpoint to the imperative not to fear other people is the exhortation to *hold Christ in your hearts in reverence as Lord.* This phrase too is built around words from Isa. 8.13, though there the word 'Lord' referred to God whereas the writer here adds 'Christ' to the text (cf. on 2.3). It is Christ the Lord whom they are urged to 'sanctify in their hearts', which means to acknowledge him to be holy in one's innermost being, 'to set him apart above all human authority' (Davids, 131). The believers' ultimate allegiance is not to any human being, not even to the emperor, but, on the contrary, to Christ as Lord.

In view of I Peter's emphasis upon reverent fear for God and not for humans it is interesting that the quote from Isa. 8.13 does not continue further. The verse in Isaiah concludes: 'He [the Lord] will be the object of your fear' (LXX), which forms a fitting contrast to the exhortation not to be afraid of 'them', in the previous verse. Perhaps the author felt that his readers would know the context of the citation and would therefore be aware of the words which followed, without his needing to quote them. More likely he felt it inappropriate to speak of 'fear' of Christ: Christ is an example to be followed, the suffering, risen and vindicated Lord, but it is God the Father who is to be the object of reverent fear (1.17; 2.17).

The exhortation to reverence Christ the Lord in their *hearts* is followed by instruction concerning the verbal testimony which Christians should *always be ready* to give. These two elements of Christian commitment are also found together in Rom. 10.9–10: believe in your heart and confess with your lips.

The word *defence* (*apologia*) was often used of the formal defence made in a legal or judicial context, though it could refer more generally to 'an argument made in one's own behalf in the face of misunderstanding or criticism' (Michaels, 188). The 'account' (*logos*) which Christians should give to *anyone* who *challenges* them might, but does not necessarily, imply a legal context. It is entirely possible that the Christians addressed by I Peter might have found themselves before the local magistrates because of accusations and charges brought by other citizens (cf. on 4.14–16). Pliny's letter to the emperor Trajan on this subject, written around 110 CE when he was governor of Bithynia, reveals that accusations were being brought against Christians, and had been for some time; though they also show that, as far as Pliny was aware, there was no official state policy on the question of whether simply being a Christian was a crime (*Letters* 10.96–97). However, many commentators suggest that what is in view here is the informal accusation and slander which Christians are apparently encountering from their contemporaries (cf. Kelly, 143; Achtemeier, 233). In either case, the description of their faith as *the hope which is in you* hardly represents the language which their accusers would have used; it is the author's terminology, and reflects the fact that for him, hope is '*the* distinguishing mark of Christian existence' (Goppelt, 244). Parallels to I Peter's instruction here are found in the Synoptic Gospels, notably in Luke 21.12–19.

3.16 They must make their defence, not with aggressive self-assertion, but *with courtesy and respect*, or 'gentleness and reverence (*phobos*)', their conduct towards other people being determined by their attitude before God, as is indicated by the reference to a *clear* or good *conscience*, which in I Peter 'involves a moral or spiritual awareness of God, and of oneself before God' (Michaels, 189; see 2.19; 3.21). The purpose of this good conduct is that in whatever way or for whatever reason they are maligned or accused, those who abuse them *may be put to shame*. The language of this verse is very similar to that of 2.12, but there the end result of the unbelievers' observation of the Christians' good deeds is that they may glorify God! The notion of shame here portrays the end-result for those whose accusations are shown to be false; even if this does not happen in the magistrates' courts, it will certainly happen on 'the day of [God's] visitation' (2.12). On the other hand, those whose faith is in God will certainly not (ultimately) be put to shame (see 2.6).

The phrase *your Christian conduct* translates a Greek phrase which literally runs: 'your behaviour (or 'way of life') in Christ'. These last two words are significant, for they show the influence on I Peter of Pauline terminology. The phrase 'in Christ' seems to have been coined by Paul, and it is used very frequently in his letters (about 164 times), as a fundamental description of what Christian life is. It appears three times in I Peter (3.16; 5.10; 5.14).

3.17   This section, which has stressed again the recurring theme of doing good even in suffering, and has encouraged the believers to offer an account of their 'hope' whenever asked, draws to a conclusion with a saying presented in a proverbial form often found in the Bible: *it is better to ... than ...* (e.g. Ps. 118.8–9; Prov. 16.19; 21.9; Mark 9.42–47; I Cor. 7.9; II Peter 2.21; see Snyder 1977). The thrust of the saying is similar to 2.20, which was addressed specifically to slaves: it is imperative to do good, even when it leads to suffering; suffering for doing evil is no credit to anyone (cf. also 4.15–16). Sayings expressing a somewhat similar idea – it is worse to inflict evil than to suffer it – are also found in Greek and Roman writers such as Plato and Cicero (see Achtemeier, 237). Michaels argues for a somewhat different interpretation which gives this verse an eschatological orientation: it is better to do good in God's sight, even though it may mean suffering now, than to suffer God's judgment for doing evil, in the future (Michaels, 191–192; 1967). However, this interpretation seems unlikely: it is easier to read the verse as a further expression, in proverbial form, of the author's emphasis on the necessity for Christians to do good, even when unjust suffering results, and not to do wrong, in which case accusation and punishment would be justified. This is clearly the point made elsewhere (cf. 2.12–14; 2.20; 4.15–16) and it is unlikely that the author would speak of God's judgment as causing 'suffering', especially since he goes on in the following verse to point to the sufferings of Christ.

The phrase *if such should be the will of God* shows (again by the mood of the verb) that suffering is possible but not inevitable. It also implies that suffering and persecution may be the will of God. For I Peter, as for other Jewish and Christian writers, God remains ultimately in control; God is the sovereign Lord of all creation, so only what is 'willed' by God can happen. This conviction was no doubt a source of assurance and comfort, even if it also raises (at least for us) certain theological difficulties (see Ch. II 4).

Christ's suffering and vindication: a basis for confidence
3.18–22

In these verses we find the third of three main christological sections in the letter. Broadly speaking, they form a logical sequence as they focus in turn on different aspects of the 'story' of Christ: in 1.18–21 we read of his being 'chosen before the foundation of the world, but revealed in this last time'; in 2.21–25 we read of his suffering and passion; here the main focus is Christ's vindication and exaltation at the right hand of God.

It is generally agreed that this passage contains traditional credal material summarizing the story and achievements of Christ, though there is less agreement over precisely the extent and form of this material. The language and structure seem to indicate that credal christological formulae are found in vv.18 and 22, while vv.19–21 (perhaps still using traditional material) are concerned with the proclamation of Christ to the spirits and the correspondence between the salvation of Noah and his family and the salvation now effected through baptism.

These verses also comprise the most difficult passage in the whole of I Peter. Their interpretation is much discussed and disputed and the larger commentaries should be consulted on the range of possibilities. Particularly difficult is the proclamation of Christ to the spirits in prison (3.19; see below).

3.18 The writer links his statements about *Christ* to the preceding verses with the introductory 'For' (omitted by the REB; cf. 2.21), not only to show Christ once again as an example of one who suffered but was vindicated, but also to demonstrate that Christ's unique work provides the sure and certain hope of vindication for his followers. *Christ suffered for our sins* is a common credal statement of early Christian faith (cf. I Cor. 15.3), although the word 'died' is more often used, and was substituted for *suffered* in many manuscripts of I Peter . The phrase *for*, or 'on behalf of', *sins* is common sacrificial language (Lev. 5.7; 6.30; Ezek. 43.21–25), though the author does not attempt to explain how Christ's death dealt with sin. But it is clearly seen as a unique, sufficient, and unrepeatable event, done *once and for all* (cf. Rom. 6.10; Heb. 9.28) by a *just* person, on behalf *of the unjust*. The purpose of his suffering was *that he might bring* you (the textual evidence favours reading you and not *us*) *to God*, an image of believers being led and reconciled to God, implying also their need to follow Christ's path (cf. 2.20; Rom. 5.2; Eph. 2.18).

There follow two balanced phrases which seem to be completed by a third phrase found in v.22: *put to death in the body . . . brought to life in the spirit . . . having entered heaven*. Together these three phrases form a rhythmic and credal summary notably similar in form to another concise christological confession in I Tim. 3.16. The contrasting terms *in the body* and *in the spirit* should not be taken to reflect a division of the person or nature of Christ into physical and spiritual 'parts'. Rather, the commentators are agreed, the terms refer to 'the whole Christ regarded from different standpoints' (Kelly, 151): from the perspective of his earthly existence, and by the judgment of sinful human beings, he was *put to death*, yet, vindicated by God and in the power of the Spirit, he was raised and *brought to life* (cf. Rom. 1.3–4).

3.19–20 Here we reach probably the most difficult verse in the whole epistle, of which there are a number of possible interpretations (see Kelly, 153; Davids, 138–41, for summaries of the difficulties and possible solutions). The most basic questions are: when and where did Christ go, what did he proclaim, and to whom – i.e. who are *the imprisoned spirits*? (Marshall, 122–29, sets out the questions and alternatives clearly.) One traditional reading, for example, links Christ's proclamation here with the announcement of the gospel to the dead in 4.6 and interprets 3.19 as a reference to Christ's 'descent into hell' (in the words of the fourth-century creed; not strictly a New Testament idea) when he announced the gospel even to those who had previously died as disobedient sinners (see Goppelt, 255–63, for a recent defence of this view). This reading may be theologically attractive, as it suggests the possibility of salvation for all, even for those who have died unrepentant. However, it is an unlikely interpretation of what the author writes here (but see on 4.6). Another unlikely interpretation, recently supported by Wayne Grudem (pp.203–39) is that Christ preached through Noah (cf. 1.11) to the disobedient people at the time of the flood, who are now spirits imprisoned in hell. Like most recent commentators, I shall broadly follow below the influential interpretation presented by William Dalton (1965/1989).

The answer to the question as to 'when' Christ *went* depends on the understanding of the Greek *en hoi*, with which v.19 opens. The most likely interpretation is not that he went *in the spirit* before his incarnation (so Grudem), nor between his death and resurrection, but that 'in his risen state, made alive *in* (or 'by') *the spirit*', Christ *went and made his proclamation to the imprisoned spirits*.

In order correctly to answer the questions concerning where Christ went and to whom he made his proclamation we need to read this section in the light of the narratives in Gen. 6–7 and the Jewish interpretation of these legends, especially in *I Enoch*, a pseudepigraphal and composite document most of which dates from 200–100BCE (see Charlesworth 1983, 5ff.). The *spirits* are not the spirits of dead human beings, but are the supernatural angelic beings (or possibly their offspring), referred to in Gen. 6.1–4, who were wicked and disobedient, *who had refused to obey* (v.20; see *I Enoch* 6–16; Reicke 1946, 90). These disobedient *spirits*, according to *I Enoch* 10 (e.g. v.13) were locked up in prison. There, according to I Peter, Christ went. The precise location of this prison and of the 'direction' in which Christ travelled are hardly of major importance, but it seems most likely that the writer implies that it was on his post-resurrection ascent, not on a descent, that Christ went to this prison; perhaps he had in mind the location of the 'second heaven', where the imprisoned spirits are kept, according to *II Enoch* 7.1–4. (Jewish cosmology pictured a number of heavens – seven in *II Enoch*; cf. II Cor. 12.2.) Like Enoch, according to the legends developed in the pseudepigrapha attributed to him, Christ made a *proclamation* to these spirits. But what did Christ proclaim? The traditional view is that he proclaimed the good news, and the possibility of salvation. However, the word I Peter uses (*kêrussô*) can imply simply a *proclamation* of whatever kind, as the REB's translation rightly suggests, and the author usually uses the verb *euangelizô*, 'to announce good news',

71

to refer to the proclamation of the gospel. The proclamation which Christ made is more plausibly seen as the announcement of his victory and sovereignty, as the author acclaims it in v.22. This is more compatible with the interpretation of the same legends found in II Peter 2.4–10 and Jude 6 (see Dalton 1979) and also fits the context in I Peter (see Kelly, 156–57): the author is not concerned here with the proclamation of the gospel to the ungodly, but rather with the victory of Christ over all hostile powers and the sure salvation for those who believe (see vv.20–21).

The author's attention moves to the sure salvation for the faithful minority in v.20, as he recalls the story of the flood and the rescue of Noah and his family. Then, *in the past*, a time of disobedience and wickedness among both humans and angelic beings (see Gen. 6; *I Enoch* 6), *God waited patiently*. Jewish writers had commented on God's patience in forbearing wickedness until the time of the flood (see Davids, 141–42) and waiting while *Noah was building the ark*. *Eight people* were saved in this ark, a figure derived from Gen. 7.13 (see also II Peter 2.5), and they were saved *through water*. Both of these points are significant for the author of I Peter: the water because it enables him to draw the link with baptism (v.21), the reference to *a few, eight in all*, because this is a link with the situation of his readers: 'Like Noah these Christians are a small, persecuted minority surrounded by a majority that is disobedient to God . . . But . . . they will be the delivered minority just as Noah and his family were, which is surely comforting in a time of suffering' (Davids, 143). For Christ, whom they follow, has been raised, vindicated, and now reigns supreme over all the spirits and powers (see v.22).

3.21   In the story of Noah the water was the means of destruction from which Noah and his family were rescued. The author of I Peter puts it somewhat differently – they were saved 'through water', not rescued from the water – because of the parallel he wants to draw with *baptism*. As elsewhere in the New Testament, the author here sees in the events and characters of Jewish history pre-representations of the things which have come to fulfilment in the last days, in Jesus Christ (cf. Rom. 5.14; I Cor. 10.1–11).

Turning explicitly to his readers the author explains: *This water*, the water of *baptism*, saves you now in a corresponding way. This is the only explicit mention of *baptism* in the letter, and the theory that the whole epistle is a kind of baptismal homily is implausible (see Ch. II 3(i)). It is also the only place in the New Testament where it is stated that baptism 'saves', though it does this only *through the resurrection of Jesus Christ*. Unlike Paul, the author does not see in baptism the believer's participation in the death and burial of Christ (Rom. 6.3–11); he does proceed to explain what baptism is, making first a negative and then a positive statement. Baptism is *not the washing away of bodily impurities* (literally, 'putting off the filth of the flesh'). This is possibly a reference to circumcision and an assertion that baptism is different (see Achtemeier, 269). The author may simply be making the rather obvious point that the purpose of baptism is not to have a wash, to cleanse the body. Or he may be asserting that it is not in baptism that people are cleansed from their fleshly impulses, important though this cleansing is (cf. 2.1, 11; Michaels, 216). This latter interpretation is perhaps strengthened by the positive point: baptism is not an act of cleansing or fleshly removal, but an *appeal made to God from a good conscience*. Once more this phrase is difficult to interpret. It might mean 'a request to God *for* a good conscience', but it is more likely that it should be understood as a 'pledge' or commitment *to God* – something which the act of baptism signified – made in integrity and in purity of heart (cf. 1.22; I Tim. 1.5). If this is right then it seems that for I Peter baptism is 'an act directed from human beings to God . . . not God's act towards them' (Michaels, 217). Baptism 'saves', then, in the sense which faith 'saves': because they both demonstrate an entrusting and a commitment of oneself to God, who alone can save, *through the resurrection of Jesus Christ*.

3.22 The mention of the resurrection of Christ brings the author back to the credal confession which he left uncompleted in v.18. Christ's exaltation *at the right hand of God* is often mentioned in the New Testament (e.g. Acts 2.33–34; Rom. 8.34); the language is derived from Ps. 110.1, which was interpreted messianically by the early church. The ascended and exalted Christ has *entered heaven* (the third of the rhythmic credal phrases begun in v.18), where he has *received the submission of angels, authorities, and powers*. This all encompassing phrase is derived from the Pauline tradition (e.g. Rom. 8.38; I Cor. 15.24; Eph. 1.20–22; Phil. 2.9–11; Col. 1.16) and acclaims the universal lordship of Christ, whom God has exalted and to whom God has made all things subject. Another psalm, Psalm 8, was an important source for this idea (see Heb. 2.5–9; I Cor. 15.24–28). For Paul and the writer of Hebrews, however, it was clear, because of the sufferings of the present evil age, that the subjection of all things to Christ had not yet happened, though it was ultimately a certainty. For the writer of I Peter, on the other hand, as for the writer of Ephesians (see Eph. 1.22) this victory is already achieved. In spite of their present experiences, therefore, the persecuted Christians of Asia Minor are assured of Christ's victory over those who at present seem to hold power. The day will surely soon come when the salvation and victory of Christ will be revealed and brought to completion by God (cf. 1.5, 7; 2.12; 4.5, 17–19).

It is always been something of a problem for Christian faith that these imminent hopes were not fulfilled. The 'powers' in the world opposed to God show no more sign of being under Christ's dominion now than they did two thousand years ago. Nevertheless, Christian hope, though needing to be rethought and articulated afresh in our very different context, may continue to serve as a basis for commitment and vision (see Ch. II 4).

Encouragement to upright living in a sinful world, for judgment will come
  4.1–6

In this passage the exhortation to live upright lives, even in suffering, in the sure hope of vindication and salvation, is reiterated, building on the affirmation of Christ's victory after suffering in the previous verses (3.13–22). While 4.1–6 is concerned with the way in which Christians are to live in a hostile and sinful world, 4.7–11 then focusses upon the kind of life required within the Christian community. As often in the letter, the believers are here reminded that their conversion involves a break with the past and a turning from sinful ways to live as God's holy children (1.13–2.3). Like the verses which preceded (esp. 3.19–21), this section also contains a number of phrases (notably in v.1 and v.6) which are difficult to interpret.

4.1   The opening verse picks up the language and themes of 3.14 and 3.18 and once again presents Christ as the model and foundation for Christian living. Again the parallel is drawn between the suffering which Christ endured and the trying situation which his followers now endure. *Since Christ endured bodily suffering* – that is, suffered even to death (cf. 2.21; 3.18) in his existence as a human being – *you also must arm yourselves with the same disposition.* The military image of 'arming' oneself is often found in early Christian writings, especially in the Pauline letters (Rom. 13.12; II Cor. 6.7; esp. Eph. 6.11–17). The word translated *disposition* should probably be taken in the sense of 'attitude', 'insight' or 'understanding' (as in Prov. 2.11; 4.1 etc.); understanding 'that produces conduct in accord with that understanding' (Goppelt, 279).

Unfortunately for us, the way the author explains this 'understanding' is difficult to interpret (Davids, 148–50 offers a clear discussion of the options). Clearly the believers' 'understanding' or *disposition* is to be the same as that which Christ himself had (cf. Phil. 2.5), but it is unclear whether the phrase *when anyone has endured bodily suffering he has finished with sin* describes the content of that attitude or the reason for holding it. Another difficulty is whether to take this as a general statement referring to *anyone* (so REB), or as a specific reference to the completed suffering of Christ (so e.g. Kelly, Michaels): 'the one who has suffered in the flesh has finished with sin'. However a clear either/or would not do justice to the thought here. For the main point is to draw a parallel between the experience of Christ and that of his suffering followers. Christ entrusted himself to God (2.23) and suffered unjustly at the hands of sinful people. His attitude was one of commitment to God. And just as Christ suffered, and thus has finished with sin – 'has finished dealing with it once and for all' (Michaels, 228; cf. Rom. 8.3; II Cor. 5.21; Heb. 9.28) – so too the suffering of the Christians indicates their break with the world, their turning from sin and their commitment to God. While for Christ the journey through suffering to glory is completed, his followers must endure for a little while yet (cf. 1.6) the sufferings which the world inflicts upon them. And the same *disposition* which was in Christ, the same commitment and entrusting of oneself to God, must motivate and direct their conduct (cf. Rom. 6.10–11).

4.2   The purpose, then, of arming themselves with the same attitude as Christ, who suffered and died to sin and lives with God, is *so that* they *may live for the rest of* their *days on earth not to satisfy human appetites, but to do what God wills*. Christians, like Christ, must ensure that they 'finish' with sin. Unlike Christ, they are still living their lives *on earth*. But just as Christ was obedient and faithful to God during his earthly life, so they too must continue to be faithful in their commitment to do God's will. As elsewhere in the epistle, they are reminded that this requires a break from their former desires, those of the sinful flesh (1.14; 2.11). This contrast is expressed in the author's characteristic style: 'not this, but that' (Michaels, 229). Indeed, in the following verse he concentrates entirely on what the will of God is *not*, whereas in 4.7–11 positive instruction is given. The reference to *human appetites* should not be taken to mean that all human, physical desires are sinful, as has all too often been implied in Christian teaching. Rather, as the next verse makes clear, the author means the over-indulgent excesses which Jewish and Christian writers frequently saw in the pagan world of the time.

4.3   Drawing a contrast between their present life as Christians and their pre-Christian (Gentile) past, the writer ironically comments that they have already *spent* quite long *enough* – any time is already too long! – *doing what pagans like to do*; literally, doing 'the will of the Gentiles/nations', which stands in contrast to 'the will of God' (v.2). In using the term 'Gentiles' the author adopts 'a thoroughly Jewish designation for those outside one's own community' (Michaels, 230). His list of 'Gentile' sins also follows stock descriptions found in Jewish and early Christian literature (e.g. Rom. 13.13; Gal. 5.19–21; 1QS 4.9–11). Jewish and Christian writers often saw the pagan world around them as hopelessly corrupt. As elsewhere the list here concentrates on excesses in sexual and alcoholic indulgence and connects such vice with idolatry (see esp. Wisd. 14.12–27). The point is not that the Christians previously took part in illegal or criminal acts, but rather that from their post-conversion perspective behaviour widely regarded as 'normal' is now seen as evil (cf. Achtemeier, 282).

4.4   As the believers once went along with this kind of behaviour, so *now*, when they refuse to do so, their Gentile contemporaries *cannot understand it*. The author's language reflects his extreme contempt for, and polemic against, what he sees as the sinful and profligate behaviour which is all around: he speaks of those who *plunge into all this reckless dissipation* (cf. Luke 15.13). The Christians' refusal to participate in such behaviour, including, of course, the many cults and religious festivals which were so prominent a part of life in the empire, and, no doubt, their criticism of such practices, caused them to be hated and regarded with suspicion. As often in the letter, the author of I Peter reveals that the Christians were subject not only to misunderstanding but also to abuse and accusation. The word *abusing* could imply blaspheming against God (cf. NRSV) but it more likely refers here to the abuse directed at the Christians themselves. Secular sources reveal that they were accused of hating the human race, of 'atheism' (that is, refusing to worship the state gods), of pursuing sinister rituals and dubious practices (see Benko

1985). Barriers of hostility and suspicion led to exaggerated polemic on both sides.

4.5   The author's message for his readers facing this situation is one of encouragement and consolation. Those who at present accuse and slander them will one day soon *have to give an account of themselves to* God (cf. Matt. 12.36). The word *account* (*logos*) is the same one used in 3.15 of the 'account' which Christians may be required to give to others. The tables will be turned: at present the Christians are accused and summoned to make their defence; soon their accusers will have to give their own account to God. The nearness of this time (cf. 4.7, 17) is implied in the words *who is ready*. The phrase *the living and the dead* was often used in early Christian literature and expresses the universal scope of God's judgment over all time and all people (Acts 10.42; II Tim. 4.1). Although in such texts it is most often Christ who is seen as the final judge, here in I Peter it is God who is the judge (1.17; 2.23; cf. Rom. 2.6; 3.6). In view of the uncertainties surrounding the interpretation of the following verse, it is important to note that here *the dead* means those who have actually, physically died.

4.6   The reference to *the living and the dead*, though a standard Christian phrase already by this time, provides the launching point for the enigmatic statement with which v.6 begins. What about the dead? How can God justly judge the dead? What follows is 'meant to provide justification for the assertions in v.5' (Achtemeier, 286), more of a 'postscript' than a central point in the argument (Michaels, 225). *That was why the gospel was preached even to the dead.* Interpreting this phrase is notoriously difficult. Traditionally it has often been connected with 3.19 and interpreted as a reference to Christ's proclamation to the spirits of the dead on his descent into hell, a proclamation made either to all the dead, or to the faithful saints of the Jewish scriptures who lived and died before his coming (see Kelly, 172–73; Reicke 1946, 205–206). However, we have already seen that 3.19 does not in all probability refer to dead human beings, nor to the proclamation of good news. Here, on the other hand, it is clear that *the dead* are indeed dead people and that *the gospel was preached* to them.

   The main questions are therefore: who exactly are the dead, and when was the gospel preached to them? Certainly the dead are human beings who are actually dead; it is not a reference to people supposedly 'spiritually' dead. Dalton's proposal, followed broadly by most recent commentaries in English, is that the dead are Christian believers who heard the gospel in their lifetime but have since died. Dalton connects this with the apparent concern among some early Christians about those who had died before Christ's return (I Thess. 4.13–18) and with those who scoff at the promise of that coming (II Peter 3.3–13; Dalton 1979, 553–55; 1965/1989, 226–29). Michaels' variation on this is to argue that the 'Christians' are in fact the righteous saints of the Jewish scriptures, regarded by I Peter as 'Christians before Christ' (cf. 1.10–12; 3.4–5), who also heard the gospel in their lifetime (Michaels does not explain quite how this came about) but have long since died (Michaels, 236–38). On either interpretation the author's purpose, once more, is to emphasize the promise of vindication for the faithful. Death was regarded by people as a sign of condemnation and an indication of the futility of the Christian hope, yet even those righteous people who had died will be vindicated and made alive at the final judgment (see below, on the latter half of v.6).

This may be the correct understanding, though it is not without difficulties, as Dalton acknowledges (1965/1989, 230). First, it feels somewhat strained to take the phrase *the gospel was preached to the dead* to mean 'to people who were alive when they heard it but now are dead' (cf. Brox, 196). Second, the gospel is said to have been proclaimed 'also', or *even, to the dead*, suggesting something different and rather less obvious than that some of those who heard the gospel have since died. Third, the tense of the verb *was preached* (aorist) may suggest 'a definite occasion' (Kelly, 173) and not a proclamation which took place over years, at various times and places. Fourth, there is no clear sign of any concern in I Peter about the fate of Christians who have died, and the concern in II Peter is with *Christian* scoffers who doubt that the Lord's return is ever going to happen. Fifth, while Dalton and others are right to insist that 3.19 and 4.6 should not be taken to describe the same event, 3.19 does clearly indicate a belief that Christ made a proclamation in a place or realm other than among living human beings on the earth; so the idea of the gospel being preached in the realm of the human dead is not inconceivable for our author. (Notably, I Cor. 15.29 surely suggests that some early Christians believed that the fate of someone who had already died could be altered.)

It is possible, then, although this view too is not without difficulties, that our author does have in mind a proclamation of the gospel made once to those who were already at the time dead, though he does not specify when, where, or by whom this was done (cf. Brox, 198–99).

The purpose of this proclamation of the gospel to the dead (however we understand it) is that they too may share in the life which God imparts. Death was often regarded in the biblical tradition as a sign of judgment for sin (Gen. 2.17; Wisd. 2.23–24; Rom. 5.12–19). Hence those who died could be seen as suffering condemnation. I Peter insists that this is a human perspective (cf. REB's footnote translation), for even those who have died will live *in the spirit* 'in the sight of God' (which is a better translation than *as God lives*). The contrasts drawn here have already been found in the letter: the contrast between human and divine perspectives (2.4) and between the 'flesh' (or *body*) and the *spirit* (3.18; cf. 4.1–2). The idea expressed here is closely paralleled in the Wisdom of Solomon:

> The souls of the just are in God's hand . . . In the eyes of the foolish they seemed to be dead; their departure was reckoned as defeat . . . But they are at peace, for though in the sight of men they may suffer punishment, they have a sure hope of immortality (Wisd. 3.1–4, REB).

In contrast to a human perspective, from which death is regarded as punishment and which mocks the faith of the righteous, I Peter holds out the assurance of life and salvation. The author does not specify those for whom this hope will be realized, just as he does not specify which of the dead heard the proclamation of the gospel. He may have in mind the 'righteous' of previous generations (as in the Wisdom of Solomon), or the Christians who have already died before the Lord's return, but if it is correct that he envisages a proclamation of the gospel to people who were dead, and since he does not specify which 'dead' he has in mind, nor how the dead will respond, we should not necessarily assume that he has such a restriction in mind (cf. Goppelt, 288–91; Knoch, 110–11). This is not to imply that he had a vision of universal salvation, but only that, as elsewhere in the letter, he does not specify the outcome of the final judgment. Christians should not be presumptuous, for God judges impartially (1.17). Certainly God's judgment will be against those who continue in sin and wickedness (4.17–18), but I Peter does not say that all who now oppose the Christians are necessarily doomed (note 2.12; 3.1–2). Clearly the author seeks throughout to encourage the believers with the assurance of their vindication, but he is notably circumspect concerning the fate of their opponents (see on 3.12).The certainty of universal judgment seems for the author to require the universal proclamation of the gospel, and may allow to all the possibility of salvation (cf. Rom. 11.30–36; 14.9).

Even if we find it hard to conceive of such things as a proclamation 'to the dead', or a journey of the risen Christ to imprisoned spirits – the author's cosmology and mythological framework may seem alien to us – we should perhaps take something from his confidence in the universal scope of Christ's work and also learn from his reluctance to specify the outcome of judgment. The author of I Peter is content to affirm that God is a righteous judge who will judge justly.

I Peter's insistence that Christian life requires a decisive break with the ways of the world perhaps has both value and risk. Positively it reminds us that we must be prepared to distance ourselves critically from the values and conduct of the world and to shape our lives according to the pattern of Christ. However, we might also wonder whether the exaggerated and stylized polemic which is used to characterize those 'outside' does not foster mutual hostility and erect unhelpful barriers which prevent communication and dialogue. In the first century context, where the Christians were often slandered and treated with suspicion and hatred, such a reaction to the outside world is understandable. Our own context perhaps demands something rather different. These questions will also loom large when we consider Jude and II Peter, where harsh polemic is directed towards people inside the Christian community.

Life in the Christian community
4.7–11

In these verses the author draws to a close the major section of instruction extending from 2.11–4.11. Having elsewhere focussed on the conduct which is necessary towards outsiders, from whom hostility is often encountered, here he gives advice concerning the inner life of the church, the conduct of Christians towards one another. His exhortation here takes up some of the ideas found already in 3.8–9. The pattern and content of the instruction in this passage also have parallels elsewhere in the New Testament. Vv.7–9 have notable points of similarity with the longer passage of instruction in James 5.7–20. The whole passage finds many parallels in Rom. 12.3–13 (notice also the appeal to right living based on the nearness of the end in Rom. 13.11–14), and vv.10–11 especially recall the Pauline teaching about gifts in the congregation (Rom. 12.6–8; I Cor. 12.4ff.). These parallels probably show that the author of I Peter is drawing on traditional forms of Christian teaching here, known already in the Roman church from where he writes. Since Paul's letter to the Romans was sent to Rome it would not be surprising if this letter formed one source for the author, although he does not quote it directly.

4.7   The author's opening assertion about the nearness of the end links this passage with what has preceded, where the reference to the one who 'stands ready to judge' (4.5) implied also the imminence of the final day. For the phrase *is upon us*, compare Mark 1.15 and Rom. 13.12. In the New Testament the nearness of the end is often used as the basis for a call to readiness, prayer, and upright behaviour (e.g. 1.13; Matt. 24.42; I Cor. 7.29–31; I Thess. 5.1–10; James 5.7–20). In order for them *to pray* with due attentiveness (cf. 'watch and pray', Mark 14.38), they must be *self-controlled and sober*. There is no specific reference here to abstinence from alcohol (otherwise Marshall 51, 142), but rather, as generally in the New Testament, to the need to be alert and clear-minded (cf. 1.13; 5.8, where the verb here translated *be sober* is rendered *be on the alert*).

4.8   Of supreme importance for the wellbeing of the Christian community (*Above all . . .*) is *love for one another*. This mutual love for the sisters and brothers must be maintained in all its strength and fervour (cf. 1.22). The motivating reason for such love given here is a proverbial saying: *because love cancels* (or, 'covers') *a multitude of sins*. The original source of this saying was probably Prov. 10.12. However the form of the saying in I Peter is closer to the Hebrew text than to the Septuagint, and since our author generally quotes from the Septuagint, many believe that he knew these words as a proverbial saying which circulated in Christian circles (cf. James 5.20; *I Clem* 49.5; see Kelly, 178). But what is the meaning of the saying? There are two main possibilities. One is that a person's love will serve to cover over their own sins; their own loving actions will be decisive in the final judgment (cf. Matt. 6.12–15; 25.31–46). The second is that love overlooks and forbears the wrongs of others, so love shown by members of the community to one another will enable sins to be 'covered up', in the sense not of being concealed illegitimately, but of being graciously overlooked, hence the translation *cancels*. Paul's comment that 'love keeps no score of wrongs' (I Cor. 13.5) expresses a similar idea. In the context of the appeal to the believers to show love towards one another, this second interpretation makes best sense. Such forbearing love will enable the community to avoid the build-up of resentment and strife which can result if people are not pre-pared to forgive the wrongs they have experienced. This Christian love is rooted in the love of God and in the forgiveness which God demonstrates.

4.9   One of the practical ways in which early Christians demon-strated generosity and love was in the offering of hospitality. Christians who travelled, whether for purposes of work or mission-ary activity (or a combination of the two), were dependent on the hospitality shown to them by other Christians in the communities which they visited. Sometimes, it seems, this generosity was abused (see *Didache* 11–13; Lucian, *Peregrinus* 13, 16). Yet the provision of hospitality was a vital means of mutual support within the growing Christian network of churches and hospitality was regarded as a virtue to be encouraged (Rom. 12.13; I Tim. 3.2; Titus 1.8; Heb. 13.2). Here the believers are urged to *be hospitable to one another without grumbling* (cf. the more general advice in Phil. 2.14). Their generosity must be freely and lovingly shown, and not offered begrudgingly or with any hint of resentment.

4.10   The discussion of *gifts* which follows is clearly influenced by Paul's distinctive language about gifts (*charismata*; Rom. 12.6–8; I Cor. 12.4ff.). In I Cor. 12 Paul emphasizes the Holy Spirit as the giver of these gifts; in Rom. 12.6–8, however, and here in I Peter 4.10–11, the Spirit is not mentioned. The word *gift, charisma*, is closely related to the word *charis*, 'grace'. Charismata, then, are the things given by grace, the gifts of grace, which, according to the New Testament, *God* bestows upon Christian people. These *varied gifts* are *given*, not for personal benefit, but for the benefit of the congregation (cf. I Cor. 14.5, 12, 26). *Each* person therefore has a responsibility to *use the gift he* or she *has received in service to others*. Hence the author urges his readers to be *good stewards* – faithful and careful managers of all that God has entrusted to them (cf. Luke 12.42–48). They are urged, literally, to be *good stewards* 'of the manifold grace of God', in other words, of the various and diverse gifts which embody the generosity and grace of God.

4.11   There is no sign here that the author is addressing only a certain group within the congregation (i.e. the leaders, whom he will address in 5.1–4). Although his discussion of gifts is much briefer than Paul's, he seems like Paul to hold the view that each person will have some gift to be used for the common good. All are being challenged to use their gift fully and responsibly. Unlike Paul, the author does not offer an extended list of gifts; he mentions only two broad areas of 'ministry', that of speaking, and that of rendering practical service (cf. Acts 6.2–4 for a similar broad division). But he does not imply that these ministries are restricted to church leaders. His address is general: 'if anyone speaks . . . if anyone gives service'. Anyone who speaks – by which is meant the various forms in which the word of God might be brought to people: teaching, prophecy, preaching etc. – should *speak as one who utters God's oracles*. The focus of this instruction is not upon the hearers, to urge them to accord the words they hear with divine status, but rather upon those who speak, that they should fulfil their task with the utmost seriousness and care. Similarly, those who *give service*, by which is meant more practical and material expressions of grace, should do so *in the strength which God supplies*. The author's well-chosen words root these two broad areas of 'ministry' in *God*, the giver of all gifts: those who speak, speak the words of God; those who serve (perhaps in ways which are physically and materially demanding) do so in the strength of God. God is the foundation and source of all such gifts and of the ability to exercise them. Therefore the ultimate purpose (the REB does not bring out the link here, but cf. NRSV) of exercising these gifts and of attributing them to God is so that *God* may *be glorified through Jesus Christ*.

This statement leads the author into a short doxology, an acclamation of God's eternal *glory and power* (the word doxology is derived from the Greek word *doxa*, 'glory'). The appearance of this doxology here, in combination with other features in the letter, has led some to propose that the epistle originally ended at this point. The other main argument concerns a supposed difference in the situation reflected in 1.1–4.11 from that presumed by 4.12–5.14. This difference, however, is supposed rather than real (see on 4.12–19; Ch. II 3(i)). Moreover, although some New Testament letters do end with a doxology (e.g. Rom. 16.27; II Peter 3.18; Jude 25) doxologies are often found at various points within a letter (e.g. Rom. 1.25; 9.5; 11.33–36; Eph. 3.20–21). This doxology marks the end of a major section in the letter (2.11–4.11), but it does not suggest that an earlier version of the epistle ended here. One question is whether *to him* refers to God or to Christ. Doxologies in the New Testament may have either as their object (e.g. God in Rom. 11.33–36; Christ in Rev. 1.5–6). Here it is most probably God: the whole of vv.10–11 are clearly God-centred (note the threefold mention of God in vv.10–11a) and the preceding phrase speaks of *God* being *glorified through Jesus Christ*. It is most natural therefore to take *to him be glory* . . . to refer also to God. Almost all New Testament doxologies ascribe *glory* to God or to Christ; here it is linked with *power*, as in Jude 25, Rev. 1.6 and 5.13 (cf. also I Peter 5.11; I Tim. 6.16). The word *amen* is a standard conclusion to a doxology in the New Testament, and expresses the writer's affirmation of the acclamation: it is valid and true.

Even though most Christians today probably do not live in real expectation of the end of the ages being imminent, they may still live with a sense of urgency; longing and hoping to see the signs of the transforming grace of God at work in the church and the world. The Christian instruction offered here, even if its setting within the context of an imminent expectation raises difficulties for us, is of clear and obvious relevance. Community life requires the exercise of forgiving love, and the belief that all have a gift to use responsibly in the service of others affirms the value of every member of every Christian community. Moreover, the purpose, according to I Peter, of exercising those gifts, however they are ranked in the eyes of others, is not self-fulfilment; it is the service of others and the glory of God, though paradoxically it may be precisely in using one's gifts in this way that fulfilment is found.

Christian endurance in a persecuted church
4.12–5.11

The beginning of the third and final main section of the epistle is marked, as was the section beginning at 2.11, with the address *dear friends*. Because here the author assumes the present reality of severe suffering – a *fiery ordeal* – it has been suggested that this portion of our text was written later and separately from the preceding parts of the letter, where suffering is spoken of more as a possibility; or perhaps that the author received fresh news of persecution which influenced his writing of the closing section of the epistle. However, recent commentators rightly reject these suggestions (see Ch. II 3(i)). The reality of suffering for the readers has been evident throughout the epistle, although the author never speaks of such suffering as inevitable (1.6; 2.19–20; 3.14–17). Here, where the writer 'gathers together his message' (Kelly, 184) and reiterates the exhortations and instruction of the letter as a whole, his expression is understandably more vivid and intense, but the situation he assumes is no different from that which has motivated his writing throughout. In 4.12–19 the need for endurance and good conduct in the face of undeserved suffering is reiterated. In 5.1–5 further instruction is given concerning the life of the community itself, with particular attention to the responsibilities of the elders. In 5.6–11 final exhortations are given, together with an assurance of salvation and vindication from God. The letter then ends with its closing greetings (5.12–14).

Enduring suffering for the sake of Christ, trusting in God 4.12–19

The first part of this final main section draws its themes from earlier in the epistle. Vv. 12–13 and 19 echo the words of 1.6–9; yet what was conveyed in the indicative mood earlier ('trusting in him now' etc.) is expressed as imperative here ('*you should rejoice* . . . and *entrust yourselves to God*' etc.). The whole passage also parallels closely the instruction found in 3.13–17. The dominant concern of the epistle – to encourage and instruct Christians facing hostility and persecution – is once more to the fore.

The author's 'language throughout [this passage] is richly informed by the Jewish Scriptures' (Michaels, 259; see further below). Moreover, there are a number of hints which suggest that the author sees an analogy between the predicament of Jerusalem during the time of the Babylonian exile (597–539 BCE) and the current trials faced by Christians in Rome, Asia Minor, and elsewhere. He describes Rome, from where he is writing, as 'Babylon' (5.13). His language about judgment beginning from the house of God (4.17) echoes Ezek. 9.6 (and perhaps Jer. 25.29) where Jerusalem and her people are punished and chastised by God through the might of the Babylonian empire (see further Isa. 13.1ff.; Ezek. 9–32; Jer. 20–50). The prophets' conviction is that judgment for the world – including the Babylonian empire (cf. Jer. 50.1ff.) – and restoration for the people of God, begins with God's judgment of his own people and their city. The author of I Peter sees in the fiery ordeal which Christians are now suffering the beginnings of God's final judgment which will encompass the whole world. The fire of Rome (64 CE) and the destruction of the Temple in Jerusalem (70 CE) may have fuelled his conviction that the time of final eschatological judgment was already beginning. An interesting parallel to his image of the *fiery ordeal* is found in Rev. 18.2–20 where the burning of evil 'Babylon' is vividly envisioned.

4.12   As so often in the letter, the author's concise instruction as to the way in which the believers should face their situation is formulated in both a negative and a positive way: *do not . . .* (v.12) *on the contrary . . .* (v.13). They are *not* to *be taken aback by the fiery ordeal . . . as though it were something extraordinary*. In the Jewish scriptures the idea of fire as a form of testing and chastening is found (e.g. Prov. 27.21; Ps. 66.10; Judith 8.25–27; Wisd. 3.5–6; cf. on 1.7). Jesus too spoke of the likelihood of persecution and suffering and of the times of woe which must precede the end (Mark 13.4–13). The scapegoating of Christians in Rome, blamed by Nero for the fire of Rome in 64CE and punished by being burned as human torches, may have added to the force (as well as the terror) of the imagery. Opposition from the world should not be a surprise (cf. I John 3.13). Unlike the Jews of the time, who were all too familiar with hostility and persecution, Gentile converts may well have been taken aback at the experience of isolation and hostility resulting from their new-found faith. However, because of their allegiance to Christ, they are now like strangers and aliens in the world (1.1; 2.11), and the world finds their behaviour incomprehensible (4.4). Yet they should not be bewildered by this, but should understand it in the light of the example and the teaching of Christ, both of which the author draws on in vv.13–14.

4.13   One reason why such suffering should not be unexpected is that Christ himself experienced the same, and Christians are called to follow in his steps (2.21; 4.1). *In so far as* their sufferings are a sharing in *Christ's sufferings*, they are ultimately a cause for joy; indeed, even now they *should rejoice* (cf. Matt. 5.12). Not all suffering can necessarily count as such, however, as the author has already made clear (2.19–20; 3.17) and will again stress (4.15–16); suffering endured as a punishment for crime and wrongdoing is of no credit to the Christian.

The idea of sharing in Christ's sufferings is a distinctively Pauline theme, and the author's use of this language, albeit in his own particular way, probably shows the influence of Pauline tradition. The closest parallels to the form of words used here are in II Cor.

1.5–7 and Phil. 3.10–11. In these references, as elsewhere, it is clear that, for Paul, sharing in the sufferings of Christ is intimately bound up with sharing in the glory and joy of his resurrection (cf. also Rom. 8.17). The anticipated joy of this future glory, which is still awaited with longing and groaning (Rom. 8.22–23), brings joy even into the present (Rom. 15.13 etc.). Here too the author urges his readers to rejoice now, yet makes it clear that this present joy will be far surpassed *when* Christ's *glory is revealed*; then their *joy will be unbounded* (cf. 1.8).

4.14 Jesus' words in the Sermon on the Mount (alluded to a number of times in the epistle) were already echoed in the call to rejoice in v.13 (Matt. 5.12). Here there is a clearer allusion to the Lord's teaching, to the 'beatitude' for those who are *reviled* and persecuted (Matt. 5.11–12; cf. Luke 6.22). *If you are reviled* (the same word as in Matt. 5.11) *for being Christians* – literally 'in the name of Christ' – *count yourselves happy* ('blessed', *makarioi*; see on 3.14). Just as Christ was rejected, reviled and taunted, so his followers may be too on his account, because they bear his name (cf. Matt. 10.22–25; Mark 9.41; 13.13). But precisely as those who are persecuted on Christ's account, they are blessed.

The author then offers a reason, an explanation, why they should indeed *count* themselves *happy*: *because the Spirit of God in all his glory rests upon you*. The words used here are drawn from Isa. 11.2. The gospel traditions record a promise of Jesus that the Holy Spirit will speak through those who are brought to trial and accused on account of their allegiance to Christ (Matt. 10.19–20; Mark 13.11). More broadly it is clear that central to early Christian faith was the belief that the Spirit of God had been poured out upon believers (Joel 2.28; Acts 2.1ff.; Rom. 8.9–11; I Cor. 12.1ff. etc.).

Most manuscripts of I Peter, though not the earliest, include a further phrase at the end of this verse: 'On their part he is blasphemed, but on your part he is glorified' (NRSV footnote). It is generally believed that this line was added to the text and is not original (but for comments, and an argument for its authenticity, see Michaels, 265–66).

4.15 'Not all who suffer', however, 'can consider themselves blessed' (Davids, 168). Suffering for doing wrong is not commendable (2.19–20). The contrast between suffering for doing wrong and suffering on account of Christ is once more drawn out, again in a 'negative followed by positive' form (vv.15–16). *If you do suffer*, the author insists, *it must not be for murder, theft, or any other crime*. These items read like something of 'a stock list' (Kelly, 188) and are not intended to imply that members of the Christian community were particularly likely to commit murder or theft, although, of course, Christians then as now were not incapable of wicked acts. The list simply reiterates the author's frequent point that Christians must not do wrong (2.12; 2.14–15; 3.17). The fourth item which the author mentions, however, seems more specific (it is marked off from the others in the Greek) and is more puzzling. The phrase *meddling in other people's business* translates one very rare Greek word which appears in Greek literature only here and occasionally in later Christian writings. Its precise meaning is therefore unclear. The REB may well be right to indicate that the author is warning his readers against being regarded as interfering busybodies; such people were certainly not popular in the Roman world, and some Cynic philosophers who sought to oversee the behaviour and morality of others were seen as 'meddlers'. The author may then be urging his readers to guard their own morality within the community but to 'mind their own business' with regard to those outside (cf. I Thess. 4.11–12; II Thess. 3.11–12; I Tim. 5.13; see Michaels, 267–68). Alternatively, the word may indicate another illegal activity, like the items that precede it, namely that of defrauding or embezzling the goods of others (see Achtemeier, 310–13).

4.16 The contrast with suffering when justly accused of some wrongdoing is, of course, suffering *as a Christian*. Here the term *Christianos* appears, one of only three occurences in the New Testament (Acts 11.26; 26.28). It originated as a label applied by (hostile) outsiders to those whom they perceived as 'supporters of Christ' and appears in the writings of Tacitus, Suetonius (Roman historians of the period) and Pliny (governor of Bithynia early in the second century). By the second century the Christians had themselves adopted the name as a self-designation. The author of I Peter seems to indicate that it is a label used by outsiders: they should not be able to 'label' you a murderer or a thief, but they may label you a *Christian*. Some debate centres around the question of whether the situation reflected here is one in which simply being a *Christian* is an official crime and if so whether this indicates a late (second-century) date for the epistle. Certainly the author seems to imply that believers could end up being dragged before the courts because of being a

Christian. However, this does not mean that being a Christian had been officially designated a crime (there is still no clear policy on this when Pliny writes to Trajan in 110CE). Other accusations could easily be made as the basis of charges, whether or not they were justified, and it is clear that at least from the time of Nero's persecution (64CE) Christians could be singled out and mistreated solely because of their faith. I Peter seems to reflect a situation in which Christians often encountered various forms of accusation, hostility, and abuse which could on occasion lead to court appearances (the Gospels, Acts, and the Pauline letters all predict or record similar experiences). Other evidence suggests that the letter was written sometime between 75–95CE (see Ch. II 2(iv)).

While suffering as a murderer or thief would be a cause for shame, suffering *as a Christian* is *no disgrace* or shame (cf. 2.6). Indeed the Gospels record the stern warning of Jesus that his followers must not be ashamed of him (Mark 8.38; Luke 9.26). On the contrary, they should 'glorify God in this name' (a rather literal rendering of the final phrase). Being labelled a *Christian* is by no means a cause for shame, but rather a means of glorifying God.

4.17   A further explanation of the time of suffering is now given. The trials which the believers are enduring are a sign that it is *the time*, the *kairos*, *for the judgment to begin*. As so often in the letter, the writer expresses his view that the end of the ages is imminent; the final judgment which will precede the end has already begun. The notion of a period of trouble and woe prior to the establishment of God's kingdom appears in both Jewish and early Christian literature. In Mark 13.8–19, for example, it is referred to as the 'birth-pangs' and as a time of 'great distress'. Moreover, rooted in Jewish literature is the idea that this judgment, like a refiner's fire, will begin *with God's own household* (cf. Ezek. 9.6; Jer. 25.29; Mal. 3.1–6; see above).

The second half of v.17 is shaped by the pattern and content of the scripture quotation which follows in v.18. Both take the form of rhetorical questions: 'if this is the case, then how much more . . . ?' If God's judgment begins with God's own people (2.9–10), if they feel the force and the distress of the refiner's fire, then how much worse will the *end* be for *those who refuse to obey the gospel of God*? Although the fate of the disobedient is not specified, the implication of the question is clearly that judgment is a more fearful and ominous threat to them than to the household of God. It is typical of I Peter to describe those who do not believe as 'disobedient' (see 2.8; 3.1), just as it describes those who believe as called to 'obedience' (1.2, 14, 22; cf. Rom. 1.5; 16.26).

4.18 A scripture quotation now makes essentially the same point (the REB, to mark this citation, has added the words *Scripture says*, as at 3.9). What is quoted is the LXX of Prov. 11.31, applied here to the context of eschatological judgment (contrast the Hebrew text, which refers to what people receive on earth). Again the fate of *the impious and sinful* is not specified, but left as an ominous question. The threat of judgment expressed here has similarities with II Thess. 1.5–10, though there the fate of the disobedient is declared: 'the penalty of eternal destruction' (1.9). While the author of I Peter clearly believes in the reality of divine judgment, and is hardly optimistic about the fate of the ungodly, he does not, as we have already seen, make definite statements about the outcome of judgment, preferring to leave that in the hands of God.

4.19 The trials which the believers are facing, then, are a sign that the final judgment is beginning. This time of judgment means suffering and distress first for the righteous, but if it is a difficult time for them, how much greater is the threat to the ungodly? The preceding two verses have made essentially this point, and the author now draws out a conclusion (*So . . .*), in the form of an exhortation to the believers.

Once again their suffering is described as *according to God's will*, a view which raises certain theological difficulties for us (see on 3.17). But the essential point is that the world is not 'out of control'; God is working his saving purposes out. *So* then, even though times are hard and suffering is near, Christians should *entrust their souls to God* (*their souls* means essentially 'themselves'; see on 1.9). The phrase *their Maker will not fail them* translates two Greek words meaning 'a faithful creator': they are told to entrust themselves 'to a faithful creator' (cf. Ps. 31.5). The form of words used here is unusual in the New Testament (the noun 'creator' appears only here), but the affirmations that God is creator of all and that God is faithful appear throughout the Bible (e.g. Gen. 1.1ff.; Deut. 7.9; Ps. 145.13; I Cor. 1.9; 8.6; 10.13). Indeed, God's faithfulness is a foundation for Christian hope (cf. Heb. 10.23; II Tim. 1.12). This verse, then, and the whole section from vv.17–19, is intended to sound for the believers a note not of warning but of assurance. Even while suffering – seen as the beginning of the eschatological judgment – they can and must trust in God. They are to entrust themselves to God *while* (or possibly 'by') *continuing to do good*. The Greek could mean either that by doing good Christians entrust themselves to God, or, more probably, as the REB translates, that they should entrust themselves to God while they continue to do good, the importance of which the author has frequently stressed (2.15; 2.20; 3.6; 3.17).

Instruction to the elders, and to the whole congregation
5.1–5

Having written about the fiery ordeal which the Christians are suffering (4.12–19) the author now turns to give instruction mainly to the church's elders but also to the whole congregation (5.1–5). The two passages are linked with the word *Now* (Gk: *oun*, 'therefore'). The reason for the connection may be that, in the author's view, responsible leadership and unity in the congregation are especially vital in a time of suffering and difficulty. A specific link may have been suggested by Ezek. 9.6 where the judgment which 'begins with God's own household' (see 4.17) starts with 'the elders'. The instruction to the elders dominates this section (vv.1–4), followed by a brief instruction to the young (v.5a), after which comes an exhortation to the whole congregation. The pattern of teaching here shows similarities with 2.13–3.12 and with 4.7–11: notice, for example, how the specific command to be submissive (2.13; 2.18; 3.1; 5.5a) is followed by a general appeal to all (3.8–9; 5.5b) and then by a quotation from scripture (3.10–12; 5.5c). Instruction relating to church leaders is frequently found towards the end of an epistle (e.g. I Cor. 16.15–16; I Thess. 5.12–15; Heb. 13.7, 17) and in 'farewell' discourses such as Acts 20.17–36 and II Timothy (cf. on II Peter 1.12–15).

5.1   The author opens with an *appeal to the elders* (cf. the 'appeal' in 2.11). (It would be better to translate 'the elders among you' rather than *of your community*, since the latter might imply that the letter is addressed to one Christian community, which it evidently is not; see 1.1–2.) These people are clearly leaders of the churches, though the apparent connection with being 'older' (see on v.5) has led to some discussion about whether a church 'office' is in view or a position of seniority. This apparent either/or is resolved when we understand that 'elders' did indeed hold a position of leadership, but a position based precisely on their seniority and social standing at the head of their households (see Campbell 1994). Elders are nowhere mentioned in the genuine Pauline letters, but appear in Acts and some New Testament epistles (e.g. Acts 14.23; 21.18; I Tim. 5; James 5.14). I Peter seems to reflect a time when 'elders' are evident as the leaders of the communities, but before these leading figures have begun to be organized further into the structure of bishops (overseers), presbyters (elders) and deacons which emerged towards the end of the first and into the early second century (see esp. the letters of Ignatius).

This verse might appear to indicate that the apostle himself is writing, with the reference to being *a witness to Christ's sufferings* (on the authorship question see 1.1 and Ch. II 2(i)). It is of course equally possible that an author writing in Peter's name added such touches to the letter, but in any case, quite apart from the unanimous testimony of the Gospels that Peter was not present at the crucifixion (Achtemeier, 323), these words are probably not meant to stress the unique experience and position of the apostle but, on the contrary, the calling and responsibilities which he and all the elders share. The term *fellow-elder* establishes a 'common bond' (Michaels, 278) between the apostle Peter and those who are elders, much as the apostle Paul often refers to people as 'fellow-workers' (Rom. 16.3 etc.). Thus they are reminded that they now continue the apostle's work; they have a responsibility for the congregations. Indeed, the phrase linked to *fellow-elder – witness to Christ's sufferings –* does not set the apostle apart as a unique eye-witness. Rather it refers to a calling which he also shares with his fellow-elders, a calling to proclaim, or testify to, the sufferings of Christ (cf. 1.10–12) and to follow in Christ's footsteps (2.21), sharing in his sufferings (4.13). Here, as in 4.13, the mention of *Christ's sufferings* is followed immediately by reference to the *glory to be revealed* (cf. Rom. 8.18). The idea is not that the apostle in some unique way *has shared* already in this *glory* (for example, at the Transfiguration, as has sometimes been suggested). Rather, once again, the emphasis is on the common hope which apostles, elders, indeed all Christians share; the hope of salvation and glory which are yet to be revealed (1.3–9; 4.13–14).

5.2–3   The common calling and the common hope which the elders share with the apostle form the basis for the instruction given in the apostle's name: *look after the flock of God, whose shepherds you are.* The image of God's people as a flock is well known from the Jewish scriptures, where we also find the image of both God and the leaders of Israel as shepherds (see esp. Jer. 23.1–4; Ezek. 34.1ff.; see on 2.25). The New Testament takes up this imagery: Jesus is the chief shepherd (see 5.4) who entrusts the care of his sheep to those who are leaders (John 21.15–17; Acts 20.28).

The way in which the elders should 'shepherd the flock' is now detailed in three pairs of symmetrical antitheses, each of which takes the 'negative-then-positive' form which we have seen so often in I Peter. Most manuscripts of I Peter introduce this list with the word (probably original here) 'overseeing', or 'exercising oversight' (*episkopoúntes*; cf. 2.25), a word closely related to the term which came to be used to describe the task of one particular leader – the *episkopos*, or bishop, who had oversight over the other leaders and church members. Firstly, then, they are to exercise their oversight *not out of compulsion, but willingly, as God would have it* (cf. II Cor. 9.7; Philemon 14; contrast I Cor. 9.16–17). Elders might sometimes have felt that they had little choice about their position within the life of the church, and might on occasion have regretted their visible position as the community's leaders, especially when hostility was encountered from those outside.

Secondly, they are *not* to fulfil their responsibilities *for gain, but out of sheer devotion* – that is, with eagerness and real enthusiasm. Since elders seem to have received remuneration for their service (see I Tim. 5.17–18; cf. Matt. 10.10; I Cor. 9.3–14), and since they probably had oversight of the money which Christians gave for charitable relief of their poorer members, the temptation to greed and self-gain was real (cf. the warnings in I Tim. 3.3, 8; 6.6–10; Titus 1.7).

Finally, their leadership must *not* involve *lording it over* their *charges*, that is, over the portion of God's people which is entrusted to their care. The warning here is against adopting a style of leadership which is domineering and authoritarian. The verb translated *lording it over* is used in Mark 10.42, where Jesus contrasts the style of leadership which is characteristic among the Gentiles with the pattern of humble service which must be adopted by any who would be leaders within the Christian community (cf. Mark 10.45). Leadership in the church should not be about domination and high position, but rather, just as Jesus offered his own way as an example of humble service, so too the elders should set *an example to the flock*. In other words, they should provide a model, a pattern, which believers can imitate (cf. I Cor. 11.1; Phil. 3.17; II Thess. 3.9; Titus 2.7).

5.4   There will, however, be a reward for faithful service on the part of the elders, but it will be received only when Christ, *the chief shepherd* (cf. Heb. 13.20), *appears*. They *will receive glory*, a reward intended for all the elders, indeed all the believers, together, according to I Peter (1.7). This eschatological reward is pictured as *a crown that never fades*. The image is of a *crown* or wreath, like those made from foliage or flowers which marked victory or achievement in the Graeco-Roman world. But unlike such worldly marks of honour and glory, this *crown* will never fade, decay, or be spoiled (cf. 1.4, 18, 23–24; cf. I. Cor. 9.25). The New Testament often uses the image of the crown to describe the believers' eschatological inheritance: e.g. 'the crown of life' (James 1.12; Rev. 2.10); 'the crown of righteousness' (II Tim. 4.8). Here it is a crown of *glory*.

5.5   An instruction is given to 'the young' (there is no reason to assume that it is only *younger men* who are addressed here) in a form very similar to that found in the household codes (cf. 2.18; 3.1; also Titus 2.2–10). It is notable that in some later Christian writings references to elders, the young, as well as women and children, are all grouped together in a kind of household code (*I Clem* 1.3; 21.6–8; Polycarp, *Philippians* 4.1–6.1). But are the *younger* people (meaning the young in the church and not those who fill a certain 'office' designated with this label) urged to *submit to the older*, or to 'the elders'? Does the writer mean the leaders within the church or more generally the people who are older? The Greek word is exactly the same, and it is unlikely that its meaning would be different between v.1 and v.5. The apparent connection between age and position in the church probably reflects the fact that the elders, who were indeed leaders within the church, were the senior members of the community (senior in terms of age, status, and probably faith; see on 5.1). Therefore we should probably translate: 'submit to the elders'.

Next follows a command to *all* – to the whole community. They are to *clothe* themselves *with humility towards one another*. The verb was used to describe the tying on of a garment such as the working apron worn by slaves and shepherds, and thus was perhaps particularly appropriate to describe the putting on of an attitude of humility (cf. Goppelt, 352; Spicq 1994, I, 404). Even though there is a structure of authority and submission, within the church and within the household, *humility* should characterize *all* members of the congregation (cf. 3.8; Eph. 5.21; *I Clem* 2.1; 13.1; 16.1). A reason for this is given, in the form of a scripture quotation. The quotation is from Prov. 3.34, with only one alteration, the change from *kurios*, Lord, to *theos*, God. The same quotation is used, with exactly the same alteration, in James 4.6, suggesting that both letters used a common Christian tradition of teaching and instruction. This 'reversal-of-fortunes language' (Davids, 185) is found in both the Jewish scriptures and the New Testament and expresses the conviction that those who are proud of their achievements and status, self-confident and self-assured, will find their fortunes overturned by God's exaltation of the humble and weak (e.g. I Sam. 2.7–8; Ps. 18.27; 31.23; 147.6; Ezek. 17.24; Luke 1.51–53; 14.11; 18.14; I Cor. 1.27–29).

Final exhortation and assurance
5.6–11

In this section the author gives his final instructions to his readers and assures them of the certainty of God's salvation. First he urges them to humility before God (vv.6–7), then to firm resistance against the devil (vv.8–9). Finally, he gives an assurance that God will keep them secure, which concludes with an acclamation of God's power (vv.10–11). Although most commentators regard v.6 as the beginning of this final section of exhortation in the epistle, they also observe that it is closely linked with v.5. Indeed, the scripture quotation of v.5c provides the basis for vv.6–7 and forms a hinge between the two sections. Vv. 5–9 show considerable similarities with another passage of exhortation in James 4.6–10, which may indicate that both authors drew on an established pattern of Christian teaching. Certainly they both reflected on some of the same verses from the Jewish scriptures.

5.6 The exhortation of v.5b concerned the need for all Christians to show humility in their conduct towards one another. The scriptural quotation in v.5c which provided a basis and motivation for this behaviour spoke generally of 'the humble', so here the author turns to the need for humility before God (cf. James 4.10). The image of the *mighty hand* of God is frequently found in the Jewish scriptures, especially in connection with God's liberation of Israel from bondage in Egypt (e.g. Ex. 3.19; 6.1; Deut. 9.26; Jer. 21.5; Ezek. 20.33–34). Like the scripture quotation in v.5 this is once more the language of 'reversal of fortunes' (see on 5.5) and it echoes a saying of Jesus found a number of times in the Synoptic Gospels: 'all who exalt themselves will be humbled, and all who humble themselves will be exalted' (Matt. 23.12; cf. 18.4; Luke 14.11; 18.14). God's exaltation of the humble will occur *in due time*, a clear reference to the last time, the final time of judgment and salvation which, for I Peter, is very close at hand (cf. 1.5).

5.7 Closely linked grammatically with the previous verse, this verse specifies further what it should mean to live humbly before God; that is, 'the positive entrusting of oneself and one's troubles to God' (Kelly, 208; cf. 4.19). Again the author's thought is rooted both in the Jewish scriptures and in the teaching of Jesus. 'Cast your burden on the LORD, and he will sustain you' (Ps. 55.22); 'God's care is for all people' (Wisd. 12.13). In the Sermon on the Mount, often echoed in the teaching of I Peter, Jesus urges people not to worry or be anxious, because their heavenly father knows their needs and cares about them (Matt. 6.25–34; cf. Luke 12.22–32; Phil. 4.6). This teaching does not encourage a naive belief that God will protect his children from all trouble and hardship – the readers of I Peter knew that that was not the case – but affirms that no hardship or suffering can ultimately separate anyone from God's love and care, which will endure and finally secure the salvation and well-being of those who entrust themselves to God (cf. Rom. 8.31–39; II Cor. 1.9–10).

5.8–9 In the present time of difficulty and distress, however, there is also the need for vigilance and endurance. The terse imperatives here sound like the instructions given to those who must face a battle; indeed, the author doubtless believed that the end-time, the last days in which he and his readers were living, would be a time of evil and suffering, a time of climactic conflict between good and evil, as the day of judgment and salvation drew near (cf. on 4.12–19). Much Jewish and Christian writing of the time expressed a similar belief (e.g. Matt. 24.4–28; II Thess. 2.3–12; 1QM, the War Scroll from Qumran). In such a time the faithful must *be on the alert* (cf. 1.13; 4.7, using the same word, there translated 'sober') and *wake up*. This second imperative recalls the instruction given by Jesus to his followers who face the trials and traumas of the end-times (Matt. 25.13; Mark 13.35, 37 etc.). Other early Christian epistles also use similar language to urge vigilance in the light of the imminent end (I Thess. 5.6; Rom. 13.11–12).

Throughout I Peter it is clear that the believers face hostility and accusation from their contemporaries. Only here is their supreme, supernatural *enemy, the devil,* mentioned. The word translated *enemy, antidikos,* denoted an adversary or accuser, originally in the court-room context (e.g Prov. 18.17). The name *devil* (Gk: *diabolos*) means 'slanderer' and is found in the LXX as the translation for the Hebrew 'Satan', meaning 'opponent' or 'adversary' (I Chron. 21.1; Job 1–2; Zech. 3.1–2). Both terms are used in the New Testament only to refer to the devil, Satan, the tempter, accuser, and supernatural arch-enemy of God and God's people, the embodiment of all that is wicked (e.g. Matt. 4.1ff.; 25.41; I Cor. 7.5; Eph. 6.11; II Thess. 2.9–10 etc.). The threat which the devil presents is graphically portrayed: he is *like a roaring lion* (cf. Ps. 22.13; II Tim. 4.17), who *prowls around* (cf. Job 1.7; 2.2) *looking for someone to devour* – a vivid image of 'a beast swallowing its prey in a gulp' (Davids, 191; cf. Jer. 51.34; Jonah 1.17). In view of this threatening presence the believers should be alert, 'for when a lion is on the prowl it is no time to sleep' (Davids, 191).

The instruction is to *stand up to him* (cf. James 4.7), to resist him, *firm in your faith*, indicating the apparent danger that 'Satan' will drag people away from the faith, a real possibility when persecution and suffering are the result of belonging to the believing community. While human accusers and opponents should encounter blessing and not resistance from the Christian community (3.9), and while those in authority, even those who are unjust, should receive due submission (2.13–14, 18), Satan should by all means be opposed and resisted (cf. Eph. 6.11–13). The difficulty of making such distinctions, if, for example, one thinks that the injustice meted out by cruel slave-owners might be labelled the wicked work of Satan, does not occur to the author, presumably because his main focus is upon the danger of losing one's faith.

The believers may perhaps be strengthened in their resolve and encouraged in their afflictions if they learn that they are not alone in their experience. So the author informs them that their *fellow-Christians in this world are going through the same kinds of suffering*. This need not imply that there was an organized empire-wide persecution of Christians at the time the epistle was written (see on 3.15; 4.16) – this was almost certainly not the case – but it shows that Christians throughout the empire also experienced the kinds of hostility and abuse which the believers in Asia Minor had to face. The networks of communication within early Christianity, through the travels undertaken for purposes of mission, work, letter-carrying etc., meant that the experiences of the sisters and brothers in various places could become known (cf. II Cor. 8.1–2; I Thess. 1.7–8; 2.14). The uncommon noun which the author uses to describe the *fellow-*

Christians – 'the brother/sister-hood' (cf. 2.17) – emphasizes the solidarity of the believers not merely within their local communities, but as one Christian community throughout the world.

5.10–11 The author concludes the main body of his letter with an assurance that, despite opposition and suffering, God's power and grace will enable the believers to stand firm and to inherit God's eternal glory. Their *suffering* will only be for a short while (cf. 1.6), since the end is surely near. *The God of all grace* (cf. 1.13) will surely not fail them; God has *called* them to *eternal glory in Christ* (note the typically Pauline phrase 'in Christ' again; see on 3.16). This is a central theme of the whole letter, reiterated here in a closing affirmation: they are a chosen people, called by God to inherit glory and salvation (see 1.2–9; 1.15; 2.9; 5.1, 4). The form of this closing affirmation is like that of the 'benedictions' found at the close of a number of New Testament epistles, except that here what God will do is expressed as firm certainty, as promise, whereas it is often found in the form of a prayer or request (cf. Rom. 15.13; I Thess. 5.23–24; Heb. 13.20–21).

Four verbs, roughly synonymous in meaning, are used to describe what God *himself* (the author adds emphasis with this word) will do. God *will restore* ('set right', or 'make ready'; e.g. II Cor. 13.11; Gal. 6.1), and *establish* ('strengthen' or 'support'; e.g. Rom. 16.25; I Thess. 3.2; James 5.8). The phrase *strengthen you on a firm foundation* translates the second two verbs, which mean 'to strengthen' (*sthenoô*; a verb unique in the New Testament) and 'to establish' or 'set on a foundation' (cf. Matt. 7.25; Col. 1.23). Together these verbs represent a strong affirmation that God *will* make them firm in their faith, strong and immoveable, able to withstand everything which the world and the devil may throw at them (cf. Eph. 6.13), like the person whose house was built on rock (Matt. 7.24–25). We may recall, whether the author intended his readers to or not, the imagery from earlier in the epistle: Christians are like living stones being built into a spiritual house, whose foundation-stone is Christ (2.4–8).

Such a strong affirmation of God's promised vindication and victory is appropriately concluded with a short doxology which praises God's might or power (see further on 4.11): *All power belongs to him*, to the God of all grace, *for ever and ever! Amen.*

Closing greetings
5.12–14

Greek letters usually ended briefly, often concluding simply with 'farewell', or 'good luck' (cf. Acts 15.29; Goppelt, 367). Paul developed a distinct and Christian pattern of letter-ending, usually comprising greetings and commendations together with a short blessing, doxology or prayer (Rom. 16; I Cor. 16.15–24; I Thess. 5.23–28; etc. contrast James 5.19–20; I John 5.20–21). I Peter broadly follows this Pauline pattern, though not in a way which would indicate direct literary dependence. This short closing section comprises a commendation of Silvanus and of the letter itself (v.12), followed by greetings from the church in Rome, from Mark, and from the author of the epistle, ostensibly Peter, and concluding with a blessing (vv.13–14).

5.12   This verse raises intriguing questions concerning the authorship and origins of the epistle (see Ch. II 2(i)). Here we are told that *this brief letter* (not brief at all, by Greek letter standards; the statement is probably an expression of 'conventional politeness', since 'letters were expected to be brief' [Kelly, 216; cf. Heb. 13.22]) was written *through Silvanus*. This *Silvanus* is probably to be identified with the Silas sent as a representative from Jerusalem to Antioch (Acts 15.22ff.) who later became a partner with Paul in some of his missionary activity (Paul refers to him as *Silvanus*; Acts 16.19–18.5; II Cor. 1.19; I Thess. 1.1; II Thess. 1.1). The varied names probably represent Greek (Silas) and Latin (Silvanus) forms of the Aramaic name She'ilah (see BAGD, 750). This man seems to have been a person of some standing in the early church and could possibly 'have belonged to a group of missionaries and teachers around Peter during the latter's last days in Rome' (Goppelt, 371), though we have no firm evidence for this. Alternatively, the *Silvanus* mentioned here may be a different person, otherwise unknown to us. But what is meant by the phrase *through Silvanus*? There are a number of possibilities:

(a) Silvanus may have been the secretary to whom the letter was dictated (we know, for example, that Paul often, if not always, used a secretary; see Rom. 16.22; I Cor. 16.21 etc.).

(b) Silvanus may have been commissioned to write the letter, on behalf of the apostle, or on behalf of the Roman church. (If this theory were correct, however, it is rather surprising that Silvanus should write the self-commendation found in this verse, unless that represents the apostle's own verification and commendation of the one entrusted with writing the epistle.)

(c) Silvanus may have been the person whose task it was to deliver the letter (Achtemeier, 349–52).

(d) If the letter is pseudonymous, written some years after Peter's death (see Ch. II 2(iv)), then either Silvanus is someone other than the Silvanus known to us elsewhere in the New Testament (Achtemeier, 351), or a later author has included in his pseudonymous letter a fictitious reference to Silvanus (and to Mark). Could there be a reason for this, other than the desire to add touches of authenticity? Goppelt suggests the explanation 'that representatives of the Roman church are passing along in the letter a tradition shaped by Peter and Silvanus' (p.370). Without being quite so precise about the idea of 'a tradition shaped by Peter and Silvanus', we may nevertheless agree that this theory fits well with the view of I Peter as a document which draws together various traditions of Christian teaching, Pauline and Jewish/Petrine (see Ch. II 3(ii)). The author therefore claims not only the authority of Peter for his teaching, but also indicates the influence and standing of Pauline co-workers (Silvanus and Mark). Silvanus possibly and Mark probably, having worked with Paul, also worked with Peter in Rome (see on v.13). I Peter therefore demonstrates that in the Roman church, after the death of the great apostles, the Pauline and Petrine/Jerusalem traditions, which had often been in conflict in earlier times (see e.g. I Cor. 1.12; 9.5; II Cor. 11.12–27; Gal. 2.11–21), were drawn increasingly together (cf. on II Peter 3.15–16). It is therefore somewhat misleading to speak of a specifically Petrine school in Rome.

Silvanus is commended, using the personal authority of the apostle (*I know . . .*), as a *trustworthy* or 'faithful' *colleague* (the Greek word is 'brother', *adelphos*, but the REB is right to indicate that this means more here than simply a fellow-Christian; cf. I Cor. 1.1; II Cor. 1.1). If the view taken in (d) above is right, the author thus indicates the influence of Silvanus (and indirectly of Paul) upon the teaching contained in the epistle and affirms, in the name of Peter, Silvanus' reliability as a witness to the gospel.

The purpose and character of the letter itself are then mentioned. It was written *to encourage* and exhort (*parakalô*, the same Greek verb used in the 'appeal' of 2.11 and 5.1). The author also affirms that he wrote *to testify* ('a strong verb which implies that his testimony carries weight' [Kelly, 216]) *that this is the true grace of God*. What precisely does he mean by *this*? Probably he is referring to the gospel message of salvation by the grace of God, and the way of life it demands, even in adversity, as it is set out in the letter. The author thus testifies both to the Christian life as founded upon the grace of God and to the epistle as a true and faithful account of these things. Consequently he urges his readers: *in this stand fast*.

5.13–14   The letter concludes with greetings, first from *your sister church in Babylon*. In fact the word *church* does not appear in the Greek text, where we find the feminine words 'the co-elect one' (cf. II John 1, 13). This could conceivably refer to a particular woman, such as the apostle's wife, but this is most unlikely. The interpretation *church* (feminine in Greek) is undoubtedly correct; ancient scribes clearly understood it in this way, for the word *church* was added to some texts of I Peter . Unfortunately the REB does not bring out the word 'co-elect' ('chosen together with you'; NRSV) in translation, though the epistle emphasizes the elect, chosen, status of the people of God (1.1–2; 2.9).

Although there are other locations which might possibly have been indicated by the name *Babylon*, it is almost certainly Rome to which the author refers (see Davids, 202; Ch. II 2(ii)). This is how the reference was understood by Papias in the second century, and a few texts of I Peter contain the word Rome instead of Babylon. The Babylonian exile was a deeply significant period in Israel's history (cf. above on 4.12–19) and by the time the book of Daniel was written (second century BCE), tales of faithful Jews in exile in Babylon had become paradigmatic for Jews seeking to remain faithful in the context of an alien and oppressive culture. After 70CE both Jewish and Christian writings adopt the name Babylon as a symbolic designation for Rome (e.g. Rev. 17.5, 18; II Esd. 3.1, 28; 15.43ff.). Thus they indicate their sense that Rome is the dominant power in the world, and that God's people are now scattered as aliens and exiles in a hostile imperial culture (cf. 1.1).

Personal greetings are also sent *from my son Mark*. The word *son* probably indicates not a biological relationship, but a close and affectionate relationship between an older and a younger Christian (cf. I Tim. 1.2; II Tim. 1.2). *Mark* is probably the John Mark mentioned in Acts 12.12, 25 and 15.39 (referred to just as John in Acts 13.5, 13). He was for a time a companion of Paul and Barnabas and is mentioned in a number of the Pauline epistles (Phileman 24; Col. 4.11; II Tim. 4.11). Eusebius also records tradition from the early second century which links Mark with Peter in Rome: Mark was a follower of Peter and he wrote down Peter's memories of what Jesus did and said (*EH* 3.15.1; 3.39.15). The greeting from *Mark* might be genuine, if Peter, or even Silvanus, were writing the epistle. Alternatively, it may reflect a later author's desire to mention esteemed and well-known Christian figures from the circle whose teaching he seeks to promote and whose authority he claims.

Finally the recipients of the letter are told to *greet one another with a loving kiss*. In the Jewish scriptures kisses are most often a sign of family relationships (e.g. Gen. 31.55; 33.4; 45.15 etc.) and in the earliest churches, in which believers regarded one another as brothers and sisters, the practice of exchanging kisses soon became traditional. Our earliest evidence for this practice comes from the letters of Paul, where we find the very similar phrase 'a holy kiss' (Rom. 16.16; I Cor. 16.20; II Cor. 13.12; I Thess. 5.26). By the mid second century the 'kiss of peace' was 'a regular feature in the Sunday eucharist at Rome' (Kelly, 221).

The closing words of the epistle are words of blessing upon the recipients of the letter, *all who belong to Christ* – literally, who are 'in Christ' (see on 3.16). Paul's letters generally end with the phrase 'the grace of the Lord Jesus be with you' (sometimes expanded; see I Cor. 16.23; II Cor. 13.13; Gal. 6.18 etc.) though he sometimes also included the wish for peace near the end of his letters (e.g. Rom. 15.33; II Cor. 13.11; cf. on 1.2). Here the author uses the traditional Jewish blessing of *peace, shalom*, given a specifically Christian colouring with the words 'in Christ'. Comparable to the greeting of peace here are Eph. 6.23, II Thess. 3.16 and III John 15. Even, or especially, in situations of suffering and conflict the blessing of *peace, shalom*, may be sought (cf. 3.11) – a desire for wholeness and well-being in relation to God and to one's neighbours.

IV

INTRODUCTION TO JUDE

1. The significance of Jude

If I and II Peter are relatively neglected amongst the writings of the New Testament, then Jude can certainly be described as 'the most neglected book in the New Testament' (Rowston 1975). The reasons for this are not hard to see: not only is Jude very brief, but it is also dominated by sustained polemic against heretical opponents (see 2(v) below) written in a style both alien and offputting to many modern readers. The best known section of Jude is its elegant closing doxology (vv.24–25). Jude is undoubtedly important as a witness to the varied and developing character of early Christianity, and to the ways in which Jewish scriptural and post-scriptural traditions were applied to a situation in which the threat from false teachers was deemed to be a pressing concern, yet its enduring theological value is questionable (see 4 below). Nevertheless, precisely because its character and content raise difficult questions – about the value and authority of scripture and how Christians today should use it – it is important to study this most neglected corner of the canon, and not only for its (considerable) historical interest (see Ch. I).

In the early church Jude seems generally to have been respected and valued. II Peter almost certainly used it as its primary source, and it is acknowledged as scripture in the Muratorian Canon from Rome around 200CE. Origen and Eusebius in the third and fourth centuries refer to some doubts about its status, which seem to have been based on Jude's use of non-canonical works (*I Enoch* and the *Assumption of Moses*; see Kelly, 223–24). Jude was no doubt valued because of its usefulness as an anti-heretical tract, providing to some extent a paradigm for the anti-heretical writings which were produced in the early Christian centuries, as the church sought to ascertain its identity and to define its 'orthodox' boundaries (see Wisse 1972).

2. Historical questions

(i) Who wrote Jude?

The letter names and identifies its author as *Jude, servant of Jesus Christ and brother of James* (v.1). There is widespread agreement that this person should be identified along with James as one of Jesus' brothers (see on v.1; Matt. 13.55; Mark 6.3). Jude's older brother James was a prominent leader in the Jerusalem church, until his execution in 62CE (see Josephus *Antiquities* 20.200) and I Cor. 9.5 refers to 'brothers of the Lord' who travel around as missionaries (see on v.1). Eusebius also records traditions concerning missionary activity in Galilee by relatives of Jesus (*EH* 1.7.14) and recounts a story about the grandsons of Jude (*EH* 3.19.1–20.6), set in the reign of Domitian (81–96CE) which, while it may be more or less unhistorical, at least points to a certain prominence for the figure of Jude in the church of the late first century and beyond (see Bauckham 1990).

The real question about authorship is whether Jude himself wrote the letter. Most scholars have suggested that he did not, and that it was written in his name some time after his death. Richard Bauckham, however, has argued that Jude's own authorship of the epistle is at least plausible, and that the writing fits well within the circles of early Palestinian Jewish Christianity, especially in its use of Palestinian Jewish traditions and literature (Bauckham, 3–16; 1990, 171–78; cf. also Charles 1993). In favour of Jude's own authorship is the oddness of someone writing in Jude's name, rather than in that of a more prominent figure, and not using the title 'brother of the Lord', which would have seemed a more impressive identification. However, it is by no means impossible that someone would have thought it appropriate to write in Jude's name, after the well-known martyrdom of James, and we have seen a certain amount of evidence for Jude's prominence (cf. also Neyrey, 30–31). An author writing in Jude's name may well have imitated the identification 'servant of Jesus Christ' found in James 1.1, especially if he wished to make something of a link with James in his own attack on those who were 'antinomians' – those who saw no need to obey the law and who lived as 'libertines' (see James 2.14–26; Sellin 1986, 211–12; further 2(v) below).

An objection often raised against the possibility of Jude's own authorship is the good quality of Greek found in the epistle (see further 3(i) below). However, the increasing recognition of the degree to which Greek language and culture had penetrated Palestine makes this a somewhat indecisive argument (cf. Charles 1991b, 118: 'perhaps it is indeed time to dispel the myth of "Galilean illiteracy"').

My own judgment is that Jude himself is unlikely to have been the author of the epistle. This conclusion, however, rests to a considerable extent on a decision about the likely date of the letter (see 2(iv) below).

(ii) Where was Jude written?

Many of the historical questions about Jude simply cannot be answered, at least not with any certainty or precision. The familiarity of the author with Jewish scriptural and post-scriptural writings, in Hebrew and possibly Aramaic as well as Greek, may point to a Palestinian origin (Knight 1995, 32), though it is equally possible that the author may have been a Jewish Christian who had previously left Palestine (perhaps because of the war of 66–72CE). Egypt and Syria have also been proposed as places of origin (see Neyrey, 29–30; Gunther 1984, who argues for an origin in Alexandria, Egypt).

(iii) To whom was Jude sent?

There is also no direct information concerning the destination of the writing. Jude does not specify its addressees, other than in general Christian terms (see v.1). It may even be questioned whether it was written to address a specific historical situation at all (Wisse 1972), though the letter does seem to reflect a concern with 'heretics' and false teachers who are a reality (in some form) in the life of the churches (see 2(v) below). All that can be gleaned from the letter itself is that the audience are likely to have been predominantly Jewish Christians familiar with the traditions to which the author refers, in an area where the authority of the brothers of the Lord (see 2(i) above) was recognized. But that does not give us much specific information, and Palestine, Syria, Egypt, and Asia Minor have all been suggested as possible destinations (Knoch, 158).

(iv) When was Jude written?

Jude has been assigned to a remarkably wide range of dates, from around 54 to after 160CE (see Bauckham 1990, 168–69). Such a diversity of opinion reflects the lack of clear evidence on this matter. If Jude himself wrote the letter, then the latest possible date is some-time in the 80s (we have no record of when Jude died), more likely sometime between 50–70 (cf. Knight 1995, 26–27). If someone wrote in his name (conceivably authorized by the old man himself, though this is mere speculation) then the range of dates is more open; yet nothing requires a date later than the end of the first century (it is most unlikely to have been written against second-century Gnostics, as has sometimes been proposed – see 2(v) below). Since II Peter appears to use Jude, and if II Peter is to be dated around the end of the first or early in the second century (see Ch. VI), then Jude must be dated sometime before this.

Arguments about the date of Jude focus particularly on vv.3 and 17 (and to some extent on vv.5 and 20; see further commentary). In these verses, it is generally argued, we see evidence that the letter stands some distance from the earliest years of the church and reflects a development towards what is known as 'early Catholicism'. James Dunn lists three features which distinguish 'early Catholicism': the fading of the parousia hope (the hope for the Lord's imminent return); increasing institutionalization; and crystal-lization of the faith into set forms (1990, 344; but note Elliott 1969). Bauckham, however, has argued that: 'None of these three features is evident in Jude' (p.8; also Charles 1993, 52–62). Certainly it may be doubted whether Jude fits so clearly into a general pattern of insti-tutionalization and early Catholicism, but it does seem to me that vv.3 and 17 reflect the perspective of second or third generation Christianity. (Jude's 'apocalyptic' character [see 3(i) below] does not require an early date.) V.17 looks back to the declarations of 'the apostles', viewing these people as 'a revered group belonging to an earlier generation' (Kelly, 281; for a different interpretation see Bauckham, 13; 1988b, 3814–15). They are for the author 'a closed group of bearers of authority for the church, whose words have already become the basic tradition of faith' (Knoch, 188; cf. *I Clem* 42). The reference in v.3 to 'the faith which was once and for all delivered to the saints' not only implies that the initial age of apostolic proclamation is past, but also reflects a later period in which there emerges an increasing emphasis upon 'the faith', as the body of tradition which is to be believed and guarded (cf. also Jude 20; I Tim. 4.6). Add to this the fact that the stereotyped polemic against opponents found in Jude finds its closest parallels in Christian literature generally dated towards the end of the first century (Pastorals; II Peter; *I Clement.*, etc.; cf. Wisse 1972, 142–43) and the most likely date for Jude would seem to be somewhere roughly between 75–90CE. However, this can be little more than an educated guess.

(v) Why was Jude written?

The letter of Jude makes clear its main aim: to urge the believers to stand firm in their faith in the face of the threat from false teachers (vv.3, 20–21). Most of the letter, however, is taken up with an attempt to demonstrate that these heretical opponents are those about whom scripture and the apostles warned and whose judgment and doom is certain. So who were these opponents and what was the nature of their threat to the church?

The problem in seeking to answer this question, of course, is that we only have the author's polemic against the false teachers from which to build up a picture of their activity and beliefs, and his polemic is surely stereotyped and exaggerated, hardly to be taken as an accurate or fair description (see Thurén 1997). When Jude describes the opponents as 'ungodly' (*asebeis;* vv.4, 15, 18), the label 'is not descriptive but judgmental' (Wisse 1972, 137). Frederik Wisse is surely right to argue that Jude describes his opponents in stock terms as the false prophets of the last days, but wrong to suggest therefore that the letter does not address a historical situation at all. So what can we learn about the so-called heretics?

Often the opponents in Jude have been described as 'libertine Gnostics' (see Sellin 1986, 206), though it is increasingly recognized that the hints in the letter hardly fit what is known of second-century Gnosticism (see Bauckham 1990, 162–65). Some therefore prefer a description such as 'libertine pre-Gnostic spirituality' (Dunn 1990, 282), indicating that Jude's opponents share some of the characteristics and tendencies later developed in Gnosticism. Even this, however, is questionable and it is better to try and understand the opponents of Jude on their own terms, without the anachronistic 'Gnostic' label.

The picture that emerges from the letter suggests that the opponents are travelling charismatic or prophetic teachers: they 'worm their way in' from outside (v.4), but they are certainly Christians who are accepted by the congregations they visit (they join in their love-feasts; v.12). They seem to claim spiritual visions in which they enter the angelic realm; perhaps they even despise the angels (v.8). They are also accused of perverting God's grace into licentiousness (v.4). This is generally interpreted as reflecting their antinomianism – their disregard for God's law and their belief that they have been liberated from such restrictions. We should be wary, however, of taking such descriptions at anything like face-value (as does e.g. Charles 1993, 48–52; see Thurén 1997). Bauckham (e.g. p.11) is perhaps rather too ready to accepts the hints, for example, of their sexual immorality. The later Gnostics were often accused of such libertinism, but their own writings often suggest the opposite: a concern for abstinence and sexual asceticism (cf. Wisse 1972, 138). It may be that Jude's opponents were influenced by a Pauline tradition which emphasized freedom from law and charismatic experience (cf. Rom. 3.8; I Cor. 13.1; 14.2; II Cor. 12.1ff.; Col. 2.16–23; Sellin 1986, 209–12; 220–22). This may help to explain Jude's link with James (v.1), for the opponents in each case may share a somewhat similar outlook (see 2(i) above; James 2.14ff.). Charles (1993, 48–52) sees the opponents as people who were once Christians but have since departed the faith. This may be Jude's view, but it seems certain that the opponents still considered themselves Christians.

Diversity and disagreement were present from the earliest days of Christianity (cf. e.g. Gal. 2.11ff.), but Jude seems to reflect a situation in which a solidifying orthodoxy (cf. vv.3, 17, 20) is concerned to oppose and exclude 'heresy' by labelling the 'false' teachers as 'despicable deviants' (cf. Pietersen 1997). Their views or arguments are hardly glimpsed in the text; instead what we find is a detailed exposition of scriptural examples intended to demonstrate that these people are the false prophets who stand in the line of Cain, and whose doom has been indicated from the earliest times. Comparable stereotypical polemic is found in the Pastoral Epistles (e.g. I Tim. 6.3–5; II Tim. 3.1ff.; see Karris 1973). A plausible scenario for Jude's attack would be the situation in the latter decades of the first century such as is reflected in the *Didache*, where warnings are given about travelling prophets and teachers who may take advantage of the material support offered by congregations (*Didache* 11–13; cf. Jude 16; Martin 1994, 75, 83–84; Sellin 1986, 222–24). The *Didache* recommends the appointment of resident leaders – bishops and deacons – and loyalty to the Gospel (*Didache* 15.1–4; cf. I Tim. 3.1ff.; Titus 1.5ff.; Horrell 1997b).

3. *Literary issues*

(i) *Style and genre*

Jude opens as a traditional ancient letter (see on vv.1–2), though it lacks any mention of specific addressees and any closing greetings, and has more the feel of a homily circulated in letter form. It may have been intended for wide distribution, perhaps as a general 'anti-heretical leaflet' (Schelke, quoted by Sellin 1986, 208).

Jude is written in a good Greek style, with a rich vocabulary much of which is unused in the rest of the New Testament. J.D. Charles (1991b; 1993, esp. 20–64) in particular has drawn attention to the literary qualities of Jude. These include its frequent use of triplets (see e.g. on v.1, v.8), catchwords to link sections of the epistle (e.g. vv.4, 15, 18), and parallelism. All this is woven into a carefully and intricately structured whole. 'In this epistle', Charles suggests, 'we are witnesses to a literary-rhetorical artist at work' (1991b, 115; see also Watson 1988).

One of the most notable features of Jude's style is the way in which the author uses scriptural types and traditions to address the circumstances of his own time. The central section of the letter (vv.5–19) may be termed a 'midrash', 'in the general sense of an exegesis of Scripture which applies it to the contemporary situation' (Bauckham, 4; see also Ellis 1978). The sources which Jude used are mentioned in the following section, and an outline of the structure of the epistle may be found in 5 below. The detailed exposition of Jude's midrash will be found in the commentary itself.

More specifically, Jude may be described as 'apocalyptic' in its mode of thought. This admittedly rather loose term describes the character of much intertestamental Jewish writing (not least that to which Jude is especially indebted; see below) and early Christian thought too. In essence, apocalyptic refers to the revelation of divine wisdom, to insight into the superhuman realm (see Rowland 1990). Characteristic features of Jewish-Christian apocalyptic shared by Jude include a focus on the cosmic and supernatural realms, with an explanation of worldly disorder in terms of cosmic and angelic/demonic rebellion; an antithesis between the ungodly and the faithful righteous; a vision of an impending eschatological judgment by God and the consummation of the divine purpose. For the apocalyptic writer, 'the world in its present form is passing away' (I Cor. 7.31) amidst woes and calamities, and the final appearance of God (or his Messiah) is at hand. (On the apocalyptic character of Jude, see further Rowston 1975, 561–62; Bauckham, 8–11; Charles 1993, 42–47.)

(ii) Sources

The most obvious of Jude's sources is the Jewish scriptures. Mostly the author refers to characters or events rather than quoting directly (e.g. vv.5–7), but he also alludes to specific passages, and when he does, reveals a knowledge of the Hebrew text (e.g. vv.12, 13, 23; Bauckham 1990, 136–37). Jude's interpretation of the scriptures, however, is heavily influenced by post-scriptural Jewish traditions and pseudepigrapha (see Charles 1993, 128–66). Most obvious, and probably most influential, is *I Enoch*, a pseudepigraphal and composite document attributed to Enoch, dating from the second to first centuries BCE (see Charlesworth 1983, 5ff.). In vv.14–15 Jude explicitly quotes a 'prophecy' of Enoch, a citation from *I Enoch* 1.9, which the author of Jude appears to know in Aramaic and which he adapts christologically (see Osburn 1977; Bauckham, 94–96). Indeed, *I Enoch* is probably Jude's 'key text', providing not only the central quotation in vv.14–15, but other allusions (e.g. in vv.6, 12–13; see Bauckham 1990, 181–216).

In v.9 Jude reveals dependence on a Jewish apocryphal legend concerning the death of Moses. Often this source is referred to as the *Assumption of Moses*, though it is most likely that Jude's material was drawn from the lost ending of a writing (current in the first century CE) known as the *Testament of Moses* (for detailed work on Jude's source see Bauckham, 65–76; 1990, 235–80).

These scriptural and post-scriptural Jewish works are Jude's most important and obvious sources. There is no apparent allusion, for example, to the Synoptic Gospels. The Pauline letters, on the other hand, have often been suggested as a further influence upon Jude's writing. Similarities of language (e.g. in vv.1–4, 19) and phraseology (e.g. cf. v.20 and Eph. 6.18) may certainly be detected, but these hardly establish a familiarity with Pauline theology or letters, and may more plausibly be attributed to shared Christian vocabulary and forms of expression. Indeed, Jude appears to draw on traditional Christian teaching (e.g. vv.20–25) and cites a prophecy which is attributed to the apostles (vv.17–19).

Finally, II Peter must be mentioned, since there is clearly a strong link between the two documents (see Ch. VI 3(ii)). However, while it has sometimes been suggested that Jude used II Peter as a source, or that they both used a common source, it seems most likely that Jude was a source for II Peter, and not vice versa.

4. *Content: themes and theology*

Jude has suffered not only from neglect but also from a degree of 'scholarly contempt' and, 'in Protestant scholarship, at least, a long tradition of theological denigration' (Bauckham 1990, 134, 155). This negative evaluation of Jude's theology is primarily due to the long section of sustained polemic (vv.4–19) which dominates the letter. This major section certainly raises difficult questions about theological appropriation (see below) but the rest of the letter should not be ignored in an appraisal of Jude's content (cf. Bauckham, 4; 1990, 156–57).

Jude's 'chief concern', according to Charles (1993, 167) is 'to strengthen and exhort the *faithful* by painting in graphic terms the fate of the *unfaithful*'. The author urges his addressees (v.1) to guard the true faith (v.3) and to continue living in this faith, grounded in God's love, empowered by the Spirit, and awaiting the Son's return (see vv. 20–21). Moreover, in view of the harsh portrayal of judgment on the 'opponents' in vv.4–19, it is also important to note the pastoral concern indicated in vv.22–23 for those who are attracted to or already involved in the dangers of false teaching. As Charles (1993, 64) notes: 'Vitriolic denunciations as well as pastoral concern are both found in the epistle.'

Both the positive appeal and the negative announcement of judgment are theologically grounded. The letter is written to people who are called, loved, and kept by *God* (v.1) – described as the Saviour to whom belongs glory, majesty, power and dominion (v.25). The gospel is fundamentally about the grace of God (v.4). On the other hand, those who abuse or pervert this grace are destined by God for punishment and doom (vv.4–19). The letter displays an interesting tension between 'divine sovereignty and human freedom' (Charles 1993, 101, 167–68). On one side is the assurance that God loves and keeps those who are called (v.1); God is *the One who is able to keep you from falling* (v.24). Yet if God is 'able to keep' then why did he not 'keep' the Christians who, as Jude's opponents, are now destined for eternal darkness (v.13)? Jude's answer seems to be that these people were marked down long ago for their judgment (v.4; cf.

v.14) – were they simply not 'chosen' to be saved? (Cf. Ch. II 4) On the other side, however, there is the *appeal* to the faithful to 'keep themselves in the love of God', and to await their salvation in prayer and hope (vv.20–21). All people have a responsibility for which they are answerable.

The foundations of Jude's message are also *christological*, though the emphasis is not upon the love or grace of Christ (these qualities are ascribed to God), nor on his saving death (it is God who is described as Saviour). What emerges clearly is that *Christ* (Messiah) is *Lord and Master* (v.4: the first reference in Christian literature to Jesus as 'Master', *despotês;* see Bauckham 1990, 283, 302–307; Charles 1993, 55–56). Also prominent in Jude is the expectation of Christ's return (vv.2, 21) and of his role in bestowing salvation (v.21) and executing judgment (vv.4, 14–15). However, it is impossible to draw a neat separation between the action of God and of Christ in Jude. In v.5, for example, it is God's deliverance of his people from Egypt which is recalled, possibly seen as executed (like the judgment which is described in vv.6–7) by Jesus as the agent of God (cf. Fossum 1987). The Lord's authority which the heretics reject (vv.4, 8) cannot be distinguished as *either* the authority of God *or* of Christ – 'the same divine authority is at stake throughout' (Bauckham 1990, 312). It is something of an exaggeration to say that 'the writer seeks to transfer to *Kyrios*-Jesus all the attributes of glory, majesty, dominion and power which are ascribed to Yahweh in the OT' (Charles 1993, 129). The doxology clearly ascribes these things to God, *through* Jesus Christ (v.25). A better summary of Jude's christology is 'that Jesus is the eschatological agent of God's salvation and judgment' (Bauckham 1990, 312). As such Jude's content and traditions reflect the influence of Palestinian Jewish-Christian apocalyptic (see 3(i) above).

Jude's theology has more of a binitarian than a trinitarian emphasis (vv.1, 24–25), except in vv.20–21, where the believers are urged to *pray in the Holy Spirit*. The only other reference to the Spirit in the letter is the negative assertion that the false teachers 'do not have the Spirit' (v.19). Clearly, then, the inspiration of the Spirit was both important and contentious for the Christians for whom Jude was written, but it is not a theme developed in the epistle.

As a positive theme Jude emphasizes God's ability to keep the faithful secure in his love, for mercy and eternal life on the last day. The more prominent negative theme concerns the condemnation which awaits the false teachers. The bulk of the letter is occupied with polemic against these people. Modern readers are likely to find this section of the letter difficult and uncongenial, and its theological value questionable. Certainly Bauckham and Charles have done much to show that Jude's polemic comprises a skilful use of scripture and scriptural traditions – a 'midrash' – with notable similarities to patterns of Jewish exegesis at the time. But the appreciation of this document in its historical and cultural setting and of its important witness to the character of early Christianity does not resolve or remove the problems concerning its theological value. Jude does not engage with the arguments or perspectives of the opponents, but labels and condemns them as the false prophets of the last days whose condemnation was foreshadowed and predicted in scripture and by the apostles (Wisse 1972; Thurén 1997). By comparing them with the classic 'stock' characters who were in Jewish tradition the prime examples of deviance and apostasy, these people are portrayed as the epitome of wickedness and evil. There is some unintended irony, moreover, in Jude's attack: Michael is presented as an example of appropriate humility who did not slander or rebuke even the devil, but remained within the bounds of his own authority (v.9). Yet the author of Jude then proceeds to slander his opponents (v.10 etc.; cf. Thurén 1997, 463)! Those who hold opinions and engage in patterns of living which the author regards as unacceptable and heretical are denounced and condemned and the faithful are warned away from such people. What we witness in Jude is a developing Christianity which is concerned to exclude deviation and so-called 'heresy', but with denunciation rather than reason. Quite apart from the question as to whether the false teachers were really as immoral as Jude portrays them to be (see 2(v) above), we might also want to question the picture of God as one who prepares eternal fire (v.7) or an eternity of blackest darkness (v.13) for those who deviate from the truth. Certainly we must acknowledge that Jude belongs to a thought-world – that of apocalyptic Judaism and early Christianity (see 3(i) above) – which is very different from our own, and which raises for us theological problems.

Our assessment of Jude need not, however, be entirely negative. Ralph Martin (1994, 85–86) suggests some points of contemporary value. First, even if Jude's 'method of rough-handling and browbeating the opposition with dire threats cannot be ours', we still do well to remember that the gospel makes moral claims and imposes responsibilities upon us, and should not be reduced to 'cheap and easy salvation'. Second, Jude's use of non-canonical writings as a source of insight may perhaps encourage us 'to enlarge our vision of the truth' and of the places where it may be found. Third, although Jude's method of using examples from the past is in many ways questionable, nevertheless it serves as a reminder that the past is an invaluable (and unavoidable) 'reservoir of meaning' with which to interpret and understand the present.

Jude represents a valuable witness to early Christian faith, and its positive message about God's ability to keep believers secure in his love may be important to Christians facing trials and pressures of diverse kinds. Yet for Christians today aware of variety and divergence within the churches (not to mention among different religions) its vision of God and God's judgment offers little towards a Christian vision for life in the church or in the world.

5. *The structure of Jude*

1–2   Letter opening: address and greetings
3–4   Introduction to the body of the letter: occasion and theme
5–23 The main body of the letter
   5–19   Midrashic interpretation of scriptural types and
           prophecies
       5–10   Three scriptural types: examples of God's
              judgment
       11–13 Three more scriptural types: wicked
              characters then and now
       14–16 The ancient prophecy of Enoch
       17–19 A modern prophecy of the apostles
   20–23 The appeal to the faithful
24–25 Closing doxology

V

COMMENTARY ON JUDE

Letter opening: address and greetings
1–2

Like the other letters of the New Testament, Jude opens in a way which broadly follows the letter-writing conventions of the period, though with specifically Jewish and Christian content. The pattern involves the identification of the sender, then the recipients, followed by greetings.

1 The sender of the letter is named as *Jude* (the Greek *Ioudas* is elsewhere in the New Testament rendered 'Judas' but here by convention as *Jude* – cf. e.g. Luke 6.16, though neither of the Judas's mentioned there is the person referred to here). This *Jude*, whether he actually wrote the letter or not, is widely agreed to be the brother of the Lord mentioned in Matt. 13.55 and Mark 6.3 (see Ch. IV 2(i); Bauckham, 21–23). He is here described, however, not as 'brother of the Lord', but as *servant* (or, 'slave') *of Jesus Christ*, a designation which indicates his call and devotion to the Lord's service. It is with the authority of one called to be a *servant of Jesus Christ* that he addresses the readers (cf. Rom. 1.1; Phil. 1.1; also I Chron. 6.49; Ps. 89.3; 105.42 etc.).

Jude is more precisely identified, however, with the words, *brother of James*. While there are a number of characters named James and Judas in the New Testament (e.g. Acts 1.13), Bauckham (p.24) rightly notes that 'after the death of James the son of Zebedee' (Mark 1.19; Acts 12.2) 'only one early Christian leader was commonly called simply "James" without the need for further identification' (e.g. Acts 12.17; I Cor. 15.7; Gal. 2.9). That was the James, brother of Jesus, who was a leader of the Jerusalem church (see also Eusebius *EH* 2.23.4–7). Moreover, the only brothers named James and Jude in the New Testament are the brothers of the Lord mentioned in Mark 6.3. Jude, or the person writing in his name, 'therefore uses this

phrase to identify himself by reference to his more famous brother'
(Bauckham, 24), thus adding to his status and authority as author (cf.
Neyrey, 45). While others may have referred to them specifically
as 'brothers of the Lord' (I Cor. 9.5; Gal. 1.19), Jude 1 and James 1.1
suggest that the brothers themselves, or those who wrote letters
in their names, avoided making this self-designation, preferring
'servant of Jesus Christ' (see Bauckham, 24). The writer of Jude may
have imitated James 1.1 in this.

There is no mention of the place or places to which the epistle is
being sent, though the problems which the epistle addresses suggest
that some particular situation is in view. The recipients are described
in three ways (on 'triplets' in Jude's style, see Charles 1991b, 122–23):
as *those* who are *called* (a typical New Testament description of
Christians); as those *who live in the love of God the Father* (the Greek
here is somewhat unusual, but clearly refers to God's love for the
believers and perhaps to the idea of their dwelling 'in God', cf. Jude
21; I John 4.16); and as those who are *kept safe for Jesus Christ* –
the Greek does not explicitly refer to his *coming*, but does imply an
eschatological sense, looking forward to the day of salvation
(Bauckham, 26; cf. I Peter 1.4–5; I Thess. 5.23). The conjunction of
similar terms in the exhortation in Jude 21 shows that 'the divine
action . . . must be met by a faithful human response' (Bauckham, 27).

2   The form of greeting in Jewish and Christian letters is effectively
a blessing upon the recipients. Unlike almost all New Testament
letters Jude does not include the word *grace* (Gk: *charis*), but the more
typically Jewish *mercy* (probably equivalent to the Hebrew *ḥeseḏ* –
see on I Peter 1.3) *and peace* (*shalom*; cf. *II Baruch* 78.2), to which Jude
also adds *love*. Also somewhat unusual among the letters of the New
Testament is the use here of *three* terms (though see I Tim. 1.2; II Tim.
1.2; II John 3); most common is the pairing 'grace and peace' used by
Paul and in I Peter 1.2 and II Peter 1.2. The verb used here expresses
the wish that these things may be bestowed upon the readers *in
fullest measure* (see further on I Peter 1.2).

Introduction to the body of the letter: occasion and theme 3–4

Following the opening address and greetings, the author now
explains the reason for his writing, indicating both the major theme

of the letter and his 'appeal' to the readers. Indeed, v.3 indicates briefly the appeal which will be made in vv.20–23, whereas v.4 outlines the reason for making this appeal, the threat from false teachers, which is the subject of vv.5–19 (see Bauckham, 29; Watson 1988, 48)

3   The recipients are addressed as *my friends,* 'beloved' (*agapêtoi*), a common form of address in early Christian writings (e.g. Rom. 12.19; James 1.16; I Peter 2.11; II Peter 3.1). There is some uncertainty as to how to understand the rest of the verse. Some suggest that the author's intention *to write to you about the salvation we share* 'in common' is the intention which has been fulfilled in the letter, even though the writer was spurred into action by a crisis which came to his attention. Others propose that an intended letter on the general subject of Christian salvation has 'been interrupted by the urgent need to deal with a particular critical situation' (Kelly, 245). We have no evidence to suggest that the general letter which seems to have been intended before the crisis was ever written. Perhaps, as Lauri Thurén (1997, 456) has recently suggested, Jude's opening remarks do not reflect a sudden crisis but are rather a typical Greek letter-opening: 'The verse seeks to apologize for not writing earlier and to introduce the issue at hand.' The letter which we have does nonetheless seem to have been motivated by a sense of some urgency in the face of a present threat from false teachers. In the light of this threat, the author appeals to his readers *to . . . struggle for the faith.* The language of struggle, of fighting, is drawn from the realm of athletic contests, and was used metaphorically in Greek and Jewish literature, as well as in the New Testament (e.g. I Cor. 9.24–27; Eph. 6.10–17; I Tim. 6.12).

The author's exhortation to struggle 'for the faith that was once (and for all) delivered to the saints' (cf. NRSV rather than REB) is rather crucial to discussions of the date of the letter. It seems to reflect a post-apostolic period (Knoch, 174) in which the author looks back to the time when the apostles (rather than *God,* as the REB suggests) delivered 'the faith' to those who believed (see Ch. IV 2(iv)). Although talk of 'the faith', of the passing on and receiving of tradition, and so on, is certainly not absent from the earliest Christian writings (e.g. I Cor. 11.2, 23; 15.3; Gal. 1.23), it is in later letters, especially the Pastoral Epistles, that an emphasis upon 'the faith' – a body of sound teaching – 'becomes much more pronounced' (Kelly, 248; I Tim. 1.3; 4.6; Titus 1.9; cf. also Jude 20).

4   The reason for this pressing appeal is that *certain individuals have wormed their way in* to threaten the life of the congregations. The language used has a definitely 'contemptuous ring' (cf. I Cor. 4.18; Gal. 2.4, 12; Kelly, 248). The persons in view are probably wandering Christian teachers, who were influential (and sometimes problematic) in early Christianity (see Matt. 7.15; II Cor. 11.4–15; II John 9–11; *Didache* 11–15; Theissen 1993, 33–59). *Scripture long ago* indicated that such people 'were designated for this condemnation' (NRSV) – precisely what the author will seek to demonstrate in vv.5–19. 'This condemnation' points forward to the fate described in vv.5–19 which will be executed at the end, at the final judgment; while the troubles which the intruders cause for the faithful believers here and now are a sign that these are the end-times (see vv.14–21; II Tim. 3.1; II Peter 3.3).

The false teachers are described as 'godless', *enemies of religion*, (cf. Rom. 5.6; I Tim. 5.9; I Peter 4.18) who *pervert* the grace of God *into licentiousness* – a term often used to describe the immoral actions, especially the sexual immorality, of those who claim the freedom to do as they like (e.g. Rom. 13.13; II Cor. 12.12; I Peter 4.3). Certainly this 'antinomianism' (lawlessness) was a real danger in early Christianity, not least as a consequence of Paul's insistence that salvation came by God's gracious act in Christ, and not by works of law, and upon freedom (I Cor. 5.1–6.20; Gal. 5.1, 13; also II Peter 2.19). Paul, however, vehemently insisted that his gospel must not be taken as a licence to sin (Rom. 3.8; 6.1ff.). What is less clear here is the extent to which the teachers whom Jude condemns were really guilty of such immorality, or whether the attack on them merely employs somewhat stereotyped polemic (see Ch. IV 2(v)). Since we only have the author's polemic, we should certainly be wary of accepting at face value his labelling of them as 'deviant', or at least recognize that this labelling reflects his own position and perspective (cf. Barclay 1995; Pietersen 1997). Through their immoral deeds, rather than necessarily through any implied doctrinal error, the author believes that the false teachers deny *Jesus Christ, our only Master and Lord.* (As the REB's footnote indicates, this phrase could be read differently, as referring to God the Master, and Jesus the Lord, but the translation given above seems more likely; cf. II Peter 2.1; Bauckham, 39–40. See further Ch. IV 4).

The main body of the letter
5–23

Midrashic interpretation of scriptural types and prophecies
5–19

In verse 5 the main body of the letter begins (cf. White 1972), divided into two main parts (with vv.17–19 marking to some degree a transition from the denunciation of the opponents to the appeal to the readers which follows in vv.20–23). In vv.5–19 the author presents a careful and detailed exposition of various scriptural types and prophecies with his own interpretations (each of which is introduced with the word *houtoi*, 'these people'), intended to demonstrate that the false and immoral teachers are destined for divine judgment. Following the work of Ellis (1978) and Bauckham (Commentary and 1990, 179–234) the structure and pattern of Jude's exposition can be set out as below. It is a pattern of interpretation which shares a good deal in common with the scriptural interpretations found at Qumran, and which reveals a knowledge of traditions known in Palestinian Judaism and Jewish Christianity (cf. on I Peter 2.4–10). Since Jude does not actually quote scripture, but refers to events, characters, and places, and to traditions later than those written in the Hebrew Bible, the term 'text' below has been placed in inverted commas (following Bauckham 1990, 181–82).

	5a	introductory statement
5b–7	'text' 1: three scriptural types
	8–10	interpretation, including secondary 'text' (v.9)
11	'text' 2: three more scriptural types
	12–13	interpretation, including further scriptural allusions
14–15	'text' 3: the ancient prophecy of Enoch
	16	interpretation
17–18	'text' 4: a modern prophecy of the apostles
	19	interpretation

Three scriptural types: examples of God's judgment
5–10

5   The writer introduces his exposition by indicating that what will follow is in fact a reminder of things his readers *already know*. Presumably they were aware, at least to some degree, of the traditions and teachings which he cites.

The first example he mentions concerns the Exodus, the paradigmatic act of God's salvation, and the subsequent punishment of *those who did not believe*. Though God acted to save *his people out of Egypt*, this did not protect them from the destruction which God brought upon them for their disobedience and grumbling (see Num. 14.1–38; 26.64–65). Elsewhere in the New Testament this same episode is used as a typological warning against sin and complacency (I Cor. 10.1–12; Heb. 3–4).

It has occasionally been suggested that the reference to a *later* destruction (Gk: *deuteron*, 'the second time') is a subtle allusion to the destruction of the Jerusalem temple in 70CE and thus an indication that the letter was written after this date. It is, however, most unlikely that this is implied here.

There are a number of textual variations in this verse, the most important of which concerns the word *Lord*. Some texts have 'Jesus' here, some have 'God', and the earliest manuscript ($\mathfrak{P}^{72}$) has 'God Christ'. While some scholars argue that 'Jesus' is the original reading (Osburn 1981; Neyrey, 61–62; Fossum 1987, who argues that Jude sees Jesus as the agent through whom God acted in the Exodus and subsequent events), it seems that *Lord* is most likely, with the other variants arising either from misreading of abbreviated sacred names, or from the ambiguity allowed by Lord – which *could* be a reference either to God or to Christ (see Landon 1996, 70–77; cf. I Cor. 10.4; I Peter 1.10–11).

6   The second example concerns the fate of the angelic beings (known as the 'Watchers') who, according to Gen. 6.1–4, lusted after human women and took them as wives. They *were not content to maintain the dominion assigned to them*; instead *they abandoned their proper dwelling-place*. Jude's interpretation of this story is dependent upon Jewish traditions, especially upon *I Enoch*, where the sins of the angels are described and also their imprisonment in *chains*, in *darkness*, where they await the *day* of *judgment* (see *I Enoch* 6–19; and

on I Peter 3.19). Indeed, *I Enoch* is probably the most important source for, and influence upon, Jude's exegesis (see Ch. IV 3(i); also on Jude 14–15).

7   The third example concerns the sins of *Sodom and Gomorrah and the neighbouring towns,* which were, in a sense, *like* the sins of *the angels. Like the angels,* these people 'indulged in sexual immorality' (NRSV) and 'went after other flesh' – i.e. non-human flesh. This last phrase is a better and more literal translation of the Greek than *indulged in unnatural lusts,* because, as the account in Gen. 19.1–26 makes clear, it was two *angels* with whom the men of Sodom wanted to have sexual intercourse. This is why the two examples in verses 6 and 7 are comparable for Jude, and why it cannot be homosexual intercourse which the author has in mind here (see Bauckham, 54): just as the angels left their proper place and indulged in sexual immorality with humans, so the men of Sodom sought to violate the proper order in creation and to have sex with angels. This was their sin – a conclusion which probably, and rightly, highlights the gap between the mythical world of the author and our own. (Jewish tradition condemns the people of Sodom and Gomorrah for their lack of hospitality, their hatred of strangers, their pride, as well as their general sexual immorality, which was only rarely (by Philo) defined as homosexual practice: see Bauckham, 54. Note e.g. Ezek. 16.49–50.) Because of this sexual immorality, according to Jude, the people of these cities are undergoing the punishment of *eternal fire,* and stand as an example, *a warning,* for all to see. The REB does not preserve the present tense of the Greek verbs here, but the author probably intended to imply that the fiery punishment was still a present and visible reality: 'in antiquity the smoking, sulphurous waste south of the Dead Sea was believed to be the aftermath of the destruction of Sodom and Gomorrah, and so regarded as visible evidence of the reality of divine judgment' (Bauckham 1990, 187; cf. Wisd. 10.7).

8   Now the author moves to the present situation which he is concerned to address (a transition marked with the term 'these [people]', used at vv.8, 10, 12, 16, 19; see Bauckham, 45). In spite of these examples of judgment, these people continue in similar sins, of which three are specified (typical of Jude's propensity to group things in threes), though they do not correspond to each of the three types mentioned in vv.5–7. These sinners are described as *dreamers;*

probably an indication that they claimed visionary experiences and saw in their dreams prophetic revelations (cf. II Cor. 12.1ff.; Col. 2.18). Jude clearly regards them as false prophets (cf. Deut. 13.2–6). They are people who *defile their bodies*; another reference to the sexual immorality of which he clearly and repeatedly accuses them. They also reject *authority*. Commentators discuss various possibilities as to what *authority* is in view here. The Greek word *kuriotês* probably indicates their rejection of 'the authority of the Lord', as is implied also in v.4. Finally, they *insult*, or slander, *celestial beings* (literally 'glories'; almost certainly a reference to angels). What exactly the author means here is hard to discern, but most probable is the view that the false teachers slandered the angels as givers of the divine law and as guardians of the created order; they refused to accept this moral order (Bauckham, 58; Knight 1995, 45).

9   As an illustrative contrast to the false teachers, who insult angels and do not accept the lordship of God, Jude cites a further 'text', almost certainly drawn from the lost ending of a (probably first-century CE) work called the *Testament of Moses* (see Ch.IV 3(ii)). The story probably ran that God sent *the archangel Michael* (cf. Dan. 12.1; Rev. 12.7) to ensure an honourable (and secretly-located; Deut. 34.6) burial for *Moses*, but *the devil* disputed Moses' worthiness for such a burial on the grounds that he had murdered an Egyptian (Ex. 2.12). Although there is some uncertainty about how to understand the phrase, it seems likely that what Jude then recounts is that Michael did not presume to condemn the devil for his slanderous accusation (cf. Bauckham, 60; REB footnote). Instead he entrusted such judgment to God, appealing to *the Lord* to assert his authority over the devil with a *rebuke* (the phrase is from Zech. 3.2). The point of the example, then, and the contrast with the intruders, is not to urge politeness even to the devil; rather it is to demonstrate that, unlike the false teachers, even the archangel Michael did not overstep the bounds of his own authority, but appealed to the moral authority of the Lord (cf. Bauckham, 61). There is perhaps some irony in the fact that Jude (unlike Michael!) surely slanders his opponents (see Ch. IV 4).

10   The attack on the false teachers is resumed (indicated by the repeated *these people . . .*). Unlike Michael, *these people* slander *whatever they do not understand*: as v.8 indicated, they reject the Lord's authority and slander the angels. Rather ironically, in view of their

claim (hinted at in v.8) to spiritual insight, all that they do understand, the author suggests, are natural instincts, like the animals.
This is surely another reference to their supposed sexual indulgence.
By these things they are destroyed (cf. NRSV; the REB's *prove their
undoing* is rather weak). That is to say, like the examples brought
forth from scripture, they incur God's judgment. The scriptural
examples are instructive 'types', prefiguring the events of the end-
times, and pointing specifically to the judgment which the corrupt
and corrupting false teachers will receive on the last day (cf. I Cor.
10.11; and on I Peter 1.10–12).

Three more scriptural types: wicked characters then and now
11–13

The second section of 'text' and interpretation is introduced in the
form of a 'woe-oracle', like those found in the prophets (e.g. Isa. 5.8,
11, 18; Amos 5.18; 6.1), the New Testament (e.g. Matt. 23.13ff.; Luke
6.24–26), and other Jewish literature (e.g. *I Enoch* 94–100). In prophetic style these verses pronounce the fate of the false teachers as something already certain and decided by God (cf. Knoch, 183).

11   In this 'woe-oracle', three scriptural characters are brought
together, each of whom illustrates, for Jude, in a typological way, the
errors of the false teachers and their certain judgment. Firstly, *they
have followed the way of Cain*, the first murderer (Gen. 4.1–16). As
throughout Jude, here the author is dependent not only on the
Jewish scriptures but also upon the interpretations of these scriptures in post-scriptural Jewish tradition (cf. Charles 1991a). For in
Jewish tradition Cain was regarded not only as a murderer, but also
as one who led others to sin, and who denied God's justice and
future judgment (Bauckham, 79–80). 'In sum', according to Charles
(1990, 116), 'Cain is the "type" and "teacher" of ungodliness'. And
his judgment was a divine curse (Gen. 4.11–12).

   In the case of *Balaam* too, it is Jewish tradition which provides Jude
with the picture of a wicked character who fell into error out of
desire for gain. In the original account Balaam the prophet steadfast-
ly refuses to curse Israel as Balak king of the Moabites urges him to,
no matter what the material inducement (Num. 22–24). In later tradition, however, Balaam was regarded as one who greedily accepted
Balak's rewards and led Israel into immorality and idolatry (see

Num. 25.1–3; 31.8, 16; Deut. 23.3–6; Neh. 13.1–2; II Peter 2.15; Rev. 2.14; Kelly, 267; Bauckham, 81–82). According to Jude, the false teachers are like *Balaam* in both ways: they lead people into immorality, and they do so out of desire *for profit*. In the early church, the right of travelling missionaries to material and financial support from the churches (Matt. 10.1–15; I Cor. 9.4–14) was certainly open to abuse by those who sought to *profit* therefrom (*Didache* 11–15; Lucian *Peregrinus* 13, 16). Since the teachers Jude attacks are regarded as intruders, this may well be an accusation hinted at here.

The third character who illustrates both the wickedness and the fate of the false teachers is *Korah*, who with Dathan and Abiram led a rebellion against Moses and Aaron (Num. 16.1ff.). Again in Jewish tradition, Korah became 'the classic example of the antinomian heretic' (Bauckham, 83). Christian writings also refer to this episode as a warning to those who cause dissension and schism (*I Clem* 51.1–4): for Korah, Dathan and Abiram suffered the fate of divine judgment – the earth opened up and swallowed them, and their 250 followers were consumed by fire (Num. 26.9–10). For Jude it is certain that the false teachers *share* Korah's *fate*. Although this may not yet be evident, it is declared with conviction, as if they were already destroyed.

12–13 Having introduced three well-known characters as classic examples of both wickedness and judgment, the author moves to his own 'interpretation'; describing the errors of the false teachers in an attempt to demonstrate that they too are worthless deceivers destined for judgment. Once again the transition to the present situation is marked by the term *these people* (cf. on v.8). They are *a danger*; more specifically, the Greek word means that they are like dangerous rocks, or a submerged reef, which can cause shipwreck (this is a more likely interpretation than the common understanding of the word as 'blemish', or 'stain'). They represent such a danger as they share in the central act of the church's fellowship – the *love-feast*, or *agapê* – where they join in the feasting without shame. Unlike good *shepherds* or worthy leaders, these people only nourish themselves (cf. Ezek. 34.2–3). These 'love-feasts' (this is the earliest use of the term *agapê* in this sense in Christian literature) were almost certainly the fellowship meals at which the Lord's supper or eucharist was celebrated. The two did not become distinct until sometime in the second century (see Townsend 1979; Marshall 1980, 110–11).

Finally the false teachers are described using four metaphors from nature, from the four regions of air, earth, sea and heavens, and probably inspired by *I Enoch* (2.1–5.4; 80.2–8; see Bauckham, 79). Like *clouds* which yield no rain, these people are all empty promise (cf. Prov. 25.14). Commentators disagree over whether the next image – *trees fruitless in autumn* – refers to a season when trees should be bearing their fruit, or to the time when they are naturally bare. Whichever is the case, this is another metaphor to illustrate the barrenness and emptiness of the false teachers' message and promise. And like fruitless trees, they too will be *uprooted* and destroyed (the reference to *dead twice over* is difficult to interpret: possibly it indicates the last judgment, referred to as 'the second death' in Rev. 2.11; 20.6, 14; 21.8. Charles 1993, 51, suggests an indication here that the opponents have renounced their faith, and thus have 'returned to the death that characterized their former life'). Just as *wild sea waves* churn up foam and debris, so what these people produce is nothing but *disgraceful deeds* (cf. Isa. 57.20). Finally, like *wandering stars*, they have abandoned their rightful place in the created order (cf. on vv.8–9) and so are destined for final judgment: *the place reserved for them is an eternity of blackest darkness.*

The ancient prophecy of Enoch
14–16

The third 'text' which Jude presents is the only one which comprises a formal quotation from a written source, and 'is probably to be seen as Jude's key text in his midrash' (Bauckham, 100; see further Osburn 1977). It is the text which most clearly elaborates the charge outlined in v.4 that the opponents are godless people destined for judgment. Indeed, for the author of Jude, the prophecy itself has these people specifically in view.

14–15   The author quotes a prophecy of *Enoch*, who as *the seventh in descent from Adam* (counting the generations inclusively, and with seven being the most sacred and perfect number) was regarded as a man of special righteousness who, according to tradition, was taken up into heaven without tasting death (Gen. 5.3–24; I Chron. 1.1–3). The quotation comes from *I Enoch* (1.9), which was highly influential in both Judaism and Christianity in this period, and is clearly regarded by the author of Jude as a source of authoritative prophecy, whether or not he viewed it actually as scripture (see Ch. IV 3(ii)).

Somewhat later, in the third and fourth centuries, some Christians found Jude's citation of a non-canonical work problematic and therefore doubted Jude's acceptability in the canon (see Kelly, 277–78). It is notable that II Peter, while dependent on Jude at many points, avoids any explicit reference to Enoch.

The citation from *I Enoch* is clearly and formally introduced, though it is uncertain whether Jude is dependent on a Greek or an Aramaic version of the text. There are, however, clearly some additions or alterations to the text from *Enoch* (see Bauckham, 94–96), the most significant of which is Jude's addition of the word *Lord*. This transforms a reference to God's coming into an expression of the Christian hope for Christ's return. The expression *I saw the Lord come* does not mean that the event is in the past, but is rather an example of the semitic 'prophetic perfect': a future event is 'seen' and thus is certain. The vision is of *the Lord* coming *with his myriads of angels* (literally 'holy ones', though angels are almost certainly what is meant here; cf. Deut. 33.2) in order to execute *judgment* upon *all* (*mankind* is unnecessary: the Greek is simply *pantôn*, 'all'). What is more specifically in view, however, is clearly a judgment of condemnation: *to convict all the godless* (some texts read 'every person' here, but the REB's reading is more likely; see Landon 1996, 117–19) *of every godless deed they had committed*. Three times here words with the root *aseb-* (meaning ungodly) are used; twice as shown in the REB translation, and thirdly in the verb rendered *committed* (the Greek verb means 'to be ungodly', or 'to act impiously'). Clearly this is a key word-group, used already in v.4 and found again in v.18, for Jude to describe the false teachers (hence the choice of this text as the key quotation): it 'crystallizes his view of the heretics' (Kelly, 277). However, the opponents are condemned not only for their deeds, but also for *every defiant word* which they dared to utter against God (cf. v.8 and their apparent rejection of the Lord's authority).

16   With the usual indicator 'these people' (though not rendered here in this way by the REB) the author begins his own explicit attack on the false teachers, in the light of the prophetic quotation. They are *grumblers and malcontents* (cf. Ex. 16.7–12; I Cor. 10.10) who *follow their* own desires (not necessarily, though possibly, sexual *lusts*; certainly desires opposed to God's will; cf. v.18). 'Their mouths are full of boastful talk' (NJB) – probably another indication of the author's view that they are arrogant and presumptuous, particularly towards God. Moreover, *they court favour*, or show favouritism

towards some – perhaps the more well-to-do members of the congregation – from whom they hope to gain, perhaps materially (cf. Lev. 19.15; and see Kelly, 279–80 and Neyrey, 82 on the origin and meaning of the words used here). Perhaps the author feels that they do this specifically in their teaching, by not teaching the way of God with its strenuous demands, but instead proclaiming an 'easy' gospel of licence and lawlessness (so Bauckham, 99–100). In Bauckham's view, Jude's main concern is with the fact that 'they are antinomians' (p. 101).

A modern prophecy of the apostles
17–19

17   The introduction to Jude's fourth 'text' and interpretation marks a definite transition. The appeal to the believers to *remember* recalls v.5, and the description of them as *my friends* ('beloved') is repeated from v.3. The same opening in v.20 leads some commentators to regard vv.17–23 as a distinct block from vv.5–16 (e.g. Kelly, Neyrey). However, while the opening phrase of v.17 does indeed mark both a break from vv.5–16 and a link with vv.20–23, it is best regarded as the final part of the midrashic section encompassing vv.5–19, though the writer moves here from Jewish scriptural types and prophecies to a prophecy *of the apostles*. The focus of vv.17–19 is still the false teachers and their condemnation; only in v.20 does the author turn wholly to exhortation of the faithful.

For many commentators, the phrase referring to 'the words spoken previously *by the apostles of our Lord Jesus Christ*' is one indication of the post-apostolic date of the letter (cf. vv. 3, 20). It appears to look back upon 'the apostles' as a definite group and to the predictions they made some time before (so Kelly, 281; Knoch, 188; otherwise Bauckham, 103–104; see Ch. IV 2(iv)).

18   The precise form of the apostolic prophecy which Jude quotes is not found elsewhere; it is closely paralleled in II Peter 3.3, but this is most likely dependent on Jude. Predictions of trouble, division, false teachers and scoffers, at the end-times, appear often in the New Testament, though the 'predictions' which are closest in form to Jude's come from letters generally dated towards the end of the first century (I Tim. 4.1–3; II Tim. 3.1–5; cf. also Acts 20.29–30; Matt. 7.15; 24.1ff.; Mark 13.1ff.; I Thess. 4.13–5.11).

The prophecy concerns *the final age*, a phrase drawn from the language of Jewish prophecy (e.g. Isa. 2.2; Jer. 30.24), referring here, as elsewhere in the New Testament, to the last days, immediately before the final judgment (e.g. I Peter 4.7, 17). In these final days there will be 'scoffers'— *those who mock at religion* and despise morality (cf. Ps. 1.1; Prov. 1.22; 14.6). The description of these scoffers is typical of Jude's accusations against the false teachers: they *follow their own* desires for ungodliness (cf. v.4, 15–16).

19 The specific application of the prophecy to the false teachers whom Jude attacks is marked, as in vv.8, 10, 12, and 16, with the term *these people*. They are accused of creating *divisions*, though since they still participate in the church's love-feasts (v.12) this presumably cannot mean that they have actually caused a complete split in the fellowship (Watson's [1988] term 'sectarians' is thus inappropriate). In fact the highly unusual word Jude uses may imply that they create divisions specifically by 'classifying' some Christians as superior to others, seeing themselves and their adherents as those who possess the Spirit in some special measure (cf. Kelly, 284; also v.8). It hardly needs to be said that the danger of such spiritual superiority is still with us. If this is the situation here, then Jude turns the tables on this claim, reversing it: the false teachers are the ones who *are worldly* (*psuchikos* – probably meaning those who 'live according to nature' [NJB], who 'follow mere natural instincts' [Bauckham, 106]; cf. v.10; I Cor. 2.14; 15.44). Contrary to their claim, they do not have the Spirit.

The appeal to the faithful
   20–23

Having completed his exposition using scripture and prophecy to demonstrate both the error and the impending judgment of the false teachers, the author now makes his appeal to the faithful believers who are the recipients of his letter. This short appeal, already anticipated in v.3, is the goal and main point of the epistle (cf. Knoch, 190, 192; Bauckham, 111).

20–21 As in v.17 the transition to a new section is marked with the introduction *But you, my friends . . .* (cf. also v.3). The author then proceeds to give four short exhortations which probably reflect established traditional Christian teaching. It may be noted, for example, that the final three injunctions 'correspond to a trinitarian formula: Holy Spirit, God, Christ' (Bauckham, 112), and also that the three great Christian themes, faith, hope (*look forward* . . .), and love (I Cor. 13.13), appear, along with exhortations to prayer and endurance (cf. Rom. 5.1ff.; I Thess. 5.17; James 5.13).

The first exhortation is that they 'build themselves up', a notable contrast to the activity of the false teachers, who pull the community apart by causing divisions (v.19). This language implies an image of the Christian community as a building or temple (cf. I Cor. 3.16; 14.4–5; Eph. 2.21; I Peter 2.5). The *foundation* for this building is their *most sacred* ('holy') *faith*: the deposit of faith, the gospel, which they received from the apostles, and which is 'most holy' because of the holy God who is its source and who calls those who respond to live in holiness (I Peter 1.16). Elsewhere the foundation of the building which is the Christian community is expressed somewhat differently – Jesus Christ in I Cor. 3.9–17; the apostles and prophets, with Christ as the cornerstone in Eph. 2.19–22 – but essentially the basis is the same as here: the gospel of Jesus Christ which the apostles first proclaimed.

The second exhortation, *to pray in the Holy Spirit* (there is no mention of *power* in the Greek text), is closely paralleled in the Pauline epistles, especially in Eph. 6.18. What it means is prayer inspired and directed by the *Spirit*, who discerns both our needs and the will of God in ways beyond our understanding (Rom. 8.26–27). Such prayer, according to the New Testament, may include, but does not exclusively imply, charismatic prayer, 'in tongues' (I Cor. 14.12–16; cf. Dunn 1975, 245–46). Again there is a notable contrast with the false teachers who, whatever their claims, do not, according to Jude, possess the Spirit (v.19).

Among the four exhortations, the only one actually to contain an imperative in the Greek is the third, *Keep yourselves in the love of God*, which should perhaps therefore be seen as the most fundamental exhortation of them all. The writer is clearly referring to God's love for his people here (rather than their love for God), though remaining in this love requires a response of obedience and faithfulness (cf. v.1; John 15.9–10). This implies the need for endurance to the end, which is the theme of the final exhortation; to '*look forward* to the *mercy* of *our Lord Jesus Christ* that leads to *eternal life*' (NRSV). The believers are urged, as so often in the New Testament, to 'wait' in hope and expectation for the coming of the Lord Jesus (e.g. I Thess.

1.10; Titus 2.13; I Peter 4.7). This is a Christian form of the Jewish hope for the day of the Lord, for a day of justice, for mercy and eternal life for the righteous (e.g. Hab 2.3–14; Wisd. 3.1–13; I Enoch 27.3–5; II Esd. 4.26–35). The REB rather avoids what is actually clear in the Greek, namely the sense that the believers are waiting for the mercy of the Lord Jesus. Though this is a somewhat unusual expression, it should not be taken to imply that the writer of Jude did not believe in the experience of grace and mercy in the here and now; rather, it indicates a focus upon the great day to come, the day of judgment and salvation, on which the believers hope to receive mercy and eternal life, while others will receive punishment (cf. vv.6, 13). Often in the New Testament it is God who is described as the final judge, though here, as in some other places, it is Christ who at his coming is portrayed in the role of judge (cf. vv.14–15; Matt. 25.31–46; II Cor. 5.10).

22–23 The author next turns to give brief instruction about how the faithful should act in relation to those who, to greater or lesser degree, have turned to what he regards as ways of error. Unfortunately there are real problems in trying to ascertain the original text here. While Jude as a whole contains a rather large number of textual variations and uncertainties (see Landon 1996), these two verses in particular constitute 'undoubtedly one of the most corrupt passages in New Testament literature' (Osburn 1972, 139). There are many variations among the textual witnesses, though they can broadly be grouped into two: a longer version containing three clauses and a shorter version containing two. The REB, like most other recently published translations, follows the Greek text published in the Nestle-Aland and United Bible Societies Greek New Testaments (basically here the reading of Codex Sinaiticus) which contains three clauses (*There are some . . . Others . . . For others*). However, it is likely that the original text is the two-clause version (translated by the REB in a footnote to v.23) contained in $\mathfrak{P}^{72}$, the oldest text of this epistle, from which the longer variations may plausibly have arisen (see Birdsall 1963; Osburn 1972; Bauckham, 108–11; Landon 1996, 131–34; against Metzger 1975, 726; Kubo 1981; Ross 1989). The text of $\mathfrak{P}^{72}$ runs:

Snatch some from the fire, but on those who dispute have mercy with fear (Bauckham, 108).

An alternative translation is given in the REB's footnote to v.23 (though it should be made clear that the alternative replaces v.22 as well):

There are some whom you should snatch from the flames. Show pity to doubting souls with fear.

All the texts then continue with the same final phrase, *hate the very clothing* etc.

The first phrase in $\mathfrak{P}^{72}$ corresponds to the REB's v.23a (but without the words *you should save*). What Jude refers to is a group of people within the church who, because of their attraction to the false teaching and sinful conduct presented by the 'heretics', stand on the brink of the eternal fire of judgment (cf. v.7). These people may be saved, if the faithful can snatch *them from the flames* (an image perhaps derived from Zech. 3.2, or Amos 4.11). Jude does not specify how they are to do this, but what may be in view is the practice outlined in the New Testament of warning and rebuking an erring believer (see Matt. 18.15–17; Gal. 6.1; I Tim. 5.20; James 5.19–20), in the hope of a repentant response.

The second phrase in $\mathfrak{P}^{72}$ corresponds to what has become two phrases, referring to two groups, in the text followed by the REB, both of which are to be treated with *pity*, or 'mercy'. I shall follow the text of $\mathfrak{P}^{72}$ and picture one group or category of people whom the author has in mind here – essentially combining the two phrases in vv.22 and 23b, as in the second sentence of the REB's footnote text: *Show pity to doubting souls with fear.* These people are described in the Greek as *diakrinomenous*, which could mean those who 'doubt', or 'waver' (as the REB translates it), or perhaps those who are 'under judgment'. More likely, however, is Bauckham's view (p.115) that it means 'those who dispute' (cf. v.9); in other words, either the false teachers or their followers, who refuse to accept what the author regards as sound apostolic teaching and do not respond to the rebuke of the faithful. This group must therefore be treated with rather more caution than the first: *show pity . . . with fear.* This probably implies fear of God (cf. I Peter 1.17; 2.17) rather than fear of them, though the need to shun contact with them is strongly expressed in the final phrase: *hate the very clothing that is contaminated with sensuality.* The Greek word *chitôn* (here translated *clothing*) referred to the garment worn next to the skin, and the image the author paints is of such clothing made filthy by contact with 'the flesh' (the words used in the Greek; cf. also Zech. 3.3–4). As the REB implies, however, it is not human flesh or bodies as such that are 'contaminating' but rather the immoral indulgence of physical desires, of which the author accuses the false teachers. He seems to intend that the faithful should avoid contact with such people, to avoid their influence, a pattern found elsewhere in the New Testament (Matt. 18.17; I Cor. 5.9–13; Titus 3.10). How then are they to be treated with mercy? This is difficult to interpret (hence Ross's suggestion that we read *elenchete*, 'reprove' or 'convict', here instead [1989, 298]). Jude does not specify what is in mind, though the mention of mercy or *pity* implies that the disputers are not simply abandoned callously to their fate. In Kelly's words (p. 289):

> Evil doers are best left to the judgment of God, but the community should not be lacking in compassion to them. Even if normal social relations should be avoided, it remains possible to 'admonish them as brothers' [see II Thess. 3.14–15], and also perhaps to offer intercessory prayer for them.

Closing doxology
24–25

Having made the appeal to his readers, after the lengthy attack on the false teachers, the author draws his letter to a close with a doxology – an acclamation of God's glory and greatness (see on I Peter 4.11). Such doxologies are frequently found in both Jewish and Christian literature, often as, or at the end of, a prayer (e.g. I Chron. 29.10–11; Eph. 3.20–21) and occasionally at the end of a letter (e.g. Rom. 16.25–27; II Peter 3.18). Jude's doxology follows broadly a traditional form (see Neyrey, 95; Bauckham, 119–21). What is unusual about Jude as an epistle, however, is that it lacks any concluding greetings or normal letter-ending (cf. e.g. I Cor. 16.19–24; I Peter 5.10–14).

24 The first part of the doxology relates to the danger posed by the false teachers who have featured so prominently throughout the short epistle. The author affirms God's ability *to keep* the faithful *from falling* into sin and error (cf. Ps. 121.3–8); by God's power they are guarded and protected until the day of salvation (cf. v.1; I Peter 1.5). The description of God as 'the one who is able' is also found in the doxologies in Rom. 16.25 and Eph. 3.20. God is able also, Jude con-

tinues, *to set you* – 'to make you stand' – *in the presence of his glory* (a reverent, Jewish way of speaking of God's very presence; Kelly, 291), *above reproach*. This last adjective literally means 'without blemish', or 'blameless', originally used of sacrificial animals presented to God (e.g. Ex. 29.1; Lev. 1.3; Num. 6.14; I Peter 1.19) and also used in the New Testament to describe the purity of those who through Christ will come before God's presence at the end 'holy and without blame or blemish' (Col. 1.22; also Eph. 1.4; 5.27). This affirmation of God's ability to save, to keep, and to purify his people thus looks forward with hope to the last day, to the completion of the process of salvation. On that day, God's people will be *jubilant*, full of great rejoicing, as God's loving purposes are finally brought to completion (cf. I Peter 1.6–9; 4.13).

As in vv.22–23, in these final verses too there are a considerable number of textual variants; $\mathfrak{P}^{72}$ preserves a somewhat different version of v.24, which may be closest to the original (see Landon 1996, 134–36).

25   After the confident affirmation of God's power to guard and to save his people, the doxology proper – the ascription of glory to God – begins in v.25. Following the usual pattern (see Neyrey, 95) it begins by specifying the one who is praised. Typical of Jewish monotheistic faith is the confession of God as *the only God*. The description of God as *our Saviour* is also derived from Judaism, particularly from the biblical phrase 'the God of our salvation', translated as *God our Saviour* in the Septuagint (e.g. Ps. 65.5; 79.9; 95.1). In the New Testament the word *Saviour* is applied both to Jesus (e.g. Luke 2.11; Acts 13.23; Phil. 3.20) and to God (e.g. Luke 1.47; I Tim. 1.1; 2.3; Titus 1.3).

The second element in the doxology ascribes honour to the one who is addressed. The 'point of a doxology is not to offer God anything which He does not already possess, but to acknowledge adoringly the blessedness which is His by right' (Kelly, 293). In their acclamation, believers only affirm what already belongs to God. Almost all doxologies include *glory*, the very radiance of God's being. Some, as here, continue with a list of divine attributes (cf. I Chron. 29.10–11); others are much shorter (e.g. Rom. 11.36; I Peter 5.11). *Majesty*, a word applied only to God in the Bible, describes God's awesome transcendence, and greatness (cf. Ps. 145.3–6; Heb. 1.3; 8.1). *Power and authority*, though almost synonymous, denote respectively God's absolute power and sovereign rule (cf. Kelly,

293). This ascription of *glory* etc. to God is made and offered *through Jesus Christ* (cf. Col. 3.17; I Peter 4.11).

Thirdly, in the traditional doxology pattern, comes an indication of time (often a brief 'forever'). Jude's doxology affirms that the attributes just mentioned are God's throughout all eternity: they were God's *before all time*, they are God's *now*, and will be so *for evermore*.

Finally, the hearers are invited to affirm the praise of God as they join in the final *Amen*. Almost certainly the congregation would have joined in this response at the end of hearing the letter read. So Jude ends, not with greetings or a conventional letter-ending, but rather as a sermon might have ended, with an affirmation of God's power to save, and of God's eternal greatness.

VI

INTRODUCTION TO II PETER

1. *The significance of II Peter*

Like Jude, II Peter is among the more neglected books in the New Testament, and, moreover, is a book whose theological value and place in the canon has not infrequently been questioned. Although it was known, at least in some circles, in the second century, it was not widely used (Bauckham, 162–63), and 'no NT document had a longer or tougher struggle to win acceptance than II Peter' (Kelly, 224). For various reasons, not least its difference from I Peter, its status was often questioned in the early church (see e.g. Kelly, 224; Martin 1994, 147–48). Eusebius accepts the first epistle of Peter as canonical, but not the second (*EH* 3.3.1–4; 3.25.1–4). Doubts were also voiced around the time of the Reformation, when some expressed the view that II Peter, along with James, Jude, Revelation etc., was of lesser value than other New Testament writings. Such criticism finds modern expression in a famous essay by Ernst Käsemann which argues that II Peter is 'perhaps the most dubious writing in the canon' (1964, 169). Certainly, like Jude and I Peter, II Peter contains material which raises difficult questions for modern Christian readers, and our assessment of its value may be somewhat ambivalent (see 4 below). Nevertheless, as this introduction will detail, it represents an attempt to present apostolic teaching to a church coming to terms with life after the generation of the apostles had passed. We may not always think that II Peter has faithfully represented the proclamation of the apostles (Käsemann's standard, or 'canon', is the Pauline doctrine of justification by faith) nor necessarily accept its way of responding to the problems and questions raised by the writer's opponents, yet this does not negate its important place within the diverse collection of writings which comprises the New Testament.

2. *Historical questions*

(i) *Who wrote II Peter?*

The letter is written in the name of Simeon Peter (1.1) and claims to be the second letter he has written (3.1). The differences in language and style between this letter and I Peter, however, have long been recognized as raising serious questions against the idea of common authorship, and for a wide range of reasons the pseudonymity of II Peter is now almost universally accepted (see Bauckham 1988a, 3722–24). Various aspects of the letter point to a date some years after the martyrdom of Peter in the 60s (see (iv) below) and its literary genre (see 3(i) below) indicates clearly that it was intended as a 'last will and testament' or farewell address to bring the absent apostle's authority and teaching into a situation which had arisen after his departure. For example, the 'predictions' uttered in Peter's name (2.1–3a; 3.3–4) are clearly shown in the letter to be already fulfilled and a present reality (2.3b–22; 3.5–16). But why was the letter written specifically in the name of Peter? Probably because he was an increasingly important figure of authority and unity in the Roman church towards the end of the first century. The martyrdom of both Peter and Paul in Rome helped to make them the two most prominent apostolic authorities for that church (see on 3.15–16; *I Clem* 5.3–7; Ignatius *Romans* 4.3). Letters were also written in Paul's name (I–II Timothy, Titus, though not necessarily from Rome) but his legacy was perhaps more ambivalent and subject to dispute (3.15–16). It is often suggested that I and II Peter were written by members of a Petrine school or circle in Rome (Soards 1988), though the evidence for such a group is rather limited. More plausible is the picture of an emerging 'orthodoxy' in Rome, for which Peter and Paul are the foundational apostles, and in which Petrine and Pauline traditions are utilized by those keen to extend the power and influence of the Roman church over congregations facing various disputes and divisions (as also in *I Clement.*).

(ii) *Where was II Peter written?*

As with Jude there is little available evidence with which to answer a number of the historical questions about II Peter. Its place of writing is not directly mentioned. While a number of possibilities have been mentioned (Egypt [Kelly, 237]; Asia Minor [Fornberg 1977, 111–48]), most commentators agree that Rome is the most likely place of origin (Knoch, 213; Bauckham, 159–62). What points to this conclusion is (a) the letter being written in the name of Peter at a time ostensibly near his death (which happened in Rome; see 2(iii) below); (b) the link with I Peter, which was written in Rome (see II Peter 3.1; Ch. II 2(ii)); and (c) the similarities between II Peter and other Roman Christian writings, notably *I Clement*. and the Shepherd of Hermas. Like *I Clement*, II Peter may plausibly be taken to reflect the growing influence and pastoral concern of the Roman church, around the end of the first century (Bauckham, 159).

(iii) To whom was II Peter sent?

II Peter does not specify its addressees, other than as Christians, and so, like Jude, has been treated as a 'catholic' letter (see Ch. I 1). However, it seems that the letter was written in response to specific problems arising in a particular area (albeit possibly a broad one). The mention of Paul's letters as subject to disputed interpretation (3.15–16) suggests an area within the scope of the Pauline mission, or at least where Paul's letters are known, but that does not narrow the possibilities much. The character of the letter would seem to indicate an audience influenced by Hellenistic language and thought, by pagan religions and myths, as well as by Judaism, in a multi-cultural and pluralistic environment (see Fornberg 1977, 111–48). Again this does not narrow the field with any great precision, and may reflect the context and background of the author as much as that of the recipients of the letter. However, these aspects of the letter's character are certainly compatible with a destination in Asia Minor, and 3.1 seems to confirm that the letter is being sent to the same recipients as I Peter, or at least to some of them, and thus to indicate that the provinces of Asia Minor were indeed its destination (Knoch, 199).

(iv) When was II Peter written?

Like Jude, II Peter has been assigned to a very wide range of dates, from the 60s to the end of the second century (see Bauckham 1988a, 3740–42). For Käsemann, II Peter provided a clear example of the church's 'decline' into 'early Catholicism', as it faced the problem of the delay in the Lord's return, and in which the Christian revelation and faith are presented as a body of doctrine, 'a piece of property' (1964, 174) passed on by those who are guardians of the apostolic tradition (see further Ch. IV 2(iv)). These features would suggest a relatively late date. However, Bauckham (151–54) has shown that II Peter does not fit quite as neatly into the category of 'early Catholicism' as Käsemann's vigorous and hostile critique suggests. Nevertheless, there are features which indicate that the letter does indeed reflect a post-apostolic situation. First, there are the indications that the letter as a whole is conceived as a 'testament' of Peter to serve as a reminder of his teaching in his absence (1.12–15; see 3(i) below). Second, 3.15–16 indicates that Paul's letters are collected together and regarded as 'scripture'. Most commentators agree that this could hardly have been the position until some time towards the end of the first century or early in the second. Third, 3.4 refers to the problem caused by the passing away of the entire first generation of Christians before the Lord's return has happened, a situation which would have arisen sometime after 80–90 CE (see Bauckham, 158). The high christology briefly reflected in 1.1 and 3.18 is consistent with a late first or early second century date. Finally, the documents which II Peter knows and uses (Pauline letters, I Peter, Jude, Gospel traditions) must have been available before II Peter was written, so indicating its somewhat later date, probably roughly contemporary with similar writings such as *I Clement*. (written *c*.96 CE). All of this evidence suggests a date for II Peter of somewhere around 90–110 CE.

(v) Why was II Peter written?

Like Jude, II Peter was written to urge believers to remain faithful to what the author regards as apostolic teaching in the face of the threat (or the attraction!) of false teaching. Because their aims are somewhat similar, the epistle of Jude provided much material which was suitable for the author's purpose and which he therefore used in the letter (see 3(ii)). However, it must not then be assumed that the two letters confront identical situations or opponents. In II Peter the specific concern is the opponents' doubts about the promise of the Lord's return on the day of judgment (1.16–21; 3.3.17), a theme which is more or less absent from Jude. The opponents of the author of II Peter 'combined scepticism about the parousia with moral libertinism' (Bauckham 1988a, 3724); apparently they denied the reality of any coming judgment and so regarded themselves as free to engage in forms of conduct which the author regards as sinful (2.10–22). As in Jude, it is hard to tell how far the harsh polemic truly reflects the conduct of the opponents. The author's main concern is that the believers are being affected by the teaching and conduct of these opponents (cf. 3.8, 11, 17 etc.) and hence he is preoccupied with the eschatological issue and its ethical implications.

It has often been suggested that these opponents were Gnostics (or 'proto-gnostics'; Caulley 1982), the second-century heretics whose teaching and ideas enjoyed considerable popularity and influence (e.g. Talbert 1966). However, recent work by Neyrey, Fornberg and Bauckham has rejected this 'Gnostic' identification and instead proposed that the opponents may have been influenced by pagan, specifically Epicurean, scepticism concerning divine justice and judgment (see Neyrey, 122–28; 1980a). It also seems likely that the opponents appealed to Paul's letters, perhaps to the Pauline teaching concerning freedom (cf. 2.19; Knoch, 210–11; hence in part the suggested 'proto-gnostic' label). However, there is little evidence in the letter to support the view that the opponents had adopted a 'realized eschatology', believing that they were already living the resurrected life here and now, as is suggested by Martin (1994, 140–44). The nature of the opposition, and the character of the letter itself, suggest a context in which the Hellenistic environment exerts an increasing influence upon the debates current within the church. Just as Jewish writers of the first century had expressed their faith in terminology and language drawn from Hellenistic culture, so II Peter is engaged in the task of translating the Christian message into 'hellenistic cultural terms' (Bauckham 1988a, 3732; Fornberg 1977).

3. Literary issues

(i) Style and genre

Although it lacks personal greetings at its beginning and end, II Peter is a genuine letter which broadly follows the rhetorical conventions of Greek letter writing (1.1–2; 3.1; 3.18; Watson 1988). It also fits into the genre of pseudonymous writing known as 'testament' or farewell address, in which a 'hero' provides a reminder of their teaching for the instruction and ethical exhortation of readers after their death (1.3–15), and warns about difficult times ahead (2.1–3a; 3.1–4). Examples of this type of pseudonymous writing are found in Judaism and early Christianity (see on 1.12–15; Bauckham, 131–35; Talbert 1966, 139–40).

The author uses a rich vocabulary and writes in a rather

'grandiose' manner, a verbose and elaborate type of Greek rhetoric known as the 'Asian' style (Reicke, 146–47). For example, the letter contains 57 words not found elsewhere in the New Testament, of which 32 are not found in the LXX either (Bauckham, 135–38).

(ii) Sources

II Peter does not quote the Jewish scriptures formally (cf. I Peter 1.24; 2.6), but it does contain a number of allusions to the LXX text (see e.g. on 2.22; 3.8; 3.13). Furthermore, although the explicit references to Jewish apocrypha and pseudepigrapha are edited out of the material adopted from Jude (see on 2.10b–22; Jude 9, 14–15), the author of II Peter knew and used Jewish interpretative traditions about Balaam (2.15–16) and perhaps drew on a Jewish apocalyptic source in 3.3–13.

Various New Testament writings should also be considered among II Peter's sources. Gospel tradition is cited in 1.16–18 and 2.20 (probably a proverbial saying), and perhaps in 1.14, 2.9, and 3.10. Paul's letters and their content are mentioned in 3.15–16, though there are few, if any, clear echoes of the Pauline correspondence in the epistle. Possible echoes are found in 2.19 (Rom. 8.21), 3.10 (I Thess. 5.2), and 3.15 (Rom. 2.4; 12.3; 15.15; I Cor. 3.10; Gal. 2.9), but these are hardly clear enough to constitute conclusive proof that the author used these texts as his source. We may cautiously suggest (and this seems intrinsically likely) that the author knew Romans, perhaps I Thessalonians, conceivably I Corinthians (see Neyrey, 133–34).

Just as the author clearly indicates his awareness of the Pauline epistles (3.15–16), so he also indicates his knowledge of I Peter (3.1). Yet, just as clear echoes of the Pauline letters are lacking, so too are clear echoes of I Peter. There are certainly places where it may plausibly be suggested that the author is influenced by I Peter (e.g. 1.1–2; 2.5; 3.9) and some scholars have argued that II Peter makes considerable use of I Peter (Boobyer 1959; Dalton 1979; cf. Fornberg 1977, 12–13). However, none of the proposed instances gives a decisive indication of literary dependence.

The most obvious literary relationship is between II Peter and Jude. A comparison of Jude 4–18 with II Peter 2.1–3.3 shows that a good deal of material is shared in common (see table). There are a number of possible explanations for these parallels: (a) that Jude and II Peter used a common oral or written source; (b) that the same

JUDE (REB)	II PETER (REB)
4 . . . people . . . marked down long ago for the sentence they are now incurring . . . licentiousness, disowning Jesus Christ, our only Master and Lord.	2.1 . . . disowning the very Master who redeemed them . . . 2 their dissolute practices . . . 3 judgment has long been in preparation for them
6 those angels . . . God is holding them, bound in darkness with everlasting chains, for judgment . . .	2.4 the angels . . . God . . . consigned them to the dark pits of hell, where they are held for judgment.
7 Sodom and Gomorrah . . . a warning	2.6 Sodom and Gomorrah . . . an object-lesson
8 defile their bodies, flout authority, and insult celestial beings	2.10 follow their abominable lusts and flout authority . . . insult celestial beings
9 Not even the archangel Michael . . . presumed to condemn him in insulting words, but said, 'May the Lord rebuke you'	2.11 angels . . . employ no insults in seeking judgment against them before the Lord
10 these people pour abuse on whatever they do not under stand . . . like brute beasts	2.12 these men are like brute beasts . . . they pour abuse on things they do not understand
12 a danger at your love-feasts with their shameless carousing	2.13 to carouse . . . while they sit with you at table they are an ugly blot
11 for profit they have plunged into Balaam's error	2.15 followed in the steps of Balaam . . . who eagerly accepted payment for doing wrong
12 clouds carried along by a wind without giving rain	2.17 springs that give no water, mists driven by a storm . . .
13 the place reserved for them is an eternity of blackest darkness	2.17 the place reserved for them is blackest darkness
16 follow their lusts . . . bombast comes rolling from their lips	2.18 they utter empty bombast . . . sensual lusts
17 my friends . . . remember the predictions made by the apostles of our Lord Jesus Christ	3.1 dear friends . . . 2 remember the predictions made . . . and the com mandment given by the Lord and Saviour through your apostles
18 They said to you: 'In the final age there will be those who mock at religion and follow their own ungodly lusts'	3.3 in the last days there will come scoffers who live self-indulgent lives; they will mock you and say . . .

author wrote both letters; (c) that Jude used II Peter as a source; (d) that II Peter used Jude as a source. Contemporary scholarship is virtually unanimous that (d) is the most likely explanation. Fornberg, Neyrey and Bauckham have studied the way in which II Peter edits and adapts Jude, and Watson (1988, 163–89) has confirmed that the direction of literary influence is from Jude to II Peter. A concise indication of the extent of the parallels may be gained from the table (see fuller detail in Perkins, 179–80; Fornberg 1977, 33–59; Watson 1988, 164–69).

4. Content: themes and theology

The aim of II Peter is to assure the faithful that God's promise of salvation (and of judgment) is certain and secure and to exhort them to live upright lives in the light of this certain truth. The author does this (a) by presenting his teaching as an apostolic writing which serves as a reminder and testimony of Peter's teaching; (b) by denouncing the false teachers with strenuous polemic; and (c) by defending the doctrine of the Lord's coming against the scoffers' criticisms.

The foundation for the author's conviction and message is profoundly theological. It is *God's* 'divine power' (1.3), his active 'word', that created and judged the world in the past (3.5–6), that provides all that the believers need to live a godly life, and that is the certain basis for the hope of salvation and the message of coming judgment. The goal of the process of salvation is described as a coming to share in the divine nature (1.4). The author refers in a distinct way to *Jesus* – as Lord and Messiah (1.8, 14; 3.18 etc.), and as Saviour (1.1; 3.18) – but a sharp separation cannot be drawn between what he says about God and about Jesus. Believers come to know both God and Jesus (1.2); Jesus is also described as 'our God and Saviour' (1.1) and is (unusually) the one to whom glory is ascribed at the close of the epistle (3.18). Moreover, the author does not appear to intend any distinction between the second coming of the Lord Jesus (1.16; 3.10) and 'the day of God' (an unusual phrase, used in 3.12). The author's christology is only glimpsed in the letter, but the hints seem to indicate a high christology in which Jesus can be described as God.

As in Jude and to a lesser extent I Peter, there is little mention of the *Spirit* in II Peter; the theological emphasis is upon God and

Christ. In fact, the Spirit is only mentioned once, in 1.21, where the origin of prophecy is attributed to the movement of the Holy Spirit.

As in the case of Jude, the theology of II Peter has drawn a certain amount of criticism, most notably in the attack by Ernst Käsemann (1964), to which I have already referred (see 1 and 2(iv) above). For Käsemann, II Peter represents a clear example of 'early Catholicism' (cf. also Dunn 1990, 350–51, 362–63), in which the apostles serve as the authorizers of an established tradition of faith, preserved and taught by a group of church officials, and where the hope for the imminent return of Christ is fading (see Ch. IV 2(iv)). For Käsemann, 'faith' in the Pauline sense has become 'the faith', which for the author of II Peter is 'mere assent to the dogmas of orthodoxy' (1964, 195). Certainly the author of II Peter claims apostolic authority for his attempt to present apostolic teaching to a post-apostolic situation; clearly he faces a situation in which the delay of the Parousia is a pressing problem; and obviously he launches into harsh condemnatory polemic against those whom he labels scoffers. But it does not perhaps do justice to the author to present him as someone who is essentially 'tradition-bound', who responds to the false teachers' challenge merely with an 'appeal for a closing of ranks and a denouncing of error' (Martin 1994, 162–63). In fact, unlike Jude (from where he lifts most of his polemical material), the author of II Peter does confront the arguments of his opponents, and is to a degree creative in his response. He appeals to God's acts in the past as the basis for his conviction as to the certainty of God's future judgment (3.5–7), but also offers two reasons for the apparent delay of that judgment: the fact that God's perspective on time is radically different from that of human beings (3.8), and second, that God's delay indicates his patience (3.9). These may or may not be satisfactory answers, but at least they take the opponents' argument into account and present a counter-argument. Moreover, the use in II Peter of Hellenistic cultural and religious terms – which for Käsemann showed 'the relapse of Christianity into Hellenistic dualism' (1964, 180) – may be viewed sympathetically as an attempt to present the Christian gospel in terms which were meaningful and current for the readers of the epistle (see on 1.3–11). Again, the attempt may or may not be judged successful, but at least it represents some form of what we might term 'contextualization', which is surely essential for any sensitive form of Christian proclamation.

There are nevertheless problems with the theology of II Peter. One is the presentation of God as one who reserves a place of blackest darkness (2.17) for the disobedient and wayward. The fiery polemic which the author uses to denounce his opponents emanates from a cultural and religious context far removed from our own, and it offers little to a contemporary understanding of the Christian gospel, or to patterns of dialogue within or outside the church. Since virtually all of II Peter's polemic is adapted from Jude, this problem has already been discussed in connection with Jude (Ch.IV 4).

A second problem concerns II Peter's answer to the problem of Parousia delay (see on 3.1–13; Bauckham 1980). While the author's attempt to acknowledge and respond to this problem should not be lightly dismissed, questions must be raised concerning the adequacy of the response today. Of course, the author's insistence that God's timescale is utterly different from that of human beings (3.8) can certainly be used by Christians today to justify holding on to a belief in a dramatic and final Parousia, a mighty intervention of God to dissolve and judge the present created order. Some believers hold the conviction that such a dramatic intervention is indeed what the Christian expects, and that it might happen on any day. Others, including myself, believe that the whole picture of God's action upon which the author of II Peter bases his conception of the Parousia has to be more radically re-thought. Our contemporary understanding of the world, and of the universe in which it is located, does not square with a picture of God who acts by dramatic intervention, whether in creation or in judgment. Moreover, there are real moral problems in conceiving of a God who acts in such dramatic fashion, yet who remained silent and apparently inactive when millions of Jews were exterminated in Nazi concentration camps, or when scores of African refugees died in makeshift camps. If we are to conceive of God at all, it seems that we must conceive of a God at work within the very basic and natural processes of the physical universe, in processes through which change occurs gradually, over huge periods of time. Prayer may perhaps bring new possibilities to reality (cf. Polkinghorne 1989), but the conception of a God who arrests the sun's movement (Josh. 10.12–13), or who suddenly and dramatically sends consuming fire (3.10; cf. I Kings 18.38), is an ancient one which can hardly stand today.

To some extent, then, we should perhaps side with the scoffers whom the author of II Peter attacks; with those who insisted that a dramatic day of the Lord was not coming (soon or otherwise) and that the processes of creation would continue in their long-term patterns (3.4). However, there remains something important in the author's critique of the scoffers. For them, the absence of impending judgment seemed to justify a licence to sin: if judgment was not going to come, then why not live in complete freedom (2.19)? The author insists that the Christian life is one in which the gifts of goodness and virtue should be cultivated (1.5–7) and that believers should live holy lives (3.11–14). The difficulty then is this: if the author's appeal depends, as it does (3.11–14), on the coming eschatological judgment, then how can his moral exhortation stand if we do not accept his eschatological framework? We should, I think, acknowledge that the Christian moral imperative does indeed rest upon a vision of hope – a hope for a new earth in which justice will be established (3.13) – and upon a conviction that God's redeeming work will not cease until that new creation is established. That faith can, I believe, stand in the modern world, without being tied to a conception of sudden divine intervention, and can provide a vision which challenges every existing injustice and inspires real change (cf. Ch. II 4).

So, like I Peter and Jude, II Peter raises certain theological problems which contemporary readers should consider carefully. However, like those other epistles, it also offers resources which are of abiding value for those who seek to work out a Christian faith which is both convincing and challenging in the contemporary world.

5. The Structure of II Peter

VII

COMMENTARY ON II PETER

Opening greetings
1.1–2

Like I Peter and Jude, II Peter opens in a way which broadly follows
the conventions of letter-writing in the period. The sender and
addressees are identified, and greetings are expressed.

1.1   The sender of the letter is identified as *Simeon Peter* (though it
was almost certainly written in his name, rather than by Peter himself: see Ch.VI 2(i)). The name *Simeon* is a Greek transliteration of a
very common Jewish (Hebrew) name, though normally the Greek
form 'Simon' was used. The appearance of *Simeon* here is striking:
elsewhere in the New Testament Peter is generally known as 'Simon
Peter', except in Acts 15.14 (where 'Simeon' also appears) and in
John 1.42, I Corinthians and Galatians (where the Aramaic name
'Cephas' is used). Perhaps the writer wished to give an impression of
authenticity (Kelly, 296), or perhaps he belonged to, or became
associated with, a circle of Jewish Christians who had known Peter
in Palestine, and thus continued to use the name 'which was current
in Palestinian Christian circles' (Bauckham, 167; cf. Acts 15.14). Peter
is described as *servant* (cf. Jude 1) *and apostle* (cf. I Peter 1.1) *of Jesus
Christ:* two terms which describe Peter's 'ministerial role' and
'authoritative commission' respectively (Kelly, 296). Both labels were
frequently used of and by Christian leaders (e.g. Rom. 1.1; I Cor. 1.1;
Gal. 1.10; Phil. 1.1).

The letter does not specify its recipients' geographical situation,
though 3.1 would seem to indicate that they are located in the same
provinces of Asia Minor (or parts thereof) to which I Peter was sent
(see I Peter 1.1). They are described instead in terms which could
apply to any Christians; as 'those who have received a faith as
precious as ours' (NRSV; cf. NAB, NJB. The REB brings out the idea
that this *faith* conveys equal rights and *privileges* to all; cf. Charles

1997, 131). The faith which the writer and readers share has been 'received' – i.e. it is given by God – and the faith of the readers is 'of equal value' (Gk: *isotimos*) to that of the writer. This may be intended to indicate that the faith of the readers (living in a post-apostolic generation) is the same and just as valuable as the faith held and proclaimed by the apostles. It may also establish a link, a sense of common ground, between the church sending the epistle and those to whom it is being sent (establishing a connection between writer and readers was a common epistolary feature; cf. Jude 3; Rev. 1.9; Bauckham, 165.)

This precious faith has been given *through the righteousness* of God in Christ. A number of commentators prefer the translation 'justice' here (*dikaiosunê* may be translated 'justice' or 'righteousness'), suggesting that the word refers to the fairness and impartiality with which God has given to all who believe – apostles and others alike. There is some uncertainty as to whether the following phrase should be understood to refer to *Jesus Christ* as *our God and Saviour* (as REB) or separately to 'our God' and '[our] Saviour Jesus Christ' (Neyrey, 143, 147–48). The former is on balance more likely, though striking. The New Testament only rarely refers to Jesus as God (e.g. John 20.28; Titus 2.13) but the practice is not uncommon from the late first and early second centuries. Similarly, the description of Jesus as *Saviour* is relatively uncommon in the New Testament, but frequent by the second century (see Bauckham, 168–69).

1.2   The greeting includes the standard phrase from early Christian epistles, *grace and peace be yours*. Exactly as in I Peter 1.2, it is formulated as a wish or a prayer, that these divine blessings may *be yours in fullest measure* (cf. also Jude 2), to which II Peter adds, reflecting its interest in the theme of 'knowledge' (*epignôsis*), *through knowledge of God and of Jesus our Lord*. In other words, through coming to know God in Christ, the believers receive the blessings of grace and peace. Unlike in v.1, here the author refers to God, and (separately) to Jesus, describing Jesus in characteristically Christian terms as *our Lord*.

A summary of the message
1.3–11

The grammatical form of the opening of v.3 makes it difficult to decide whether it should be read as a continuation of v.2, or as an introduction to what follows in v.5. Vv. 3–4 probably serve as something of a transition, but it seems best, with a number of commentators and translations, to take vv.3–11 as a new and distinct block of text. The whole section seems to reflect the pattern of a 'farewell speech', which follows 'a standard homiletic pattern in Jewish and early Christian literature' (Bauckham, 173; Watson 1988, 96. Boobyer 1959, 40–42, suggests that I Peter 1.3–9 may have influenced the author here). Thus the writer first recalls God's saving acts (vv.3–4), then exhorts his readers to ethical living (vv.5–10) in view of the eschatological hope of salvation (v.11). Moreover, as Neyrey shows in some detail (pp.113–16), this opening summary mentions a number of themes which are developed further in the letter as a whole. The passage is rich in terminology widely used in Hellenistic philosophical and religious discourse.

1.3   It is uncertain from the text whether 'his' *divine power* (which is what the Greek says) should be understood as referring to Jesus' or God's power. Bauckham (p.191) sees the whole passage as 'christological' in its focus and suggests that a reference to Jesus is most likely here (p.177). Neyrey (p.155–56) regards the divine power as God's. On balance I think the REB is probably correct to interpret with *God's*. However, it should not be supposed that any neat or clear distinction between the activity of God and of Christ can be drawn. Similar questions arise over the phrases *him who called us* (v.3) and *he has given us his promises* (v.4; cf. Kelly, 300–301).

Through *God's divine power* the believers (*us* refers to the readers, to all Christians, and not to a specific group such as the apostles) have been given everything necessary for *life and true religion* (*eusebeia*). This term *eusebeia* is a 'characteristically Hellenistic term' generally denoting piety towards the gods (see Bauckham, 178). It is used little in the LXX and New Testament (only in Acts, the Pastorals, and II Peter) and describes life directed properly and dutifully towards God (hence the common translation 'godliness'). This generous bestowal by God is given *through the knowledge* (*epignôsis*: cf. 1.2, 8; 2.20) *of him who called us* (generally a description of God in the New Testament, though here possibly of Christ). The phrase *glory and goodness*, a standard combination in Hellenistic writers, describes God's honour, power, and excellence: the word translated *goodness* here is *aretê*, rendered 'virtue' in v.5 (see below). There is perhaps a link to be drawn between the two occurences of the word: God's 'excellence and goodness' are to be imitated by those who live in loyalty to him (cf. Neyrey, 151, 156).

1.4 *In this way* (i.e. through God's glory and goodness), God's precious and very great *promises* have been *given* to *us*. They have been given for a purpose, a purpose which is expressed in terms of both an 'escape from' and a 'sharing in' (the latter comes first in the Greek text). The shift from *us* to *you* here may reflect the transition to moral exhortation, urging right living upon his readers, which the author is about to make in v.5. The end result of God's gracious action is expressed in a phrase which has been of considerable theological influence. The REB's translation, *that you . . . may come to share in the very being of God*, perhaps points rather too much in the direction of a notion of 'divinization'; the NRSV's 'become participants of the divine nature' is probably better. The idea and terminology are well known in Greek religious and philosophical thought, and are found also in Hellenistic Jewish writings. Here the author seems to be expressing the belief that after death (or the return of Christ), Christians will share the immortality and incorruptibility of God's nature (see Bauckham, 179–82). Some comparison (though not a precise one) may be noted with Paul's teaching that Christians all become 'sons' of God, 'in Christ' the firstborn Son (Rom. 8.14–17; I Cor. 15.42–57; Gal. 4.4–7).

First, however, the believers must *escape the corruption* which is in *the world* because of *lust* (Gk: *epithumia*, meaning 'desire', not necessarily evil, though here clearly wicked or 'sinful desire'; cf. I Peter 1.14; 2.11; 4.3; Eph. 4.22). When does this *escape* happen? Certainly it begins at conversion and baptism (so Kelly, 302), but it is not completed until one's physical death or the return of Christ (cf. Bauckham, 183).

1.5–7 This saving work of God forms the basis for an ethical appeal, made in the form of a 'virtue list', a pattern which is found often in the New Testament and elsewhere (see Charles 1997). A number of the terms used are particular favourites in Stoic-Hellenistic ethical philosophy. The list here proceeds step by step to a climactic conclusion (cf. Wisd. 6.17–20; Rom. 5.3–5). A notable parallel in early Christian literature is found in Hermas *Visions* 3.8.7, which also begins with 'faith' and ends with 'love' (cf. also II Cor. 8.7). These are two of the three classic Christian virtues (I Cor. 13.13) along with hope, which appears here in the form of 'endurance' (*hypomenê*; see below).

Every effort should be made to cultivate and produce the virtues which are listed. The REB's translation, *to add virtue to your faith* etc., is, in Bauckham's words, 'not what the Greek says' (p.184). A better translation would be: 'make every effort by your faith to produce virtue, and by virtue knowledge, etc.' Each virtue is the basis for producing the next (Bauckham, 172, 184). The first and most fundamental is *faith*, faith in and fidelity to the gospel. Next is *virtue* (*aretê*; cf. v.3), a favourite term of Greek moral philosophy and meaning essentially moral excellence and uprightness. *Knowledge* might seem a strange 'virtue', but here most likely refers to the important quality of 'discernment of God's will and purpose' (Kelly, 306). The Greek word here is *gnôsis*, rather than *epignôsis*, the term which II Peter uses for the 'coming to know' which is conversion (see on 1.2, 3). *Self-control* is another virtue highly valued and frequently mentioned in Hellenistic ethics, as is *fortitude* (*hypomenê*: patience, endurance, or steadfastness). *Piety* (*eusebeia*) is also a well-known virtue in Hellenistic writing (see on v.3, where the REB translates it 'true religion'). *Brotherly affection* (*philadelphia*) is used in Greek literature for the kinship love between brothers and sisters (see Neyrey, 161). The early Christians described one another (and God) in familial terms and regarded one another as brothers and sisters (cf. I Peter 1.22). Above the virtue of *philadelphia*, however, comes *love, agapê*, the supreme Christian virtue which encompasses all the rest (cf. I Cor. 13.1ff.). *Agapê* describes a generous, active love, a love which may be shown even to enemies (Matt. 5.44) and which unites God and humans. For the Christian it is a love grounded in, and brought forth in response to, the generous love of God in Christ (see Spicq 1994, I, 8–19).

1.8   The result of *these gifts*, or virtues, where they are present and increasing among a Christian community, is expressed in terms of avoiding a negative: 'they will cause you not to be idle/ineffective or unfruitful' (the REB translates using positive terms: *you will grow actively and effectively*). Here, as often in II Peter (cf. e.g. 1.9), we find a pairing of two terms which are close in meaning – 'idle and unfruitful'. Most commentators interpret the text along the lines implied by the REB's translation: that the virtues will lead to or produce an increasing *knowledge of our Lord Jesus Christ*. It is also possible (and perhaps more likely) that the writer means that cultivating the virtues he has listed is necessary in order for the knowledge of Christ which the believers already have (from their conversion) to bear fruit in their lives (cf. Kelly, 307–308).

1.9   On the other hand, almost as a warning, the negative expression of the same idea is that *anyone who lacks* the virtues listed is 'blind and short-sighted'. The combination of these two terms is odd (how can you be blind and short-sighted?) and the word for 'short-sighted' is extremely rare. The REB's translation *wilfully blind* reflects the suggestion of some commentators (e.g. Kelly, 308) that the description is of someone who deliberately closes or contracts their eyes. It is probably more likely that the author is simply using for effect two words close in meaning (as he does elsewhere; cf. 1.8). The metaphor of short-sightedness is certainly appropriate to the idea of a person who has *forgotten that his past sins were washed away*, i.e. who can no longer (or refuses to) look back to that crucial time of conversion. This cleansing from sins, an expression established in the Jewish scriptures (e.g. Lev. 16.30; Ps. 51.2), took place in the washing of baptism, which marked a break from former ways and the beginning of a new life in Christ (cf. Acts 22.16; I Cor. 6.11; Col. 3.1–17).

1.10–11   In view of all this, the writer urges the *friends* (*adelphoi* – brothers and sisters) to whom he writes to eager and earnest commitment to Christian living, which will *establish* (almost with a semi-legal sense of 'ratify', or 'confirm') their calling and election by God. Here again we find two closely related terms side by side – *called and chosen* – used in the New Testament to describe the status and responsibilities of those whom God has graciously elected (e.g. Rom. 11.28–29; Eph. 1.18; 4.1; I Thess. 1.4). (On the problem of those not elected, or apparently elected to a fate of judgment, see on I Peter 2.8; Rom. 9–11.) Living in the right way (vv.5–8), in the gracious provision which God has made (vv.3–4), will ensure that *you never stumble* (possibly in the sense of falling into sin, but more likely that of missing the goal of one's election, 'the disaster of not reaching final salvation' [Bauckham, 191; cf. Kelly, 309]). Instead, the writer affirms in a note of assurance, *your entry into the eternal kingdom of our Lord and Saviour Jesus Christ* will be richly provided. The section thus comes full circle, as the author again (cf. vv.3–4) depicts the lavish generosity of God. The description of the *kingdom* as Christ's is relatively unusual in the New Testament (the kingdom of God is more common), and the exact phrase *our Lord and Saviour Jesus Christ* occurs only in II Peter (though cf. Luke 2.11; Phil. 3.20). This probably reflects the increasingly high christology which emerged during the late first and early second centuries (cf. on v.1 with the reference to Jesus as God).

One of the striking features of this passage, a feature encountered elsewhere in II Peter as well, is its clear and widespread use of Hellenistic religious-philosophical ideas and terms. This has led to the accusation that II Peter has corrupted the gospel and lapsed into Hellenistic dualism (see Käsemann 1964). Certainly the author has adopted and adapted ideas and language from his cultural environment (as some Jewish writers had done before him), but it may be questioned whether he has thereby lost sight of the true character of the Christian gospel. The task of 'translating' the gospel into new and particular contexts has always faced the church, and it is surely right to express the faith in terms which people can identify and understand (cf. Bauckham, 183–84). Then and now the difficult question is: how far can the gospel's message and language be translated and contextualized before it ceases to be the gospel (see Ch.VI 4)?

The reason for writing: leaving a reminder

1.12–15

After the summary of the message in the form of a farewell speech, this section clearly indicates the purpose of the epistle: to serve as Peter's 'testament', that is, as a record and reminder of his teaching after his death. Such testaments were a 'recognized literary genre' (Kelly, 311) with standard features, notably two which appear here: (i) the 'hero' knows that death is approaching and (ii) wishes his teaching to be remembered (Bauckham, 194; further Neyrey, 163–64; Knoch, 251–54). Examples appear in the Jewish scriptures (Gen. 49.1ff.; Deut. 31.14–30 etc.), the New Testament (Acts 20.17–38; II Tim. 3.1–4.8), and pseudepigraphal literature (such as the *Testaments of the Twelve Patriarchs*; see Charlesworth 1983). Most scholars agree, moreover, that this passage gives a clear indication of pseudonymity, and possibly one which the readers of the epistle would have recognized (see Bauckham, 202–203; 1988d; see Ch. I 3(i)). An unnamed author is writing in the name of Peter a letter which is to serve as a permanent reminder of apostolic teaching and tradition for readers living after the death of the apostle, in an era when the church feels the need for texts stamped with apostolic authority (cf. Käsemann 1964).

1.12 Because of the need to follow the right way to attain salvation (vv.3–11; the REB omits to translate the 'therefore' with which v.12 begins) 'Peter' *will keep on reminding* the readers *of all this* – a reference to the matters concerning God's saving purposes and the appropriate human response, summed up in vv.3–11 and defended against accusations in the rest of the epistle. Three times in this passage the idea of reminding is mentioned, a clear indication of the purpose envisaged by the author for the letter: to uphold what he regards as genuine apostolic teaching (vv.12, 13, 15; see Neyrey, 166–67). The future tense used (*I will keep on reminding . . .*) indicates the ongoing function which the letter is intended to perform after the apostle's death; perhaps it also hints that this is not the first communication sent in his name (cf. 3.1).

In what may be a touch of politeness, the author affirms that the readers *know* this teaching already (cf. Jude 5), and *are well grounded in the truth* they *possess*. (The New Testament often refers to the gospel as *the truth*; e.g. Gal. 5.7; Eph. 1.13; 4.21; Col. 1.5; II Thess. 2.10.) Those who are addressed, then, are affirmed as faithful believers who know the truth, but who need reminders and encouragement in the face of the threat of false teaching.

1.13   Even if the readers know and adhere to 'the truth', 'Peter' considers it *right* to provide this 'reminder' (literally, 'to stir you up', or 'rouse you', 'with a reminder'). The assertion 'I consider it right', as indeed the whole passage, bears close similarity to other farewell addresses (notably that attributed to Moses by Josephus in *Antiquities* 4.177ff.; Kelly, 312; Bauckham, 194, 198). The setting down of the 'speech' (i.e. the letter) as a reminder is presented as something done by the apostle just before his death. The phrase *as long as I still lodge in this body* translates the metaphorical description found in the Greek and quite commonly employed at that time: the body is a *skēnōma*, a 'tent-like dwelling' (cf. II Cor. 5.1–4).

1.14   As is typical in farewell speeches, the hero in whose name the real author is writing somehow knows that the time of departure is near. Again the image of the body as a 'tent' is used, as death is here described metaphorically as 'the putting off of my tent', i.e. discarding the body as one's dwelling (cf. II Cor. 5.3–4). The apostle's knowledge that he must *soon* die corresponds with what the *Lord Jesus Christ* made clear or revealed to him. Commentators have discussed various possibilities as to the revelation or prophecy to which the author here refers (see Bauckham, 200–201). Many have suggested that the saying of Jesus recorded in John 21.18 is the most likely basis for the statement here. This tradition might have been known to the author and readers as a prophecy of Jesus concerning the death of Peter. Kelly (p.314) objects that John 21.18 says nothing about the timing of that death, but the passage does indicate that it will occur when Peter is old. It is possible, as Kelly suggests, that no specific source need be sought for the revelation of Jesus to Peter; the author and readers would have known of Peter's martyrdom (cf. *I Clem* 5.4) and it 'came naturally to Christians to believe that heroes of the faith received premonitions of their approaching martyrdom' (Kelly, 314). Certainty about such matters is impossible, but on balance the wording of this verse does perhaps suggest that some tradition about a prophecy of Jesus concerning Peter's death was known to the author of the epistle.

1.15   Here is further indication both of the pseudonymity of the epistle and of the purpose which it is intended to fulfil. Peter *will do* his *utmost to ensure that* his teaching is available after his death (described again in metaphorical terms, as an *exodos,* an exit or departure). It is clearly implied both that the apostle is indeed already dead, and that the epistle serves as the means by which his teaching can be called *to mind*. It is of course open to debate whether and to what extent the teaching of the epistle is in fact Peter's (see Ch.I 3(i)).

The reliability of apostolic and scriptural testimony
1.16–21

In view of the accusations which opponents and sceptics are making (see further chapters 2–3), the author now begins to defend the veracity of what he presents as the apostolic message, specifically the message about the return of Christ in judgment and glory. In essence the author argues that the apostolic teaching about the return of Christ is rooted in eyewitness testimony to the Transfiguration and in the prophetic message of the scriptures. Neyrey (170–71; 1980b; also Watson 1988, 102–106) has suggested that the form of the argument reveals its character as a defence and refutation of opponents' charges (*it was not ... rather ...* vv.16, 21; cf. 3.9).

1.16   'Peter' insists that the message made known by the apostles (note the change from 'I' to 'we' from v.15 to v.16, 'we' being the apostles as a group) was *not* based on *cleverly concocted tales*. The style of the insistence seems to imply that the opponents, perhaps influenced by a rational scepticism such as is found in Epicureanism (see Neyrey 1980a), did regard the teaching (specifically about the Lord's return, as we shall see) as nothing but a human myth (see 3.3–4). The author may also be polemically characterizing the opponents' teachings as human 'myths' (cf. 2.3; Kelly, 316; I Tim. 1.4; 4.7; II Tim. 4.4; Titus 1.14). The message the apostles proclaimed was about *the power of our Lord Jesus Christ and his coming*. The terms *power* and *coming* (Gk: *parousia*) refer to the *power* which Christ, as the risen and glorified Lord, has received from God, and to his second *coming* in majesty and victory on the last day. Thus the particular message to which the author here refers concerns the glorious return of Christ. He seeks to show that, far from being a *cleverly concocted* myth, this 'aspect of the apostles' teaching . . . is soundly based on what the apostles witnessed' (Bauckham, 216). The apostles were 'eyewitnesses' of *his majesty* at the Transfiguration (see below on vv.17–18), 'which is taken as a foreshadowing of Christ's Second Coming in glory' (Kelly, 317). Clearly for the author the Transfiguration confirms the truth of Christ's future return in glory, and the apostles as witnesses to this event base their proclamation not on myths but on historical truth.

1.17 The scene recalled here, which the apostles (Peter, James and John, according to the Synoptic Gospels; see Mark 9.2 and parallels) witnessed, is that known as the Transfiguration (most commentators agree on this point). On this occasion, Jesus *was invested with honour and glory by God the Father* (for the phrase *honour and glory*, see Ps. 8.5; Heb. 2.7, 9, etc. The reference to God as *Father* points forward to the calling of Jesus as *Son*, which follows below). The apostles glimpsed then the *glory* bestowed upon Jesus by God, an anticipation of the vision which all will see at his final coming. The impersonal description, *there came to him from the sublime Presence a voice*, reflects a (Jewish) concern to retain a proper sense of God's transcendence (God does not speak directly) and a typically Jewish avoidance of the divine name (the reference to *the sublime Presence*, or 'the Majestic Glory' [NRSV] is in effect an honorific term for God).

The words which the voice is said to have uttered are similar, though not identical, to those recorded in the Synoptic accounts of the Transfiguration (II Peter is closest to Matt. 17.5) and the baptism of Jesus (Matt. 3.17 and parallels). The differences might indicate that the tradition which the author knew was independent from that of the synoptic accounts (see Bauckham, 205–10), though the concise summary given hardly yields enough evidence to establish this. Early Christian letters only rarely refer explicitly to the gospel traditions, and when they do the practice is to allude or echo rather than to quote word for word (cf. I Cor. 7.10–11; 9.14; Thompson 1991, 37–63). II Peter 1.17 in fact represents an unusually direct citation of gospel tradition (perhaps an indication of its relatively late date; cf. 3.16; Ch.VI 2(iv)).

The voice acclaims Jesus as God's *Son*, perhaps with echoes of Ps. 2.7, which speaks of a king begotten as God's son and appointed as ruler over the nations (note also the 'holy hill' in Ps. 2.6 and v.18 below) and which was interpreted messianically in Judaism and early Christianity (see e.g. Acts 13.33; Heb. 1.5; 5.5). Differing slightly from the Synoptic accounts, II Peter has *my Beloved* as a separate title for Jesus (rather than 'my beloved Son'; see Bauckham, 207–209). The phrase *on whom my favour rests* is paralleled only (and not precisely) in Matthew's Transfiguration account (Matt. 17.5) and in the accounts of Jesus' baptism (Matt. 3.17 and parallels). The phrase perhaps derives from Isa. 42.1 (cf. Luke 9.35; Matt. 12.18). Thus Jesus is acclaimed as the one appointed and anointed by God as his unique agent and kingly ruler.

1.18 The author stresses that the apostles heard this declaration; *we ourselves* is emphatic. The Synoptics speak of a 'voice from the cloud' (Mark 9.7 and parallels); here we have *this voice . . . from heaven*. Perhaps this is one hint at a gradual 'sacralizing' of the tradition about the Transfiguration: this certainly seems evident in the difference between 'a high mountain' (Matt. 17.1; Mark 9.2) and *the sacred mountain* (cf. Ps. 2.6; mountains have particular significance in the Bible as the site of divine revelation: e.g. Sinai/Horeb [see Ex. 3.1ff.]; Zion [Ps. 2.6; 50.2 etc.]). Moreover, in Mark's account Peter's inappropriate reaction to the transfiguration of Jesus is explicitly described as a response to being terrified and not knowing what to say (Mark 9.6). This description is toned down somewhat in Luke (9.33) and omitted altogether in Matthew (see 17.4–5). No hint of Peter's awkward terror appears here in II Peter either.

1.19 A number of questions arise over the translation and interpretation of this verse and its link with what precedes. One question concerns which prophecy/ies the author has in mind (literally the phrase is 'the prophetic word'). Is he referring to the Transfiguration as a prophecy of the return of Christ (so Neyrey, 178–80; 1980b, 514–16; Perkins, 176)? Is this 'the prophetic word', *to which you will do well to attend*? Most commentators think that a reference to the prophets of the Jewish scriptures is intended, and this seems a more likely interpretation (hence the REB's translation: *the message of the prophets*). But in this case does the author mean certain specific prophecies contained within the Jewish scriptures (so Fornberg 1977, 82–83), or the scriptures as a whole, in their prophetic witness to Christ? On balance the latter is probably to be preferred.

A further question is whether the author means that the Transfiguration *confirms the message of the prophets*. This is the most common interpretation among commentators and translators, and it offers a clear link between vv.16–18 and vv.19–21: the prophetic message of the Jewish scriptures is confirmed, or becomes more sure (Gk: *bebaioteron*), in the light of the Transfiguration. It seems more likely grammatically, however, that the author begins a fresh point here, affirming the reliability of scriptural prophecy. As the NAB translates: 'Moreover, we possess the prophetic message that is altogether reliable' (Gk: *bebaioteron*; cf. Reicke, 158; Bauckham, 223; BAGD, 138). So, again in the light of accusations made against his teaching, the author now affirms that the apostolic message is rooted not only in eyewitness testimony but also in the reliable prophecy of scripture (cf. Watson 1988, 104).

People should therefore *attend* to the prophetic message, since it serves as a *lamp shining in a murky* (or 'dark') *place* (cf. Ps. 119.105). Like a lamp, prophecy offers valuable illumination and guidance, but it is partial and incomplete, and is no longer needed when the full light of day dawns (cf. I Cor. 13.8–12). The image of day breaking is a reference to Christ's return, a 'day' of light and salvation, but also of judgment (cf. Rom. 13.12; Jude 6; II Peter 3.10). Christ himself is metaphorically described as *the morning star* (the planet Venus which the ancients recognized as the herald of the dawn). The image of the Messiah as a star derives from Num. 24.17, which was interpreted messianically in Judaism and early Christianity (see Kelly, 322; Bauckham, 226; Rev. 22.16; cf. Luke 1.78; Matt. 4.16). But if this image here refers to the final, glorious return of Christ, why does the author describe it as the time when *the morning star rises* 'in your hearts' (a more literal rendering than *to illuminate your minds*)? The reason is that the focus here is on the significance of the Parousia for individual believers (cf. Knoch, 257), though the cosmic scope of the event is not lost sight of (cf. 3.4–13): for them it will be a day of illumination, revelation and transformation.

1.20–21 Now the author makes a response to a second accusation of the opponents, namely 'that the Old Testament prophecy upon which the apostles base their teaching of the parousia is a matter of the prophet's own interpretation and impulse, not the inspiration of the Holy Spirit' (Watson 1988, 105; cf. Bauckham, 228). The introductory phrase *But first note this* (used again in 3.3) indicates that an important proposition follows (i.e. *first* is meant in the sense of importance, not of temporal priority). But the proposition is difficult to interpret. The author most likely intends a reference to scriptural writings: hence the best translation is 'no prophecy of scripture' rather than the more general *no prophetic writing*. Also unclear is the remainder of the statement. It may mean either 'no prophecy of scripture *is a matter for private interpretation*', or 'no prophecy of scripture derives from the prophet's own interpretation'. The former rendering, which is followed by most commentators and translators, implies that the author's point is this: 'no individual is entitled to interpret prophecy, or scripture generally, according to his personal whim. It is precisely this . . . that the trouble-makers are guilty of' (Kelly, 324; cf. 3.16). Thus: 'The notion of the official Church as the appointed guardian of scripture is evidently taking shape' (Kelly, 324; cf. also Knight 1995, 62). One of the problems with this interpretation, however, is that v.21 does not make this point (see below). It is therefore perhaps preferable (though the matter is rather finely balanced) to follow Bauckham (pp.229–33) and adopt the second interpretation (though one difficulty for this interpretation is 3.16, where the accusation against the opponents is that they distort and misinterpret the scriptures). On this reading the author is countering an accusation that the prophets of old gave their own human interpretations to the visions which they saw, so their words need not be regarded as coming from God. On the contrary, the author insists (v.21), no prophecy ever came through *human initiative; rather,* moved by *the Holy Spirit people spoke as messengers of God.* This view of genuine prophecy as resulting from a compulsion to speak God's word and not, as in false prophecy, from the prophet's own initiative, is common in the Jewish scriptures (e.g. Jer. 1.4–10; 20.7–10; 23.16; Ezek. 13.3). Just as the author of II Peter insisted that the voice at the Transfiguration was the voice of God (vv.17–18) so he insists here that the words of the prophets also came from God. Both sources for the apostolic teaching are reliable records of God's word, contrary to the opponents' accusations.

We should bear in mind, however, that any account of an event, even by eyewitnesses, is an interpretation, and that this account is presented by someone writing in Peter's name some years after his death. It is not exactly self-evident that the Transfiguration is a confirmation of Christ's second coming. Moreover, any word of scripture must be interpreted, and does not yield only one possible meaning. And the claim that a particular teaching is God's word is always a claim made by a human being, and is therefore open to question. Such sceptical points should not be taken as a denial of the truth of the apostolic teaching which the author presents; but they should make us aware that he is making certain claims and seeking to exclude others, presented and no doubt argued for by his opponents. He is presenting a certain interpretation of apostolic teaching as the only authorized and approved one. Then, as well as now, an important question remains: how much diversity of inter-pretation, belief and practice can be encompassed within the church?

God's judgment on the false teachers
2.1–22

In chapter 2 the author turns from defence to attack, indicating how the false teachers are destined for God's judgment, at the same time affirming that God's judgment will occur soon, despite the opponents' assertion that it will never come and that the promise is false (see 3.3ff.). In chapter 3 he turns to a more detailed defence of the teaching about the Lord's return. From 2.1–3.3, II Peter clearly takes up and adapts material from Jude 4–19 (see Ch.IV 3(ii)). Jude's use of scriptural material to demonstrate the certainty of the doom which awaits his opponents suits II Peter's purpose well. The use of Jude by II Peter might also reflect the fact that Jude was regarded as authoritative by the author and readers of II Peter (cf. Watson 1988, 106 n.160).

A prediction of false teachers

2.1–3a

In a 'testament' or farewell address the departing hero normally makes predictions about future times, and in New Testament examples we find predictions specifically about false teachers (Acts 20.29–30; II Tim. 3.1–5; 4.3–4; cf. Matt. 24.11; Mark 13.5, 22). Writing in Peter's name, the author 'predicts' the appearance of false teachers in the future (cf. 3.2–3; Jude 17–18), though they are clearly a reality at the time of writing (see 2.12–22). He thus seeks to label his opponents as the false teachers whom the apostles predicted (cf. Ch. IV 2(v)). These verses introduce the polemic which follows, and mention most of the important topics which will be dealt with in the rest of the letter (see Neyrey, 186–87).

Although a new section begins here, the author links it carefully with what has preceded. Following the mention of the prophets of scripture (1.19–21), he begins with a mention of the false prophets who also existed back then (2.1), before moving on to the false teachers of the present. And while the apostles did not pass on 'cleverly concocted tales' (1.16), the opponents' teaching is nothing but 'sheer fabrication' (2.3).

2.1 Along with the true prophets who spoke God's word (1.21) *in the past there were also false prophets among the people* (i.e. the people of Israel). The reality and danger of false prophets is often mentioned in the Jewish scriptures (e.g. Deut. 13.1–5; 18.20; Ezek. 13.1ff.; Micah 3.5–12) and their characteristics may be summarized: they 'speak on their own authority, preach freedom from fear and judgment, but are condemned by God' (Neyrey, 190). Correspondingly, *you also will have* (note the future tense here and elsewhere in these verses, which are written as a prediction of Peter's) *false teachers among you*. It is notable that the author calls them false *teachers* and not false *prophets*, perhaps because they did not claim prophetic or charismatic inspiration (against Cavallin 1979; contrast Jude: see Ch.IV 2(v)), or to emphasize the fact that they propagate a message, a teaching which leads others astray. They *will introduce* (perhaps with the pejorative sense, 'bring in secretly') *their destructive views*. This is perhaps a hint that the opponents are not itinerant travelling teachers, but members within the congregations (contrast Jude 4; so Bauckham, 239). Their *views* (Gk: *haireseis*, probably here in the sense of particular teachings, rather than 'divisions'; cf. Knoch, 260; I Cor.

11.19; Gal. 5.20) lead to destruction – i.e. to judgment (though this may be the very thing that the opponents deny).

By their denial of the Lord's judgment and their licentious immorality, the false teachers deny *the Master* (cf. Jude 4). Christ is their master because, in language used to describe the purchasing of slaves, he has *redeemed* or 'bought' *them* (cf. I Cor. 6.20; 7.23; Rev. 14.3–4). Yet by *disowning* all this, the false teachers will bring upon themselves divinely-ordained *destruction* which, despite their scepticism (see 3.3–10), will be *swift* and soon (*tachinê*, translated *swift* here, *soon* in 1.14). This stark assertion is the theme of what follows in the rest of the chapter.

2.2   As a further 'prediction' of what must presumably already be the case, 'Peter' warns that *many* will follow the *dissolute* or licentious *practices* which the false teachers introduce (the accusation of licentiousness, sexual indulgence, and freedom from morality, recurs through the chapter: see 2.10, 12, 14, 18–19 etc.). And so, through these people, *the way of truth will be brought into disrepute*. The term *way* (cf. 2.15, 21) is common in Jewish and Christian writings as a description of a whole way of life: either following that which God commands and approves or following paths of wickedness and destruction (Ps. 1.6; 5.8; 119.1; Prov. 1.15; *Didache* 1–6; *Barnabas* 18–20; 1QS 3.20–21). Christianity is referred to simply as 'the Way' in Acts 9.2; 19.9, 23; 24.14, 22 etc. According to the author, the behaviour encouraged by the false teachers damages the reputation and honour of the community (and therefore of God; see Neyrey, 189, 193). The phrase used here echoes Isa. 52.5 (LXX). The author's concern is often encountered in the New Testament, that the conduct of Christians should, as far as possible, gain the respect of outsiders (e.g. I Thess. 4.12; I Tim. 3.7; 6.1; Titus 2.5; I Peter 2.12).

2.3a   The false teachers' activities are apparently motivated by *greed*, perhaps reflecting the fact that they receive payment in *money* or in kind from the churches (cf. 2.14; Jude 11, 16). However, the accusation of greed was typical in polemics and we should be wary of taking it at face value (Neyrey, 192; Watson 1988, 109). The author here turns the false teachers' accusation back on themselves: they accuse the apostles (and those who represent them now) of basing their teaching on 'cleverly concocted tales' (1.16). On the contrary, the author charges, it is the false teachers who exploit people with *sheer fabrications*.

The certainty of divine judgment
2.3b–10a

Although v.3b is closely connected grammatically with v.3a it is best (with REB, Bauckham, Neyrey) to see it as the introduction to the next stage in the argument, a transition marked by the change from future to present tense verbs (cf. 3.3 and 3.5). The author shifts from 'prophecy' in Peter's name, to a focus on the opponents in the present, showing how the apostles' prophecies are now being fulfilled (cf. II Tim. 3.1–9). Verse 3b provides a 'statement' for which vv.4–10a offer a 'proof' (cf. Neyrey, 195–96; Watson 1988, 111). In fact the whole of vv.4–10a comprises one long sentence in the Greek, structured in the form: 'If . . . and if . . . and if . . . then . . .' (a form not shown in the REB's translation, but see e.g. NRSV). On the basis of events in the past, an affirmation about the certainty of God's judgment in the present and future is made. Later in the letter the problem of the delay of the coming judgment will be faced, here it is the certainty of God's judgment which is demonstrated, in the face of mocking doubt.

In these verses II Peter uses material from Jude 6–8 (see Ch. VI 3(ii)), though it is heavily reshaped, with some material omitted and new subjects included. Like Jude, II Peter reveals an acquaintance not only with the Jewish scriptures but also with Jewish traditions of interpretation. Jude is most concerned to warn about the dreadful consequences of deviating from the right way (see Jude 5) whereas II Peter stresses the danger of denying the reality of God's judgment. II Peter omits Jude's example of the Exodus and wilderness wanderings (Jude 5) and lists his examples in chronological order. II Peter cites three examples of judgment (the sinful angels, the ancient world at the time of the flood, Sodom and Gomorrah) and two of preservation (Noah and Lot). Unlike Jude, therefore, II Peter does not focus only on God's judgment of the wicked, but includes also the theme of God's deliverance of the righteous (note the stark and emphatic contrasts: *did not spare* . . .[vv.4–5] *rescued* [v.7]). In this II Peter shows similarities with (and possibly the influence of) a tradition encountered elsewhere which uses a number of the same examples employed here, in which God's justice is defended and his rescue of the righteous and condemnation of the wicked are anticipated and affirmed (see Sirach 16.6–23; Wisd. 10.1ff.; cf. also I Peter 1.6–9; 4.17–19, etc., possibly an influence on II Peter).

2.3b The form of the author's assertion probably reflects the opponents' claim that God's judgment is 'idle' and 'asleep' (Neyrey 1980a, 415–16; cf. 3.3–9). Elijah taunted the followers of Baal that their god was asleep (I Kings 18.27), while the Psalmist affirmed that Israel's God 'never slumbers, never sleeps' (Ps. 121.4), though in a time of affliction he could call upon God to awake (Ps. 44.23; cf. Isa. 51.9). Epicureanism, which may have been an influence upon the opponents in II Peter, was known for its denial of divine judgment and providence (see Neyrey 1980a). In the face of such doubt, and its consequent moral laxity, the author affirms that the *judgment* pronounced on such people long ago 'is not idle'; their *destruction* 'is not asleep'. Implicit behind such personalized references to judgment and destruction lies God, whose action they represent.

2.4 To prove this assertion, the author now begins a long sentence which argues that since God acted in judgment and deliverance in the past, then he will certainly not fail to do so in the future. The first example, based on Jude 6 and originally on Gen. 6.1–4, is that of *the angels who sinned*, that is the angelic beings (the 'Watchers') who lusted after human women (see on Jude 6). These *angels God did not spare, but consigned them to dark pits* (or perhaps 'chains of darkness': there is a textual uncertainty here). The verb rendered *consigned to hell* literally means 'to consign to Tartarus', a place known from Greek mythology as the lowest place in the underworld (where the Titans were thrown) and referred to also by Hellenistic Jewish writers. There the sinful angels *are held for judgment*, that is, for the final judgment on the last day.

2.5 The second example is that of the Flood (linked with the story of the Watchers e.g. in *I Enoch*; see Bauckham, 249). Repeating the verb used in v.4 – *he did not spare* – the author recounts God's judgment in bringing a *flood* upon *the world in ancient times*, for it was a world of *godless people* (a term which recurs in 2.6 and 3.7). The judgment which the flood represents is sometimes seen as a precursor of the final judgment (e.g. Matt. 24.37–39). For the author of II Peter it provides an example not only of judgment but also of deliverance: for God protected *Noah . . . with seven others*. Noah is referred to as 'the eighth one', implying seven others. The reason for this slightly odd expression may be that some symbolic importance was seen in the reference to 'the eighth one', perhaps signifying the eighth day as the day of new creation after the seven days of creation, or the

Christian celebration of the eighth day, Sunday, as the day of resurrection (see Bauckham, 250). Genesis does not refer to Noah as a 'preacher' of *righteousness* (cf. Gen. 6.9) but the idea became well established in Jewish tradition. The influence of I Peter 3.20 might be detected in the choice of this example by the author of II Peter (note the reference there to eight persons), but the idea need not have come from this source (cf. Wisd. 10.4).

2.6 The third example of judgment, again drawn from Jude (v.7), is God's condemnation of *the cities of Sodom and Gomorrah*. According to Jewish tradition only *ashes* were left of them (Kelly, 333) and the smouldering waste south of the Dead Sea was thought to be enduring evidence of their destruction (see on Jude 7). Thus they serve as *an object-lesson*, or a warning example, *for the ungodly in future days* (or, 'of the fate in store for ungodly people'; see Kelly, 333, on the textual variation here).

Elsewhere too the Flood and the fate of Sodom and Gomorrah are mentioned together as two prime examples of divine judgment (Luke 17.26–30), representing the pattern of destruction by water and fire, mentioned in II Peter 3.5–7 (Bauckham, 252). Bauckham (p.252) also makes the interesting observation that II Peter seems consistently to omit Jude's references to the eternity of punishment (II Peter 2.4, 6, 17; Jude 6, 7, 13), though the reason for this is not clear.

2.7–8 As in the story of the Flood, so here too there is a counterpart to the theme of destruction: the deliverance of *Lot, a good* ('righteous') *man*. Again the author's view owes more to Jewish tradition than to the Genesis account, in which Lot is not entirely blameless (Gen. 19.4–38). Abraham's plea on behalf of the righteous in Sodom (Gen. 18.23–32) was interpreted as a reference to Lot, who came to be described, as here, as a righteous man (Wisd. 10.6; 19.17). The description of Lot's distress – witnessing the evil ways of those among whom he lived – is perhaps meant to echo the experience of II Peter's readers. V. 8 elaborates in parentheses (cf. NRSV; NAB etc.) the inner torment which Lot is supposed to have suffered.

2.9 The conclusion to which the long sentence has been leading is at last reached. This conclusion is a two-fold moral concerning divine justice, on the one hand for the righteous, on the other, for the wicked. If God has done all the things listed above, then certainly he *knows how* (and by implication is able) *to rescue the godly from their trials* – namely, the afflictions which, like Lot, they suffer through living in an evil world (cf. Sirach 33.1; Wisd. 10.9; I Peter 1.6). There may be an echo here of the Lord's prayer (Matt. 6.13: 'do not bring us to the time of trial, but rescue us' [NRSV]).

On the other hand, God will certainly *keep the wicked under punishment until the day of judgment.* There is some debate as to whether to understand the verse in this way – with the sense of a present punishment which precedes the punishment to be meted out on the day of judgment – or whether it should be translated 'keep the wicked to be punished on the day of judgment'. On balance the latter is perhaps to be preferred (see Bauckham, 254).

2.10a   Although the REB breaks its paragraph at the end of v.9, most commentators and translations rightly see v.10a as a continuation and amplification of the statement in v.9. Elaborating the assertion that God will judge the wicked, and using phrases from Jude 7 and 8, the author singles out 'especially' *those who follow their abominable lusts and flout authority.* Clearly pointing to the trouble-makers in his own time, the author summarizes their sins as indulgence of the flesh in corrupt and depraved desires and as despising the authority of the Lord (see on Jude 8). The two are connected: from the author's perspective the opponents deny the reality of God's judgment, mocking the idea that it will ever come, and thus count themselves free to act as they please without fear.

While drawing much of his material from Jude, the author of II Peter introduces the idea of deliverance for the righteous alongside that of condemnation for the wicked. Both aspects are relevant as a defence of God's justice, in a situation where the wicked seem to go unpunished and the righteous suffer. Yet is the author's conviction about the reality and imminence of God's judgment plausible today? No such judgment has come, and we might question whether this is the message of the Christian gospel anyway. Even so, as contemporary readers we may do well to hold on to a sense of God's justice, unfashionable though it may be, to a sense of God's outrage and anger at injustice, and to a sense of our ethical responsibilities. Nevertheless, the images of God's condemnation and punishment found here raise, as they did in Jude, questions about the gap between the author's conception of God and our own, and so raise difficult questions about the value and use of this material today (see Ch.IV 4).

Denunciation of the false teachers
  2.10b–22

The whole of this section comprises 'a loosely structured series of denunciations of the false teachers' (Bauckham, 259) based in part on Jude 8–16. Kelly (p.337) describes it as 'the most violent and colourfully expressed tirade in the NT'. As vilifying polemic it gives little clear or precise indication of the views or conduct of the author's opponents (cf. Knoch, 266). Verses 10b–18 draw primarily on Jude as their source, but Jude is then left to one side until 3.2. In 2.19–22 the author adopts and adapts a series of proverbial sayings. The material from Jude, as elsewhere in this letter, is freely adapted to the author's purpose. Notably, the clear references to apocryphal writings, especially *I Enoch*, are omitted (see Jude 9, 14–15), perhaps because the author (and his readers) did not know these writings, or because he disapproved of them or doubted their authority.

2.10b–11   The false teachers, in their presumptuous disregard for the divinely-established order, are *reckless and headstrong*, for *they are not afraid to insult celestial beings* (Gk: *doxas*, see on Jude 8, from where this phrase comes). Most commentators agree that these *celestial beings* are fallen or evil angels (cf. 2.4: *the angels who sinned*). The false teachers fail to show proper regard for the power of these spiritual beings; they *insult* them by mocking or denying the idea that they could have any influence or hold any danger. This is consistent with the 'sceptical rationalism' which seems to characterize their views (see Bauckham, 262–63). Adapting the idea from Jude 9, without making the explicit reference to the apocryphal story about Michael and Moses' body, the author contrasts this recklessness with the attitude of the *angels*. Though they are stronger and more powerful than the evil *celestial beings*, the *angels* do not bring a slanderous *judgment against them* (i.e. the evil celestial beings) 'from the Lord'. The REB's rendering *before the Lord* reflects the wording in some texts, but probably not the original. The change likely shows a scribe or scribes concerned to avoid the idea that God might make a 'slanderous judgment'. But the point the author is making is that even the angels do not use insults (unlike the false teachers) when they pronounce God's judgment.

2.12–13   Expanding an image from Jude 10, the author now compares the false teachers (not necessarily all *men*, see on v.14) to *brute*

beasts, mere creatures of instinct, born to be caught and killed. The idea
that certain types of animal were born to be slaughtered and eaten
was common in the ancient world (Bauckham, 263). The opponents
are like irrational or dumb beasts as, continuing the theme from
vv.10–11, they 'insult' *(pour abuse upon) things they do not understand*.
This is probably meant to refer back to their insulting of the evil *celestial beings* (v.10). If this is correct it may affect the interpretation of
the final phrase of the verse which, literally translated, runs: 'in their
destruction, they also will be destroyed' (cf. NAB). Most translations
and commentators, like the REB, take 'their destruction' to refer to
the beasts. Kelly (p.339), for example, writes of 'a destruction similar
in its finality to that which befalls wild beasts'. It is more likely, however, that the author is referring to the destruction of the evil angels;
his claim is that 'the false teachers will share the fate of the powers of
evil who will be eliminated at the day of judgment' (Bauckham, 264)

A further indication of the false teachers' destiny at the final judgment is given in the form of a statement about their 'just deserts':
suffering hurt for the hurt they have inflicted. The REB brings out the
word-play which is apparent in the Greek, though difficult to retain
in a translation. Their 'reward' for doing wrong (Gk: *adikias*) is to
suffer harm (Gk: *adikoumenoi*) themselves.

The moral depravity of which the author accuses his opponents is
shown in the fact that not only do they *carouse*, or revel in indulgence, but they do so shamelessly *in broad daylight*. Revelling
was bad enough, but doing so in the daytime was a clear mark of
degeneracy (cf. Eccles. 10.16; Isa. 5.11). This they regard as *pleasure*
(often seen as a cardinal vice; see Neyrey, 214).

The false teachers are clearly still involved in the fellowship of the
church and in its common meals, for the author describes them as
'feasting with you', sitting *with you at table* (the same verb used in
Jude 12). Yet while they do this they are 'spots and blemishes' (the
word 'spots', *spiloi*, is adapted from Jude's description in v.12 of the
false teachers as 'dangerous rocks', *spilades*). A comparison of the
Greek words used here and in 3.14 shows the false teachers to be
precisely what the church should be without: they are spots and
blemishes (*spiloi . . . mômoi*), the believers are urged in 3.14 to be a
community without spot or blemish (*aspiloi . . . amômetoi*). The
opponents are a polluting presence in what should be a pure community (cf. Neyrey, 212–13) as *they revel in their deceits*. This last word
is probably a deliberate pun by the author, though one which carries
'stinging irony' (Kelly, 341): in Jude 12, on which the author draws

here, there is a reference to love-feasts (*agapais*), which the author of II Peter has changed to *deceits* (*apatais*). Defiled by the licentious behaviour of the false teachers, the meal together is a mockery of a true *agapê*, and can only be labelled a 'deception' (cf. I Cor. 11.20).

2.14   The long string of abuse continues: *they have eyes for nothing but loose women*, i.e. they are 'always looking for a woman with whom to commit adultery' (BAGD, 526). The exaggerated and stereotypical character of the polemic in this chapter should make us wary of taking this accusation too literally: it does not necessarily imply that all of the author's opponents were men (cf. vv.12, 17, which need not be translated *these men*, but rather 'these people'). Nor does it quite give a firm basis for saying that the opponents did not regard illicit sexual relations and divorce as sinful (as does Knoch, 267), though there may be an element of truth in this (cf. I Cor. 5.1ff.; 6.12–20; 7.10–16; Rev. 2.14, 20–22). Clearly the author's view, hardly a 'neutral' perspective, is that they *never* cease *from sin*.

Moving on to the impact which the false teachers have on others within the church, the author accuses them of luring or enticing people (a metaphor derived from baiting and catching in fishing or hunting; cf. Neyrey, 215). The author does not actually state to what they are lured, though the REB's *to their ruin* would certainly be what he implies. Those who are susceptible are the *unstable*, especially new converts (cf. 2.18–19), hence the author's aim to establish further the readers' grounding in the truth (1.12). On the other hand, the false teachers are 'well-trained' (a metaphor from athletics); they are *experts*, yet not in right ways (cf. v.15) but in *greed* (cf. on 2.3a)! The abuse culminates in the exclamation, *God's curse is on them*; they are, literally, 'children of a curse', a typically Hebrew form of expression (see on I Peter 1.14).

2.15   In all this sinful behaviour, the false teachers *have abandoned the straight road*, or 'right way', (a common metaphor for the path of obedience to God; see on 2.2; I Sam. 12.23; Hos. 14.10; Ps. 107.7; Acts 13.10). In doing so, they have *gone astray*, a verb which was often used of 'being corrupted either spiritually or morally' (Kelly, 343).

From Jude's trio of wicked characters – Cain, Balaam, and Korah (Jude 11) – the author of II Peter selects just Balaam, and develops further the analogy between Balaam (as presented in Jewish tradition; see Neyrey, 211–12) and the false teachers. Rather than following 'the right way' (*hodos*), the false teachers *have followed* 'the way' (*hodos*) of *Balaam son of Bosor* (cf. Jude 11: 'the way of Cain'). The name of Balaam's father is in fact Beor (see Num. 22.5; 24.3 etc.); the name *Bosor* is found nowhere else but here. The reason for the change is unknown, though one suggestion is a pun on the Hebrew word *basar*, meaning 'flesh': 'Balaam's immoral character would be indicated by calling him "son of flesh"' (Bauckham, 267–68). The author chooses the example of Balaam to focus on the false teachers' greed, for it was Balaam's greed for profit which became well-known as his sin: he *eagerly accepted payment for doing wrong* (the same phrase used in v.13). Actually, the Numbers narrative records Balaam refusing to do what Balak wished, no matter what the financial inducement (Num. 22–24; see on Jude 11). Balaam agrees to go with Balak's embassies only when God urges him to (Num. 22.20–21), yet apparently God is still angry with him for going (Num. 22.22).

2.16   The account of Balaam's journey in Num. 22.22–35 is the basis for this verse. Balaam's donkey sees an angel of the Lord (unseen by Balaam) repeatedly blocking the way, and so tries to abort the journey, receiving beatings from Balaam for her actions. Eventually the Lord gives the donkey a voice to speak in protest at this treatment, after which Balaam sees and speaks with the angel and realizes what has been happening. Nevertheless, the angel still urges Balaam to continue on the journey (Num. 22.34–35). The author of II Peter, following Jewish interpretations of this story, sees the donkey as rebuking Balaam for *his offence* – i.e. the *offence* of being greedy for material gain from doing wrong, though this sin of Balaam's is not mentioned in Numbers. This is an ironic and 'humilating outcome' (Kelly, 343), for the prophet who utters God's words (see esp. Num. 23–24) is shamed by *a dumb beast*. For the author of II Peter the two aspects of Balaam's behaviour are connected: his wickedness in seeking to profit from wrongdoing, and his madness in thinking that he could get away with it and escape God's judgment. Both of these faults, the author implies, characterize the false teachers as well.

2.17   After a slight pause, appropriately marked by a paragraph break, the verbal attack continues, beginning once again with the accusatory '*These* people . . .'. Taking up language from Jude 12, the author describes the false teachers as *springs that give no water, mists driven by a storm*. In the context of a dry climate where water is precious and rainfall welcomed, these are clear images of 'bitter disappointment to the thirsty traveller or anxious farmer' (Kelly, 345).

The mist or haze referred to does not bring rain, but only signals heat to come, and is easily dispersed by the wind or the sun (cf. Wisd. 2.4). So the author argues that the false teachers promise much – the 'water' of life-giving teaching – but their promises are empty and deceptive. Drawing another phrase from Jude (v.13), though without the same context and omitting the phrase 'an eternity', the author describes *the place reserved for* these false teachers as *blackest darkness*.

2.18   Developing the theme of empty promise, the author derides the words of the false teachers as mere *empty bombast* – 'high-sounding but empty talk' (NJB). The parallels of language between 1.3–4 and 2.18–20 serve to contrast God's generous giving and assured promises declared in the apostolic gospel with the empty and deceptive promises of which the false teachers speak (cf. Bauckham, 276–77). Yet their talk is clearly enticing to some (the language of 'baiting', as in 2.14). With the promise of freedom from moral restraint and from divine judgment (see v.19) *people* become ensnared in *sensual lusts* (cf. 1.4; 2.10; 3.3) *and debauchery* (cf. 2.2, 7). And the people who are vulnerable to this trap are new converts, not established in the faith, *who have only just begun to escape* (or, have only recently escaped) from 'those who live in error'. This last phrase is a literal rendering of the author's description of the pagans among whom the readers live. Other Jewish and Christian writers also use the terminology of 'error' or 'going astray' to denote the idolatry and ignorance of those who do not acknowledge God (e.g. Wisd. 12.24; 13.1–10; Rom. 1.27; Titus 3.3; cf. 2.15).

2.19   The false teachers *promise freedom,* but freedom from what? Many suggestions have been made (see Bauckham, 275) but most likely, as far as we can tell from the author's viewpoint, is that the false teachers derided any notion of coming judgment, consequently linking freedom from judgment with freedom from moral restraint (cf. Bauckham, 280). The message of freedom from divine retribution was also found in Epicureanism, perhaps an influence on the opponents in II Peter (see Neyrey 1980a, 418–19). Paul's proclamation of Christian freedom could also certainly be misunderstood as a licence to sin (see Rom. 3.8; 6.1ff.; Gal. 5.13). Perhaps the false teachers derived inspiration from what the author regards as a distorted reading of Paul's letters, hence his comment in 3.16 (Knoch, 269). Just as Paul insisted that Christian freedom meant freedom *from* sin, not licence to sin (Rom. 6.1ff.), so the author of II Peter maintains that the freedom the false teachers promise is not freedom at all, since in reality they are *slaves of corruption* (cf. 1.4; 2.12).

To illustrate this point the author quotes a proverbial saying which was widely quoted in later centuries: *people are the slaves of whatever* (or, 'whoever') *has mastered them*. The imagery derives from 'the ancient practice of enslaving an enemy defeated in battle' (Kelly, 347). The author's point is that by succumbing to sensual desires and sinful indulgence, far from being free, the false teachers and their followers have become slaves to these things. A similar idea is expressed by Stoic-Cynic thinkers, for whom it was slavery to be subject to any desires or needs: freedom was found in indifference to external conditions and relationships, and in being content with a few basics necessary to life (Epictetus *Discourses* 2.19.24; 3.22.45–49; 4.1.1–23, 128–31).

2.20 The first part of v.20 is expressed in a conditional form (For *if . . .*), with the resulting situation stated in the latter part of the verse and elaborated further in vv.21–22. The people in view are those who, having *escaped the world's defilements* (cf. 1.4) *through coming to know our Lord and Saviour Jesus Christ* (cf. 1.2), become *entangled* in these things *again* and defeated (or *mastered*) by them (the same verb used in v.19b). A question is whether *they* refers to the false teachers or to those who are drawn to their teaching. It may be unnecessary and inappropriate to make a sharp distinction, but it is probably best to see the prime focus of the author's warning as those who are being enticed away from their new-found faith, back into pagan ways (v.18; cf. Kelly, 347–48; Knoch, 270). For any such people, and certainly also for the false teachers, 'their last condition is worse than their first' (NAB; cf. also NRSV). This phrase is almost identical to words attributed to Jesus in Matt. 12.45/Luke 11.26. It was probably a form of proverbial saying (cf. Matt. 27.64) which Christians adapted in order to describe (and warn against) apostasy – turning away from the faith (Kelly, 348).

The danger of apostasy was clearly a reality in the early church; as has always been the case, people sometimes turned away from something to which they were once converted. A horror of apostasy and vivid declarations of the grievous state in which apostates find themselves are found both here and in Hebrews (6.4–6; 10.26). Gradually a system of penitence for post-baptismal sin and even for apostasy evolved; but apostasy remained a particularly serious offence (see Kelly, 349).

2.21 This verse takes the form of a *Better . . . than* saying, a form often found in Jewish and Christian writings (see on I Peter 3.17; Snyder 1977). The phrase *the right way*, or 'way of righteousness', is a typically Jewish-Christian description of the ethical 'way' of life which God requires and approves (see on 2.2; 2.15; Prov. 21.16 [LXX]; Matt. 21.32). A similar idea is conveyed in the words *the sacred commandment*, which probably refers not to a specific law or command but to the instruction embodied in the law as a whole, to live a holy life (see on I Peter 1.15–16; Rom. 7.12). Against the lawless behaviour of the false teachers, the author presents the truly Christian way as a way of ethical and upright living. This holy way of living is what was 'passed on' (NRSV; cf. 1.12–16; Jude 3) by the apostles and their successors. The clear declaration of the verse is that those who turn back from the faith are in a worse state than those who never found it at all.

2.22 The situation of such people is illustrated with a *proverb*, which *in their case has proved true*. The sayings which follow were originally two separate proverbs, but were probably known by the author as one, possibly from some Jewish-Hellenistic collection of proverbs. The first proverb, concerning *the dog* returning *to its vomit*, is based on Prov. 26.11. The second is probably derived from *The Story of Ahiqar*, an ancient story adopted by Jews and containing a series of proverbs and sayings (see Charlesworth 1985, 487–88; Charles 1913, 772; Bauckham, 279–80). Both dogs and pigs were regarded by Jews as dirty and despicable animals (cf. Neyrey, 221–22) and both proverbs depict an animal getting rid of some filth only to return to it. For the author this illustrates the apostasy of the false teachers and all who follow them, turning away from the true faith and reverting to the immorality of their pagan past (cf. 2.12, where the false teachers are described as 'brute beasts').

As with much of the polemic of Jude and II Peter, we may feel awkwardly conscious of the gap between the author's thought-world and our own. In keeping with the culture of the time, the author is vigorously defending the honour of his group and their God against what he sees as the slanderous attacks of the false teachers (see Neyrey, 218–19); he warns the false teachers and their followers of the dire state in which they will find themselves. On the one hand, we may feel that his harsh polemic and stern warnings are out of line with our own conception of God and our way of understanding the Christian faith. For example, a conversation with someone who has 'lost their faith' is more likely to involve sympathy and understanding than stark warnings of judgment and proverbs about dogs returning to their vomit! Most contemporary Christians, unless they have a strongly sectarian world-view, would not describe their non-Christian neighbours as people who live in filth and error. On the other hand, however, we may do well to hold on to the author's warning that Christian living is not a matter of free licence and self-indulgence; there is a 'way of righteousness', a 'holy command-ment', to be followed.

The Day of the Lord will come
3.1–13

A reminder of prophecy concerning the last days
3.1–4

After a lengthy passage attacking the false teachers, the author now returns to defending apostolic teaching (specifically about the Lord's return) against the objections of the sceptics. With a clear reiteration of his (assumed) identity as the apostle Peter, he 'predicts' what is already the case. In chapter 2 a 'prediction' of false teachers (vv.1–3a) was followed by a denunciation of them as a present reality (vv.3b–22); here too it is clear that the scoffers who are 'predicted' to come (vv.1–4) are already present (v.5). In this introduction to the last major section, the author again takes up material from Jude (17–18) concerning the scoffers of the last days. Jude, however, was not concerned to confront doubts about the parousia hope, and so does not provide material for the author to use specifically on this subject. The author of II Peter perhaps used a Jewish apocalypse as a source (see Bauckham, 283–85).

3.1   As in Jude 17 and 20 the author turns from polemic against opponents to appeal to his readers with the address *dear friends* (cf. Neyrey, 227). He indicates that *this is now* his *second letter* to them, so reiterating the apostolic identity of the implied author, Peter. Most commentators agree that the first letter must be I Peter, which was presumably known to the readers of II Peter. There is little sign that the author has used I Peter as a source in the writing of II Peter (cf.

Ch.VI 3(ii)), though he may have known it, and there are some notable overlaps of themes and ideas (e.g. the need for holy living in the light of the coming judgment: see I Peter 1.13–17; 4.1–19 etc.; cf. Dalton 1979). The specific theme of the prophets and apostles, mentioned here in v.2, is paralleled in I Peter 1.10–12. Both letters, the author explicitly states, serve as 'reminders' from the apostle (cf. II Peter 1.12–15) which are intended to keep their readers pure in their thinking – to prevent them being led astray by the immoral desires which the false teachers follow.

3.2   The author adapts and expands upon words from Jude 17, urging his readers to *remember the predictions made by God's own prophets* (literally, 'the holy prophets'), *and the commandment given by the Lord and Saviour through your apostles.* Whereas Jude 17 refers only to the words of the apostles, II Peter (as in 1.16–21) mentions both prophets (by which he means the prophets of the Jewish scriptures – see on 1.19–21) and apostles. The phrase *your apostles* may be intended to refer to the apostles who founded the churches to which the readers belong (cf. I Peter 1.12). These apostles passed on *the commandment* of *the Lord*: not a specific or particular commandment, but the Christian way of upright and holy living (see on 2.21). As in 1.16–21 the testimony of the prophets of scripture together with that of the apostles is presented as the reliable foundation for orthodox Christian faith and life.

3.3–4   One particular teaching is singled out as of especial importance and relevance (the same phrase, *first of all note this,* was used in the opening of 1.20). Following Jude 18 closely the author quotes a prophecy attributed to the apostles which predicts that *in the last days there will come scoffers.* Predictions of difficult times ahead, and specifically of the appearance of opponents in the form of false teachers or scoffers, are found in a number of farewell speeches in the New Testament (see on Jude 18; II Peter 2.1–3a; cf. esp. Acts 20.29–30; II Tim. 3.1–5). There is some irony in this passage, for the very people who scoff at the idea of the Lord's return (see below) are, in the author's view, proof of its nearness (Fornberg 1977, 61). The phrase *in the last days* is common in the LXX; the author has altered Jude's wording to a more familiar form (see e.g. Gen. 19.1; Hos. 3.5; Ezek. 38.16; Dan. 2.28 etc.). The description of the *scoffers* is made emphatic by a word-repetition in the Greek: literally, 'scoffers [will come] with scoffing'. These scoffers (clearly the false teachers who have already been derided in chapter 2) 'follow their own desires' (cf. Jude 16, 18).

The content of their 'mocking' is then cited. The form of the rhetorical question (*what has happened to . . . ?* literally, 'where is . . . ?') is common in the Jewish scriptures as an expression of the doubts or taunts which enemies or scoffers express (e.g. Ps. 42.3, 10: 'where is your God?'). Particularly relevant parallels are found in places where the prophets confront those who mock the reality of God's judgment (Mal. 2.17; Jer. 17.15). The specific question which the scoffers raise concerns *his promised coming*. Evidently they express doubts about the return of the Lord. Their argument is clear: *our fathers have been laid to rest, but still everything goes on exactly as it has done since the world began*. Most commentators agree that 'the fathers' (which is what the Greek says) refers to the first generation of Christians (Knoch, 275; Bauckham, 290; etc.). The death of the first generation of believers was understandably problematic for the early Christians (cf. I Thess. 4.13–5.11), especially given the words of Jesus which apparently promise that at least some of that generation would not die before seeing his return in glory (Matt. 16.28; Mark 9.1 etc.). This is perhaps the specific promise (cf. 1.4) which gives rise to the taunts and doubts of the opponents. This questioning might reflect a crucial time, then, towards the end of the first-century, when the first generation of believers had all died, yet the Lord had not returned (see Bauckham, 292–93). According to the opponents, there is no sign that God will ever intervene decisively in the world – everything just carries on the same. It is this objection to which the author responds first, in vv.5–7, before turning in vv.8–10 to the question about the timing / delay of the Lord's return.

Response to the accusation of God's inactivity: the active word of God
3.5–7

In response to the assertion that the world simply carries on as it always has done, without dramatic divine intervention, the author presents essentially a three-fold argument in which points one and two are the basis for his third assertion. Firstly, the creation itself only came about through the word of God; secondly, everything has not continued without disturbance – there was a time, the time of the flood, when the creation was destroyed, by God's word and with water; thirdly, there will come a time, already decreed by God's word, when the created order will again be judged and destroyed by God, this time with fire. The author apparently envisages three great periods of cosmic history: the time before the flood; the period from the flood until the second great and final judgment; and the age of the world to come, in which justice will prevail (3.13; cf. Bauckham, 299).

3.5   *In maintaining* their view, the opponents *forget* two main points. There is a notable contrast between the opponents' forgetting and the author's concern to remind (cf. 1.12–15; 3.1–2). Firstly *they forget* that the creation of *heavens and earth long ago* was accomplished *by God's word* (cf. Gen. 1.3ff.; Ps. 33.6; Heb. 11.3), *out of water and with water*. The idea of creation *out of water* expresses the ancient Near Eastern view, reflected in Genesis 1, that the world emerged out of a watery chaos. The waters were separated and held back, in order for dry land to emerge. The words *with water* are more difficult, but should probably be understood in the sense, 'by means of water': 'water was, in a loose sense, the instrument of creation, since it was by separating and gathering the waters that God created the world' (Bauckham, 297). Most fundamentally, however, it was *by God's word* that creation took place.

3.6   The second point that the opponents forget is that it was also through God's word, and by means of water, that this original created order was annihilated. This striking idea of the destruction and replacement of the first heavens and earth, which goes beyond the Genesis account of the destruction of all living things in the Flood, is implied in the contrast between *heavens and earth long ago* (v.5 – cf. *the first world*, v.6), and *the present heavens and earth* (v.7). Only righteous Noah, his family, and those animals with them in the ark survived (cf. 2.5; I Peter 3.20; Gen. 6–8).

It is difficult to decide exactly to what the opening Greek words of v.6 – *di' hôn*, 'through which' (plural) – are meant to refer (cf. NRSV; NAB etc.). Most likely is the implication 'through God's word and through water' (so e.g. Knoch, 278; Kelly, 360; Bauckham, 298). Unfortunately the REB refers only to *water*, so missing the implied reference to the word of God which was active both in creation and in the destruction brought about by the flood. The explicit reference to destruction *by water* emphasizes both the parallel with the idea of creation 'by water' (v.5) and also the contrast with the second great destruction, which will be 'by fire' (v.7).

3.7   These two great acts of creation and judgment, accomplished *by God's word*, provide for the author a firm basis for certainty about what will happen in the future. By the same word of God *the present heavens and earth are being reserved for burning; they are being kept* (cf. 2.4, 9) *until the day of judgment*. The idea of a final fiery end may owe something to the influence of ancient Iranian (Zoroastrian) religion, and the notion that the world was periodically dissolved and renewed by fire was taught in Stoicism. An ancient idea of recurrent destructions by flood and fire alternately is also evidenced (see Bauckham, 300–301). II Peter's basic source, however, is Jewish scriptural and post-scriptural tradition, where the themes of destruction and judgment by flood and fire are well-known (cf. 2.5–6; Luke 17.27–29). The idea of judgment by fire is clearly expressed in the prophets (e.g. Isa. 66.15–16; Mal. 4.1). However, as Kelly (pp.360–61) notes, 'the idea that the world will be finally annihilated by fire appears only in II Peter in the NT, and is indeed in its fully developed form not biblical at all', though the theme is found in Jewish apocalyptic and in some later Christian literature. However, II Peter's main concern, as it is for the biblical prophets, is with the fire as a judgment of destruction upon *the godless* (Isa. 30.30; 66.15–16; Nahum 1.6; Zeph 1.18; 3.8). As Noah and his family were kept safe through the flood (cf. 2.5; I Peter 3.20), so the righteous will be preserved in the final fiery judgment (cf. I Peter 4.12–19). *The godless*, on the other hand, *will be destroyed*. It is precisely the reality of this judgment that the 'scoffers' deny, and thus they fail to perceive the need to live holy lives (3.11–14).

Response to the accusation of indefinite delay: God's patience
  3.8–10

3.8   Next the author deals with the scoffers' question cited in v.4a: *What has happened to his promised coming?* The same verb (*forget*) appears in v.5 and v.8, indicating the beginning of each of the two main parts of the author's response to the scoffers' objections. However, there is also a contrast: in v.5 the author is concerned with what *they forget* (that is, the scoffers), whereas in v.8 he addresses his *dear friends* directly (*here is something . . . you must not forget*). This surely shows that the faithful, as well as the opponents, were disturbed and puzzled about the apparent delay in the Lord's promised return (against Talbert 1966). The author is concerned as much to reassure them as to counter the argument of his opponents (Kelly, 361).

His first response to this question of delay is based on Ps. 90.4, and indicates that God's perspective on time is very different from that of human beings; from God's viewpoint a long time span may appear very short, and vice versa. Unlike some other Jewish and later Christian writings, the author of II Peter does not attach any particular significance to the idea of 'a thousand years' (cf. Fornberg 1977, 69–70); he is simply concerned to show, as the two balanced clauses indicate, that God does not reckon time in the same way as human beings, limited as they are in their lifespan and outlook. Nor does this point necessarily reveal that the author has abandoned any sense of imminent expectation (cf. 1.19; 3.14). However, while it offers one 'answer' to the apparent problem of delay, it certainly at the same time removes the possibility of any conviction as to the timetable from the perspective of human history. As Käsemann suggests: 'If we ascribe to God a time-scale different from our own, we are no longer in a position to maintain seriously the "soon" of the apocalyptic believer, but are compelled to refrain from any utterance about the time of the Parousia' (1964, 194).

3.9 The author's second response to the problem of delay is to reveal a reason for delay on God's part. The opening words of this verse may well be influenced by Hab. 2.3, a classic source for reflection upon the problem of eschatological delay in both Judaism and early Christianity (Bauckham, 310; Heb. 10.37). Here the author explicitly argues against the implication of v.4, using an argument in the form *not . . . but* (cf. Watson 1988, 130). *It is not that the Lord is slow in keeping his promise* – contrary to the accusation the scoffers make and which is their reason for denying that the promise will ever be fulfilled at all. Their perspective on the reckoning of 'slowness' is misguided; the Lord is not *slow, as some suppose,* or, more literally, 'as some consider slowness'. The author accepts that, from a human point of view, there is some delay in the expected fulfillment of the promise, but insists that this human perspective is the wrong one to adopt. The delay is due not to God's 'slowness', or impotence *but* to his patience – a fundamental attribute of God in Jewish and Christian thought, rooted originally in the statement of Ex. 34.6–7 (see e.g. Num. 14.18; Neh. 9.17; Ps. 86.15 etc.; Bauckham, 312). For God does not will that *any should be lost, but that all should come to repentance* (cf. Ezek. 18.23, 32; 33.11). Since the author has already specified that God's patience is towards *you* – i.e. the Christian readers of the epistle – he is probably thinking in this context of all Christians, especially those who are currently erring and opposing the true faith (so Bauckham, 313). However, the idea may legitimately be applied to God's desire for all people to repent and be saved (Acts 17.30–31; Rom. 11.32).

The basic problem which II Peter here confronts was an issue for pagans, as well as for Jews and Christians. Plutarch, for example, writes in response to those who argue that God's slowness undermines a belief in providence (*On the Delays of the Divine Vengeance*; Kelly, 362; Neyrey 1980a). The primary source and background for II Peter, however, is Jewish writing and thought (see Bauckham 1980).

3.10   Although God is a God of patience, he is also a God of justice; mercy and justice being two basic attributes of God (see Neyrey, 241–42). People should therefore not treat God's patient waiting as an excuse for sin. The present is certainly a time of delay, *but the day of the Lord* (cf. e.g. Amos 5.18–20; Joel 1.15; 2.11) *will come like a thief*. The verb 'it will come' is the first word of this verse, placed for emphasis and contrast with what has preceded (perhaps also a further allusion to Hab. 2.3). The comparison of the Lord's coming with the unexpected visit of a *thief* originates in the sayings of Jesus (Matt. 24.43; Luke 12.39) and was taken up into early Christian teaching about 'the End' (I Thess. 5.2–4; Rev. 3.3; 16.15). *On that day the heavens will disappear* (cf. Matt. 5.18; 24.35 and parallels) *with a great rushing* (or 'roaring') *sound,* the onomatopoeic word in Greek indicating perhaps the roaring flames of the fire, or the thunderous roar of God's voice (cf. Ps. 18.13–15; Amos 1.2; Joel 3.16). There is some debate about what is meant by *the elements* (*stoicheia*; cf. on v.12). The possibilities are (i) the four elements of which the ancients believed all physical things were composed: water, air, fire, and earth; (ii) the heavenly bodies: sun, moon and stars; (iii) spiritual powers (cf. Gal. 4.3; Col. 2.8, 20). The second, perhaps linked with the third, since the cosmic bodies were often thought to be controlled by spiritual powers, seems most likely. The essential point, however, is that the whole creation – heavens, celestial powers, and earth – will all pass away (so Knoch, 282). For the notion of a fiery end see on 3.7.

The final clause of the verse is very difficult. Literally translated it reads: 'and the earth and the works in it will be found'. There are a number of textual variants, probably reflecting attempts to supply a reasonable sense, since the verb 'will be found' seems so odd. Some scholars, for similar reasons, have suggested amending the text. However, there is no good reason to believe that the text said anything other than what is translated above. This could conceivably have been meant as a question ('the earth and the works it contains – will they be found?' Kelly, 364) but most likely is the indicative sense 'will be found'. Although a somewhat unusual sense for the word, it is best taken as a divine passive, meaning, 'will be discovered by God', or revealed, uncovered, brought to light (see e.g. Bauckham, 316–21; Watson 1988, 133; Neyrey, 243). All the deeds and works of human beings will be laid bare before God (cf. on v.14). So, just as v.7 concluded on a note about judgment, and vv.11–14 focus on the moral implications of the coming day, here too the author's focus is on the day of the Lord as a day of *judgment* – an implication which the REB makes explicit.

An appeal for holy living in view of the coming end and the new beginning
3.11–13

As was conventional at the end of apostolic letters and testaments, the author now begins to focus on exhortation, on the moral implications of his teaching. In doing this he takes up central topics from the opening of the letter (1.3–11) concerning the kind of lives which the believers should lead (Watson 1988, 134). His appeal is based not only on the threat of judgment and the dissolution of the old creation, but also on the promise of a new creation in which justice will dwell.

3.11   In view of the coming end and the final judgment, described in v.10, the believers should live their lives in a certain way, in holiness and godliness, *devout and dedicated*. The plural forms used in the Greek are difficult to render in an acceptable English translation, but they perhaps indicate that the author is thinking of concrete acts and practices (Knoch, 284). We might paraphrase: 'in holy actions and godly deeds' (cf. I Peter 1.15–16; 3.1–2; II Peter 1.3, 6–7).

3.12   As often in the New Testament (see on Jude 21) the believers are urged to 'await eagerly', to *look forward to, the coming of the day of God*. There is perhaps here another echo of Hab. 2.3 ('wait for it / him'; cf. 3.9–10). Certainly the theme of expectant waiting is prominent in these verses: the verb 'to await' or 'expect' appears three times in vv.12–14. The exact phrase *the day of God* is very unusual (cf. only Rev. 16.14; more usual is 'the day of the Lord': see on v.10; I Cor. 5.5; I Thess. 5.2; II Thess. 2.2), and the word *coming* (Gk: *parousia*) elsewhere in the New Testament always has a personal reference – e.g. 'the coming of the Son of Man' (Matt. 24.27, 37–39). However, this is an insufficient basis for suggesting, as Kelly (p.367) does, that the author intends a distinction between Christ's return and the final 'day of God'; on the contrary, they are one and the same (cf. Bauckham, 325).

As well as awaiting the day with eager expectation, the believers are also urged *to hasten it on*. In v.9 it was stated that God was delaying the day in order to give time for repentance; the corollary of this idea is that repentance and holy living may bring the day nearer (an idea found also in Rabbinic Judaism; cf. also II Esd. 4.38–39; Acts 3.19–20; *2 Clem* 12.6–13.1; Bauckham, 325). God remains in sovereign control, but just as lack of repentance leads her to gracious patience, so repentance and holy living may hasten the end, and the arrival of the kingdom for which Jews and Christians have long prayed (Matt. 6.10).

It is because of the will and action of God, to be enacted on *that day*, and not as a result of any natural cyclical process (as some Stoics thought), that the great fiery end will occur (cf. Kelly, 367–68). The description of the dissolution of the universe in flames corresponds with vv.7 and 10; the verb 'to dissolve' (*luô*) appears in vv.10, 11 and 12 (translated 'fall apart' in v.12 in the REB). The phrase *will melt the elements in flames* may echo a version of Isa. 34.4 found in some texts of the LXX which reads: 'all the powers of the heavens will melt'. This may add some weight to the interpretation of *the elements* as the heavenly bodies or cosmic powers (see on v.10).

3.13   The repeated description of the fiery end prepares the way for the contrasting statement of v.13 (a contrast brought out, e.g., in the NRSV: 'But . . .'). Christians should be encouraged to live holy lives not only in view of the coming destruction and its accompanying judgment, but also, and perhaps more fundamentally, by the hope of *new heavens and a new earth*. It is this that *we look forward to* (the verb 'await' again; see vv.12 and 14). This hope and expectation is based upon God's *promise*, recorded originally in the prophecies of scripture (Isa. 65.17; 66,22) and taken up in Jewish apocalyptic (e.g. *I Enoch* 72.1) and early Christianity (Rev. 21.1). The work of God is complete renewal (Isa. 43.19; Matt. 19.28; Rom. 8.21; II Cor. 5.17; Rev. 21.5). In contrast to the present world, characterized by corruption (1.4), lawlessness and godlessness (2.5–7), the new creation is described, in what Charles Bigg (p.299) calls a 'beautiful phrase', as a place 'in which righteousness has its home', or *justice* is *established* (cf. Isa. 32.16). Fundamental to the biblical portrayal of God is his righteousness, and fundamental to the biblical hope is the establishment of righteousness/justice (e.g. Gen. 18.19; Lev. 19.15; Isa. 9.7; 11.4–5; Ps. 9.8; 11.7; Matt. 5.6; Rom. 14.17). This hope expresses the longing of the weak and powerless, of all who are denied justice and who experience hostility and rejection from the world, that God may act to replace injustice with righteousness (cf. Matt. 5.3–12; Luke 6.20ff.).

This major section of the epistle (3.1–13) raises serious interpretative questions for modern readers (see Ch.VI (4). Who was right: the author or the scoffers? The author's conviction about the coming day of the Lord is based on beliefs about the structure and formation of the universe and about dramatic interventions by God which many would now regard as reflecting an ancient mythological world-view. And 2,000 years after the time when the first Christians were earnestly expecting the day of the Lord, we must acknowledge that their sense of 'soon' was misguided – it is still the case that *everything goes on as it always has done*! Many modern theologians who wish to sustain a faith in the Christian God maintain that God does not exercise will over the world through dramatic interventions (cf. e.g. Wiles 1986). Perhaps we should resist the urge to side entirely with either the author or the scoffers. Certainly we need to continue the task of revising and articulating afresh our understanding of God and of God's interaction with the world, not only in the light of the Bible, but also using the resources of our traditions, our intellects, and our experiences in the world. Our ideas about God, judgment, and so on, may need to be very different from those of the author of II Peter. Yet, in opposition to the 'scoffers', we may wish still to proclaim the hope that God will continue the work of redemption and transformation until the creation becomes a place in which justice is at home; and we should insist that the vision of hope should inspire us to holy and committed living in the present. Revising our picture of judgment or its timetable is no reason for an abandonment of morality. On the contrary, the vision of a world in which justice dwells should serve as an inspiration to walk in the light of that vision, however distant its fulfillment may be, and however fragile the achievements.

Closing exhortations
3.14–18

The author now draws his letter to an end, presenting final exhortations and warnings, and closing with a short doxology. The lack of personal greetings (as in Jude, but contrast e.g. I Peter 5.12–14) is unusual. The major themes of the letter are here succinctly reiterated, together with the new subject of Paul's letters and their use and abuse within the church.

3.14   The introductory words of this verse ('Therefore, beloved') indicate a new paragraph and a drawing together of conclusions and implications based upon the preceding teaching about the end. Since the believers live *in expectation of all this* ('awaiting these things'; the verb 'await' again, as in vv.12 and 13) – where *all this* refers to the coming judgment and the hope of a new heavens and a new earth – they should live now in a way appropriate for those who are to inhabit a new world in which righteousness will dwell. The vision of the end should act as an inspiration for holy living in the present. They are urged to 'strive', to 'be eager', to *do* their *utmost* (cf. 1.10, 15) *to be found at peace with him*, or 'in his sight', i.e. when God comes to judge. The verb *to be found* may echo and contrast with 3.10, where there is a sense of threat in the idea of the earth and all its works being 'found', or laid bare, before God at the end. Here the believers are urged to be found *at peace*, which may mean reconciled to God (so Bauckham, 327; Kelly, 370), or in that state of wholeness and holiness which is salvation (cf. Isa. 32.17; Ps. 34.14; 85.10; Neyrey, 250). The two ideas are, of course, not entirely separable.

What the believers are urged to be is *unblemished and above reproach*. These words originally described the required condition of sacrificial animals and were applied also to Christ, the perfect sacrifice (see on I Peter 1.19; Jude 24; also Heb. 9.14). Those who offered sacrifices, similarly, had to be 'without blemish' (Lev. 21.16–21). The terms thus came to refer to moral purity and perfection. The words used here are the same as appear in I Peter 1.19, and similar phrases appear frequently in early Christian literature, often in a context which describes the state in which Christians should be in readiness for the Lord's return (Eph. 1.4; 5.27; Phil. 2.15; Col. 1.22; I Tim. 6.14).

3.15–16   In contrast to the false teachers and sceptics, who regard the delay in the Lord's return as 'slowness' (3.9), the readers of the epistle are urged to regard *our Lord's patience* (an echo of 3.9, and possibly of Rom. 2.4) positively, as *an opportunity for salvation*. The time of delay is a time in which people have the chance to be reconciled to God and so *to be found at peace* (v.14).

This teaching (meaning the whole of vv.14–15a), the author urges, is the same as *Paul said when he wrote to you*. The subject of Paul and his letters is a new one, and it is probably introduced for two reasons. One is that the 'author wishes to point out that his own teaching (specifically in 3.14–15a) is in harmony with Paul's because Paul was an important authority for his readers' (Bauckham, 328). The writer claims authority not only by writing in Peter's name, but also by aligning his teaching with Paul's. He claims to be a faithful witness to the message of the biblical prophets (1.19–21) and of the apostles (1.16–18; 3.1). This passage clearly reflects a time some distance from that when Paul and Peter seemed to represent distinctive and sometimes conflicting strands within early Christianity (cf. I Cor. 1.12; 9.1–6; Gal. 2.11–16), though the extent of their difference and disagreement should not be exaggerated (I Cor. 3.22; 15.3–5; Gal. 1.18–2.10). Now Peter and Paul are 'venerated together as the joint leaders and heroes of the apostolic Church' (Kelly, 370; cf. Acts; *I Clem* 5.3–7; Ignatius *Romans* 4.3). The second reason for introducing the subject of Paul is that the false teachers also used Paul's letters, though in a way which the author regards as 'distortion' (see below on v.16).

Paul is referred to as *our dear friend and brother*, that is, as one whom the apostles regard as a colleague and leader in the church (cf. Eph. 6.21; Col. 4.7; I Thess. 3.2; I Peter 5.12). He wrote *with the wisdom God gave him* – a phrase which finds echoes in Paul's own descriptions of the wisdom he teaches (I Cor. 2.6–16) and of the grace given him by God (Rom. 15.15; I Cor. 3.10; Gal. 2.9). His letters are recognized and regarded as inspired.

The indication that what Paul *wrote to you* is *the same* as *he does in all his other letters* would seem to suggest that the readers are located in a certain geographical area and received a certain letter (or letters) from Paul. Scholars have long discussed which letter(s) the author may have had in mind (see Bauckham, 329–30). If the readers are located in Asia Minor (see I Peter 1.1; II Peter 3.1) then Galatians, Colossians and Ephesians are perhaps most likely (though the latter two are often thought not to have been written by Paul himself). However, since Paul's letters probably began to circulate and be used more widely from quite an early date, and since we have no precise information regarding the content or character of the letter(s) in mind, it is best to leave this an open question. In any case, the author states that, whichever of the Pauline letters they possessed, the teaching would be *the same . . . wherever he speaks about this*. About what? Most likely about the need to live a holy life in view of the coming end, a theme which does indeed appear in the majority of Paul's letters (e.g. Rom. 13.11–14; I Thess. 5.4–11; note also the parallels between II Peter's references to God's patience and judgment and Rom. 2.4–6). It may not be insignificant to note that Romans and I Thessalonians are the two letters which the author of II Peter seems most likely to have known (Neyrey, 134, 250).

There follows a candid acknowledgment that Paul's letters *contain some obscure passages*, i.e. passages which are difficult to interpret. The *ignorant* (or 'uninstructed') *and unstable* – a description with a clear hint of condemnation, and probably aimed at the false teachers and their followers (cf. 2.14) – *misinterpret* or distort these writings. The author does not tell us how, in his view, they misinterpreted Paul. Although there are a number of possibilities, it seems most likely that they took Paul's teaching on justification by faith as a basis for liberty and freedom from law, in a way which neglected the need for moral and holy living (see 2.19). Paul himself had to confront similar misinterpretations of his gospel (Rom. 3.8; 6.15; I Cor. 6.12; 10.23; Gal. 5.13). The result of their misinterpretation, and its consequent immorality, is *ruin*, or destruction, at the final judgment.

Paul's letters have clearly begun to be regarded as a collection of writings which are inspired and authoritative, and which may be set alongside *the other scriptures*. This must confirm the relatively late date (and hence also the pseudonymity) of the epistle, reflecting a period perhaps towards the end of the first or early in the second century when the Gospel traditions and Pauline letters were acquiring a status comparable to that of the Jewish scriptures, through their use in the life and worship of the church (cf. I Tim. 5.18). Although the formalization of a New Testament canon was still some way off, a movement in that direction had begun (cf. Knight 1995. 71).

3.17   With a final note of conclusion – *So, dear friends* – the author summarizes the purpose and content of his letter, written in Peter's name: to serve as a means of 'forewarning' the readers about the false teachers who would arise in the last days, and who are, in fact, already a reality as he writes. The readers should hold on to Peter's teaching, so as not to be carried away by the *errors* of the lawless, *unprincipled*, people who are now among them. They must make every effort to maintain their *own safe foothold* and not to fall away. The letter aims to sustain their stability in the truth (1.12), in face of the enticement into error which threatens the unstable (2.14–15; 3.16).

3.18   The final exhortation, echoing themes from 1.2–11, is that they should *grow in grace and in the knowledge of our Lord and Saviour Jesus Christ.*

The author's closing words comprise a doxology, an exclamation of praise often found in Jewish and Christian writings, sometimes, but not always, at or near the end of a letter (see on I Peter 4.11; 5.11; Jude 24–25). Although it broadly follows the conventional pattern of New Testament doxologies, II Peter's doxology is unusual, though not unique, in being addressed to Christ rather than God (other examples are II Tim. 4.18; Rev. 1.5–6). It is notable that 1.17 refers to God's bestowal of honour and glory upon Jesus at the transfiguration, and that 1.1 refers to Christ as 'our God and Saviour'. In contrast to Jude 24–25, II Peter's doxology does not expand the acclamations beyond the basic *glory*. II Peter's reference to time is also more concise than Jude's, and employs the unusual phrase 'both now and to the day of eternity' (NRSV); more usual is the phrase 'for ever' (e.g. I Peter 5.11). II Peter's distinctive wording probably reflects the theme of the great 'day' which will dawn (1.19), a theme so prominent in the letter (3.7–13). The Lord's return will mark the dawn of the day of eternity, the beginning of a new age of righteousness, a 'day' in the Lord's timescale which cannot be reckoned according to human measurements of time (cf. 3.8).